Philosophy as Therapeia

ROYAL INSTITUTE OF PHILOSOPHY SUPPLEMENT: 66

EDITED BY

Clare Carlisle & Jonardon Ganeri

CAMBRIDGE
UNIVERSITY PRESS

PUBLISHED BY THE PRESS SYNDICATE OF THE UNIVERSITY OF CAMBRIDGE
The Pitt Building, Trumpington Street, Cambridge, CB2 1RP,
United Kingdom

CAMBRIDGE UNIVERSITY PRESS
The Edinburgh Building, Cambridge CB2 8RU, United Kingdom
32 Avenue of the Americas, New York, NY 10013–2473, USA
477 Williamstown Road Port Melbourne, VIC 3207, Australia
Ruiz de Alarcon 13, 28014 Madrid, Spain
Dock House, The Waterfront, Cape Town 8001, South Africa

Printed in the United Kingdom at the University Press, Cambridge
Typeset by Techset Composition Ltd, Salisbury, UK

A catalogue record for this book is available from the British Library

ISBN 9780521165150
ISSN 1358-2461

Contents

Notes on Contributors

Keith Ansell Pearson

Keith Ansell Pearson is Professor of Philosophy at the University of Warwick. His research interests are in 19th and 20th century European philosophy. He has published studies of Nietzsche, Bergson, and Deleuze, as well as introductions and edited volumes, and has served on the editorial boards of *Nietzsche-Studien* and *Journal of Nietzsche Studies*.

David Burton

David Burton is Senior Lecturer in the Department of Theology and Religious Studies at Canterbury Christ Church University. His doctoral dissertation was on epistemological and ontological issues in Madhyamaka Buddhism, and he has interests in religious language, comparative philosophy, and the philosophy of religion. Along with a number of articles, he has published two books: *Buddhism, Knowledge and Liberation: A Philosophical Study* (Ashgate, 2004), and *Emptiness Appraised: A Critical Study of Nāgārjuna's Philosophy* (RoutledgeCurzon, 1999).

Clare Carlisle

Clare Carlisle is Lecturer in Philosophy at the University of Liverpool. Her research interests include Kierkegaard, the philosophy of habit, philosophy of religion, and Buddhist philosophy. Among her publications are *Kierkegaard's Philosophy of Becoming* (State University of New York Press, 2005), *Kierkegaard's 'Fear and Trembling': A Reader's Guide* (Continuum, 2010), and the first English translation of Félix Ravaisson's *Of Habit* (Continuum, 2008).

Stephen R. L. Clark

Stephen R. L. Clark is Professor of Philosophy at the University of Liverpool. His research interests include Plotinus, animals, science fiction and philosophy of religion. Among his many books, the most recent are *Understanding Faith: Religious Belief and its Place in Society* (Imprint Academic, 2009), *Biology and Christian Ethics* (Peking, 2006) and *G. K. Chesterton: Thinking Backward, Looking Forward* (Templeton Foundation Press, 2006).

Notes on Contributors

Jonardon Ganeri

Jonardon Ganeri is Professor of Philosophy at the University of Sussex. His books include *The Concealed Art of the Soul: Theories of Self and Practices of Truth in Indian Ethics and Epistemology* (Clarendon Press, 2007) and *Philosophy in Classical India: The Proper Work of Reason* (Routledge, 2001). His interests include the Hindu-Buddhist dialogue in Classical India, Indian philosophy in Early Modernity, and theories of reason and philosophies of mind and self.

Martin Ganeri O. P.

Martin Ganeri O. P. is Prior, Blackfriars, Cambridge. He is Lecturer in Theology, Heythrop College, University of London. He has worked extensively on the theologies of Thomas Aquinas and Rāmānuja.

Christopher W. Gowans

Christopher W. Gowans is Professor of Philosophy in the Philosophy Department at Fordham University in New York City. His areas of research are contemporary moral philosophy, Buddhism and Hellenistic philosophy, and Buddhist moral and political philosophy. He has published *Philosophy of the Buddha* (Routledge, 2003) and *Innocence Lost: An Examination of Inescapable Moral Wrongdoing* (Oxford, 1994).

Logi Gunnarsson

Logi Gunnarsson is Professor of Philosophy at TU Dortmund University, Germany. He is the author of *Making Moral Sense: Beyond Habermas and Gauthier* (Cambridge University Press, 2000) and *Philosophy of Personal Identity and Multiple Personality* (Routledge, 2010).

Garry L. Hagberg

Garry L. Hagberg is Professor of Philosophy at the University of East Anglia, and has for some years served as the James H. Ottaway Professor of Philosophy and Aesthetics at Bard College. His books include *Describing Ourselves: Wittgenstein and Autobiographical Consciousness* (Oxford University Press, 2008), and an edited collection, *Art and Ethical Criticism* (Blackwell, 2008). He is joint editor of the journal *Philosophy and Literature*, and co-edited *The Blackwell Companion to the Philosophy of Literature* (Blackwell, 2009).

Michael Hampe

Michael Hampe is Chair of Philosophy at Swiss Federal Institute of Technology Zürich, and President of the Spinoza-Foundation. He studied philosophy and biology at Heidelberg and Cambridge. After professorships in Dublin, Kassel and Bamberg he teaches early modern philosophy and history of cosmology in Zürich.

Jayandra Soni

Jayandra Soni is Lecturer in the Department of Indology and Tibetology, Philipps-Universität Marburg, Germany. He holds Ph.D.'s from Benaras Hindu University and McMaster University, and has published widely on Śaiva Siddhānta, Jaina philosophy and other aspects of Indian thought.

Kate Wharton

Kate Wharton is a full-time researcher on inter-religious affairs for the Archbishop of Canterbury. She completed her Ph.D. thesis, *Philosophy as a Practice of Freedom in Ancient India and Ancient Greece*, at the School of Oriental and African Studies, in London in 2008, and offers courses on Hindu and Buddhist Philosophy for Birkbeck College, London.

Introduction

'Empty are the words of that philosopher who offers therapy for no human suffering. For just as there is no use in medical expertise if it does not give therapy for bodily diseases, so too there is no use in philosophy if it does not expel the suffering of the soul.' The philosopher Epicurus (341–271 BCE) gave famous voice to a conception of philosophy as a cure or remedy for the maladies of the human soul, and this recurring theme in Hellenistic thought has been the subject of two important recent studies.[1] What has not until now received a comparable degree of attention is just how prominent an idea it has been across a whole spectrum of philosophical tradition. Scholars of Buddhism have known for some time that a medical analogy features strongly in Buddhist conceptions of philosophical practice, but this fact has rarely been the object of explicit discussion. The idea that philosophy should be therapeutic, indeed that this is philosophy's first function, was indeed widely spread in India, and the analogy between philosophy and medicine was put to important use in several other, non-Buddhist, Indian schools. In the West, too, this conception of philosophy has displayed a great resilience, persisting long past the Hellenistic age. It can and will be argued that medieval scholasticism, a mode of philosophizing now so often and often so naively criticised, should be understood as therapeutic in intent. If that is right it is important, because it allows us to see continuities between ancient, medieval and early modern thought where too often discontinuities alone are emphasised. For Spinoza too thought of philosophy as therapeutic, and after him Nietzsche and Wittgenstein. So the conception of philosophy as therapeia allows for, and even necessitates, a new reading of the history of philosophy, one in which deep continuities come into vision which have been obscured, a reading which also contradicts those who have wanted to maintain that philosophy is a peculiarly European cultural product, and instead affirms its identity as a global intellectual practice.[2]

[1] Richard Sorabji, *Emotion and Peace of Mind: From Stoic Agitation to Christian Temptation* (Oxford: Clarendon Press, 2000), and, Martha Nussbaum, *The Therapy of Desire: Theory and Practice in Hellenistic Ethics* (Princeton, NJ: Princeton University Press, 1994).

[2] The idea that philosophy is peculiarly European is most explicitly articulated by Hegel, Husserl, and Heidegger. It is true that European philosophy and Indian philosophy are intellectual disciplines with different

doi:10.1017/S135824610999021X

With this in mind, we have assembled together here a set of new essays, all specially commissioned for our volume. We begin where the studies by Nussbaum and Sorabji leave off, with discussions of the therapeutic model from two leading voices in Buddhist philosophy. One of these studies, by Christopher Gowans, an expert in both Hellenistic and early Buddhist philosophy, focusses on the many similarities between Hellenistic and Buddhist uses of the model. The other, by David Burton, goes deeply into the Buddhist sources, including Tibetan along with later Indian contributions. As per their brief, neither writer merely documents, both instead putting challenging questions to the literature they survey. For it was our intention that the volume contain a thorough examination both of the scope and of the *limits* of the medicinal model. Kate Wharton, emphasising a disanalogy, very creatively plays with the use of two educational metaphors, juxtaposing the maieutic Socrates with the Vedic teacher who gestates his students; and Stephen Clark, in a complementary way, traces the original meaning of the word "therapeia" to an idea of service. These two essays press us to think through the value we now habitually attach to notions of autonomy. Jayandra Soni uses the therapeutic paradigm to demonstrate that the school of Yoga philosophy has far more in common with a Hellenistic school than its contemporary image would lead one to think.

The chapter by Martin Ganeri is a pivotal one. He argues precisely that scholasticism embodies a therapeutic conception of philosophy, and does so by bringing into dialogue two great scholastic thinkers, Aquinas and Rāmānuja. His chapter thus simultaneously displays the two dimensions of continuity that this volume aims to demonstrate, those that obtain *within* and *across* philosophical traditions. With a view to tracing this continuity through the work of more modern thinkers, we invited experts on Spinoza, Nietzsche, William James and Wittgenstein to examine how these philosophers take up the theme. Michael Hampe has shown how Spinoza was able to rejuvenate the conception of philosophy as therapeia and finesse difficulties in earlier formulations. Keith Ansell Pearson has written for this volume on Nietzsche, and contributes to the growing body of work on Nietzsche as a therapeutic philosopher with a new reading of Nietzsche's *Dawn* or *Daybreak*. In an age when thoughts about immortality—whether in the shape of the hope for an after-life, or in the form of a fear of endless

---

histories and methods; the fallacy in the argument consists in the false assumption that the term 'philosophy' denotes a species and not the genus.

re-birth—no longer serve to animate the lives we try to lead, philosophical reflection is what awakens us to our condition. The question is, can it also help us find ways to live in the face of these acknowledgements? Logi Gunnarsson writes about William James, casting new light on this thinker at a moment of philosophical crisis in his intellectual life. Gunnarsson uses his study of James to make the important point that the maladies of the soul for which philosophy might be held up as a cure are sometimes not everyday emotional turmoils but difficulties of a peculiarly philosophical sort; for James they arose from a confrontation with the possibility that there is no freedom of will, and are not themselves susceptible to further reflection. Implicit in Jonardon Ganeri's chapter is the sense that it is our inability to think of ourselves without fear in relationship to different cultures, nations or religions which gives shape to a distinctively contemporary malaise, to which philosophy renders a service in the fashioning of new sorts of cosmopolitan identity. We seem to need either to domesticate or else to deride what is alien, too bound by what is our own to be able to let it 'inform' us. With some of the above concerns, Wittgenstein too might have agreed. Garry Hagberg has written a very provocative and stimulating chapter on Wittgenstein, drawing attention to a previously unnoticed affinity between Wittgenstein's interest in architecture and his conception of the role and function of philosophy, an affinity that the 'philosophy as therapiea' model makes visible.

Among the central themes our contributors explore, then, are:

- What are the 'illnesses' that afflict us as subjects, for which philosophy might provide a remedy?
- What is the content of the medical analogy? Is the medicine a curative, a tonic, or a prophylactic?
- Why do both Sextus Empiricus and Nāgārjuna regard the medicine that is philosophy to be an emetic, purging itself as well as the disease?
- What is the relationship between thinking well and the integrity of the self?
- Is there a tension between philosophy as treatment and the autonomy of the subject? Can those who suffer cure themselves?
- To what extent must a philosophical 'treatment' be adapted to fit the needs of the particular individual? Is there a risk that, in locating the cause of suffering in all that individualises human beings, the cure deprives individuals of their individuality?

Our contributors have considerably eased our editorial labour by providing material for the ensuing summaries of their contributions.

Together, these summaries constitute a synopsis of all the many interwoven strands of investigation. Our volume owes its existence to the Royal Institute of Philosophy, who supported the idea by awarding us one of its annual conferences, and we would like to thank Anthony O'Hear and James Garvey for their help and patience. That conference took place in Liverpool on June 19–21, 2008, an enjoyable gathering and an indispensible preparatory event for this volume. The University of Liverpool provided additional support, for which we are grateful.

The Chapters in this Volume

Medical analogies are regularly appealed to in both Indian Buddhist and Hellenistic philosophy. In one form, the analogy states that just as medicine cures bodily diseases and brings about physical health, so philosophy cures mental diseases and brings about psychological health. Christopher Gowans provides a very thorough and helpful survey of the main uses of medical analogies in Theravāda and Mahāyāna schools of Indian Buddhism, as well as in the Epicurean, Stoic and Pyrrhonian Sceptical schools of Hellenistic philosophy. He argues that philosophers have had good reasons to invoke these analogies, but also thinks that there are limitations to their use. The limitations Gowans identifies derive in the first instance from the radical conceptions of psychological health invoked by what he calls 'tranquillity philosophies,' which represent psychological health as requiring the elimination of emotional life. Even if desirable, Gowans contends that it is implausible that emotions like anger can be eliminated just by changing one's beliefs.

Michael Hampe, on the other hand, finds in the work of Spinoza a new affirmation of the analogy. Conversant with Hellenistic thought, Spinoza was nevertheless sensitive to difficulties of the sort Gowans has highlighted. Fundamental to Spinoza's approach is a distinction between *technical* and *practical knowledge*, or between a technical and practical approach to one's own life. For Aristotle, technical knowledge deals with the correct means of achieving a given objective, and practical knowledge is knowledge of ends as such. A technical approach to life will view an existence led without pain and suffering as the means to another end, such as the satisfaction of desire. A practical approach to life, meanwhile, will seek to achieve an existence that is an end in itself, the realisation of a way of life in which action and experience need not be directed towards anything other than that life. At the end of the *Ethics*, in a statement setting out the aim of his deliberations, Spinoza criticises the technical approach to life: 'Blessedness (*beatitudo*) is not the reward of virtue, but virtue itself; neither do we rejoice therein, because we control our lusts, but, contrariwise, because we rejoice therein, we are able to control our lusts.' The practice or therapy outlined by Spinoza consists firstly in deconditioning the human mind in a way that results in a removal of contingent judgements of things and ideals – a process akin to techniques of 'de-imaging' found in meditative practices. In the second phase of Spinoza's philosophical therapy, the mind should reason solely on the basis of 'common notions.' Because that which can be understood by means of common notions necessarily relates to the true nature of a being, those who draw conclusions solely with the aid of true common notions can no longer suffer and necessarily realise their true nature. Thus the method of converting all mental operations into inferential ones becomes for him a therapeutic strategy. Hampe finishes his chapter with the worry that Spinoza's philosophical therapy ends up eliminating all that is individual to a human life. This, as later chapters in this volume show, is a theme very much in the foreground of Indian explorations of the paradigm.

Spinoza's *Ethics* is, in a useful phrase Martin Ganeri introduces to describe the *Summa* of Aquinas and the *Śrī Bhāṣya* of Rāmānuja, a 'pedagogy for happiness:' a text so constructed as to make the active process of reading into work the reader does on him- or herself. Martin Ganeri's contention is that it is a virtue of the conception of philosophy as therapeia that it can lead us to be less blind to the importance of scholasticism, especially scholastic insights into the relationship between text and reader. The scholastic approach challenges us to retrieve the idea that philosophy is transformative through pedagogical reading. Martin Ganeri analyses those structural features of the *Śrī Bhāṣya* and the *Summa* that lend them their therapeutic potential; and it is striking indeed that the *Ethics* of Spinoza and the *Tractatus* of Wittgenstein, works of two European thinkers most closely associated with an advocacy of the 'philosophy as therapeia' model, are also the two texts in modern European philosophy most nearly to conform to this structure (the elaborate matrix-like structures of Pāli Abhidharma texts, which make them so hard on a modern reader, display a similar type of textuality).

An important theme in the idea of philosophy as therapeia is that philosophical practice—including activities of reading and thinking—engages us in projects of self-formation. Garry Hagberg's chapter, drawing on Wittgenstein, develops a way of describing the role of narrative in self-understanding, looking into the distinctive kind of work a self-narrator undertakes. Wittgenstein notes the deep similarity in work that unites the thinker and the draughtsman: the draughtsman strives to 'represent all the interrelations between things,' and the thinker—the philosopher—can be seen to hold strikingly similar aspirations. Hagberg suggests that a relational embeddedness makes remembered and retrospectively-described experience what it is, so that the task of clarifying relations emerges as essential to autobiographical undertakings and acts of self-constitution. As Wittgenstein himself says, 'Working in philosophy—like work in architecture in many respects—is really more a working on oneself. On one's way of seeing things.' This likening of the thinker to the draughtsman echoes a theme in earlier chapters, that the almost cartographical structure of texts like the *Ethics*, the *Summa* and the *Śrī Bhāṣya* is a source of their therapeutic potential for the reader.

In *Tractatus* 6.45 Wittgenstein famously writes, 'To view the world *sub specie aeternitatis* is to view it as a whole—a limited whole.' To see all of the connections between elements perspicuously is to see the macrocosm as such a whole, and one might seek to trace the therapeutic value of philosophy to this source. Stephen Clark, in a careful re-appraisal of the notion of 'therapy' in Plato and his successors, observes that the original therapy with which philosophy is to be identified is to love and serve the lord. But isn't there something wrong with accepting divine requirements because they are divine—aren't we subject to the Euthyphro Dilemma, which supposedly makes it impossible to think that an act is right if it is divinely required? This, argues Clark, is to misunderstand Plato and the problem that Euthyphro actually faced, which was how to deal with his father's crime. The conclusion that Euthyphro reaches is that it is indeed his task to please the gods, but by doing what is right, by manifesting the beauty that is the focus of contemplative love; specifically by being willing to submit himself, his father and his family to *objective* judgement, that is, to a judgement which approximates that of an impartial, omniscient witness. To serve the gods is to live as the gods prefer, and that is to be stripped of our attachment to all lesser goods. The best that most of us can manage is to practice civic virtue: not to be greedy, cowardly or unkindly. But all these precepts rest on a perception of divine beauty, on waking up to reality, to God, who is the contemplative love we serve. Learning to detach ourselves from sensory illusions, to live in the understanding that each of us is a version of reality, an entity wholly dependent on its membership of that real world and without any special status, is both an epistemological and a moral exercise. We serve the gods by pleasing them.

We please them by sharing, sometimes, in their life, and dismissing the charms that bind us to our sensual, solitary delusions.

In Vedic pedagogy, observes Kate Wharton, education begins with a ritual initiation, an *upanayana*, in which the student is metaphorically reborn from the womb of the teacher, memorising sacred verses by replicating his teacher's recitations. Wharton contrasts this image of replication with the image of midwifery that Socrates uses to describe his educational method. Socrates claims to be barren of wisdom, not passing down knowledge but instead watching over the birth of his students' ideas. Both the Brahminical and the Socratic systems of education claim to *free* the student, but they affirm very different forms of freedom. Wharton contrasts those philosophical practices of freedom that are founded on a value of trust (*śraddhā*) with those that rest on testing and examination (*elenchus*). She asks difficult questions of the Socratic principle of limitless questioning and its ensuing *aporia*, a state akin to being cast adrift in a chaotic sea, and defends in its stead an alternative conception, in which to be free is to have confidence that one is fully surrounded by the truth.

Jonardon Ganeri finds in several philosophical traditions a common thought: that philosophy teaches us to consider our lives as if they are works of art, and provides us with the methods needed to fashion a life accordingly. He contrasts the model of sculpting, which one finds in Plotinus, with the model of weaving in Plutarch. He moves on to observe how a template with four constituents had wide circulation in both medical and philosophical contexts in ancient India, of which the four 'noble truths' of the Buddha is but one instance. The four constituents are: the disease, the cause of disease, the cure, and the state of health which ensues. Jonardon Ganeri observes, however, that a voice dissident to the medicinal model comes in the form of someone who says that a life is complete at every moment. He finds such a voice in Marcus Aurelius and Rabindranath Tagore. Drawing on a discussion in the *Mahābhārata*, he argues that Indians are not the 'nay-sayers' mischaracterised by Nietzsche, their appeal to notions like nirvāṇa and mokṣa being as regulative ideals in lives led in the here and now.

Keith Ansell Pearson contributes to an emerging trend in modern scholarship which connects Nietzsche to traditions of therapy in philosophy. He does so by focusing on *Dawn*, Nietzsche's future-oriented text of 1881. Ansell Pearson describes how *Dawn* revitalises ancient philosophical concerns for a modern age, by offering a teaching for *mortal* souls who wish to be liberated from the fear and anguish of existence. Having lost the dream of the soul's immortality, philosophy for Nietzsche continues to offer consolation in the form of 'new sublimities'. Stressing the Epicurean aspect of Nietzsche's thinking at this time, Ansell Pearson examines that task of purification of the higher feelings which Nietzsche thinks modern spirits need to perform.

William James, observes Logi Gunnarsson, distinguishes *philosophical melancholy* from any psychiatric disorder. Philosophical melancholy is produced by philosophical reflection. It is characterized by the judgment that life is not worth living, by a tendency to suicide, and by sentiments such as a feeling of uncanniness. So philosophical melancholy is not an unfortunate philosophical condition but rather involves an existential crisis, threatening to a person's life. In the late 1860s and early 1870s, James had a psychological and biographical crisis. However, as Gunnarsson argues, he also understood himself as being subject to philosophical melancholy. James took this condition to be generated by the assumption that theoretical reason alone can settle various philosophical issues, such as the question of free will. Contrary to widespread interpretations of James, his solution was not to decide the matter by an arbitrary act of will. Rather, he thought that emotions had an integral role to play in discovering the right solution to pressing philosophical questions, and maintained that the cure to philosophical melancholy is to give up the assumption that theoretical reason alone can solve these questions. Gunnarsson considers whether James succeeds in presenting an effective cure to philosophical melancholy, and whether certain form of this 'disease' may even be a condition worth preserving.

In James' refusal to allow that further reflection can cure the melancholy produced by philosophy's inability to decide if there is free-will or not, there is an important echo in the Buddha's famous refusal to enter into debate about a number of philosophical dilemmas (and in James' ensuing claim that 'our passional nature not only lawfully may, but must, decide an option between propositions, whenever it is a genuine option that cannot by its nature be decided on intellectual grounds,' there are intriguing resonances with Indian moral theorists' appeal to *ātmatuṣṭi* in the same circumstances). David Burton focusses on three significant features of Buddhist philosophical therapy. First, Buddhist philosophical thinking claims that various 'diseases' of our belief-desire psychology are the maladies that require treatment. Second, it maintains that successful therapy needs to address the entrenched dispositions that inform our views, desires, and emotions. Third, it acknowledges that the therapy will vary according to the specific needs and difficulties of the individual. Burton responds to the worry, presented by Gowans and others, whether Buddhist philosophical therapy misdiagnoses the human predicament and espouses a misguided goal of emotional detachment, and whether it neglects the physiological, social, political, and economic causes of suffering by concentrating too heavily on personal cognitive therapies. These are important challenges, which future work in Buddhist philosophy will certainly need to engage with; and they receive further support from many of the essays in the volume.

Rounding off our volume with his scholarly study, Jayandra Soni argues that the doctrines of the Indian school of Yoga should be recast as a form of philosophical therapeia. By so invoking the 'philosophy as therapeia' paradigm, Jayandra Soni here reclaims Patañjali as a serious and important *philosopher*, and not merely, as he has come to be seen in Europe, the inventor of a physical work-out regime or a set of breathing excercises. Soni shows that 'yoga' is properly defined as the restriction or arrest of the modifications and fluctuations of the psyche, and that the aim of philosophy, according to the school, is to show how suffering may be minimised if not completely eradicated through practices of discrimination. It is Yogic *asaṃprajñāta-samādhi*[3] rather than Sceptic *epoché*[4] which leads to this tranquillity and freedom from distress, or else it is discriminative knowledge of *vyaktāvyaktajña*[5] in the related Sāṃkhya account. Motivating the Yoga theory is the idea that what is sought is not merely temporary relief from everyday affliction but a more permanent ground for psychological well-being. To establish his case, Soni needs to read the texts with a careful philological eye; and while this makes his article a little hard-going for a non-specialist, our volume would not have been complete without the corrective it affords to popular misconceptions. Correcting deeply entrenched misconceptions, as we see time and again, is difficult philosophical medicine.

3 A focussed psychological state not involving any meditational aid.
4 Suspension of judgement.
5 Knowledge of what is evolved, what is unevolved, and of the one who knows.

Medical Analogies in Buddhist and Hellenistic Thought: Tranquillity and Anger

CHRISTOPHER W. GOWANS

Medical analogies are commonly invoked in both Indian Buddhist dharma and Hellenistic philosophy. In the Pāli Canon, nirvana (or, in Pāli, *nibbāna*) is depicted as a form of health, and the Buddha is portrayed as a doctor who helps us attain it.[1] Much later in the tradition, Śāntideva described the Buddha's teaching as 'the sole medicine for the ailments of the world, the mine of all success and happiness.'[2] Cicero expressed the view of many Hellenistic philosophers when he said that philosophy is 'a medical science for the mind.' He thought we should 'hand ourselves over to philosophy, and let ourselves be healed.' 'For as long as these ills [of the mind] remain,' he wrote, 'we cannot attain to happiness.'[3] There are many different forms of medical analogy in these two traditions, but the most general form may be stated as follows: just as medicine cures bodily diseases and brings about physical health, so Buddhist dharma or Hellenistic philosophy cures mental diseases and brings about psychological health—where psychological health is understood as the highest form of happiness or well-being. Insofar as Buddhist dharma involves philosophy, as it does, both renditions of the analogy may be said to declare that philosophy cures mental diseases and brings about psychological health. This feature of the analogy—philosophy as analogous to medical treatment—has attracted considerable attention.[4]

[1] For example, see Bhikkhu Ñāṇamoli and Bhikkhu Bodhi, eds. and trs., *The Middle Length Discourses of the Buddha* (Boston: Wisdom Publications, 1995), pp. 614–6 and 867 (I 510–12 and II 260). For ancient texts, ordinary pagination is followed by standardized pagination (in parentheses).

[2] Śāntideva, *The Bodhicaryāvatāra*, Kate Crosby and Andrew Skilton, trs. (Oxford: Oxford University Press, 1995), p. 143 (10.57).

[3] Cicero, *Cicero and the Emotions: Tusculan Disputations 3 and 4*, Margaret Graver, tr. (Chicago: University of Chicago Press, 2002), pp. 5 and 70 (3.6 and 4.84).

[4] For example, with respect to Buddhism, see Richard Gombrich, *Theravāda Buddhism: A Social History from Ancient Benares to Modern*

doi:10.1017/S1358246109990221

My thesis in this chapter is that in both Indian Buddhism and Hellenistic philosophy the medical analogy in its various forms has some importance, but not as much importance as its intuitive appeal and the frequency with which it was invoked might lead one to suspect. There are good reasons why these traditions were drawn to the analogy. However, there are significant disanalogies between medical practice and physical health on the one hand, and philosophy and psychological health as understood in these traditions on the other. These differences turn on three central features of Buddhism and Hellenistic philosophy: their radical conceptions of psychological health; the inevitable moral questions these conceptions raise; and the assumption that attaining psychological health requires modifying or eliminating beliefs in response to rational argument (at least to some extent), in order to attain wisdom.

The Meaning of the General Form of the Medical Analogy

Any assertion of medical analogies presupposes some understanding of medicine in the primary sense. In both India and the Mediterranean world, in the time periods we are considering, there were on-going traditions of medicine that may be interpreted, from a contemporary standpoint, as involving, on the one hand, an array of religious, ethical, and magical approaches and, on the other hand, emerging empirically-based techniques (emphasizing empirical observations in understanding diseases, their causes and their remedies). In both contexts, the practice of medicine was both more fluid and less autonomous than in modern Western medicine. It is hard to know how effective these ancient medical practices were, but presumably claims of expertise were made on their behalf, however well-founded, and the assertion of the medical analogies obviously presupposes respect for at least some of these

---

Colombo (London: Routledge, 1988), pp. 2 and 59, and with respect to Hellenistic philosophy, see Martha Nussbaum, *The Therapy of Desire: Theory and Practice in Hellenistic Ethics* (Princeton, NJ: Princeton University Press, 1994) and Julia Annas, 'Philosophical Therapy, Ancient and Modern,' in Mark G. Kuczewski and Ronald Polansky, eds., *Bioethics: Ancient Themes in Contemporary Issues* (Cambridge, MA: The MIT Press, 2000), pp. 109–127. They are briefly compared in Thomas McEvilley, *The Shape of Ancient Thought: Comparative Studies in Greek and Indian Philosophies* (New York: Allsworth Press, 2002), pp. 596–7.

claims. There were, in fact, significant interactions between medical practice and both Buddhism and Greco-Roman philosophy.[5] These interactions probably played some role in the development of the medical analogies.

The practice of medicine employs the contrary concepts of physical disease and health. To some extent, these concepts were, and still are, contested. However, there is likely to be considerable overlap in their referents, consistent with considerable diversity in their meaning and interpretation. Physical disease (including injury) presumably refers to such things as: physical pain that is abnormal, excessive, or chronic; failures or disruptions of basic bodily functions; and conditions that threaten premature death. Physical health, by contrast, involves the absence of these things and perhaps, more positively, some notion of well-being characterized as an optimal bodily condition. These ideas of disease and health inevitably depend on some beliefs about what is normal for the species. It is reasonable to suppose that ancient medical practices, in India and the Mediterranean world, assumed some such understanding of disease and health, and claimed to have some expertise in promoting health by preventing or curing disease. This expertise must have rested on some purported understanding of the causal conditions of disease and health, and skill in influencing these conditions so as to promote health.

If we think of medical practice in these terms, then the general form of the medical analogies (hereafter, the medical analogy) may be understood as making two points: first, there are some analogous concepts of disease and health in the mental or psychological realm, and second, Buddhist dharma or Hellenistic philosophy has an analogous expertise in promoting this state of health, an expertise that involves some knowledge of the causal conditions of disease and health, and some skill in affecting these conditions in ways that promote health. In fact, in Buddhism and the Hellenistic schools, both of these claims were regularly made.

[5] In the case of Buddhism, see Kenneth G. Zysk, *Asceticism and Healing in Ancient India: Medicine in the Buddhist Monastery*, Corrected Edition (Delhi: Motilal Banarsidass Publishers, 1998). In the case of Hellenistic philosophy, see Ludwig Edelstein, 'The Relation of Ancient Philosophy to Medicine,' in *Ancient Medicine: Selected Papers of Ludwig Edelstein*, Owsei Temkin and C. Lilian, eds. (Baltimore: Johns Hopkins University Press, 1967), pp. 349–66 and James Longrigg, *Greek Rational Medicine: Philosophy and Medicine from Alcmaeon to the Alexandrians* (London: Routledge, 1993).

There are, however, some complications. One is that both of these traditions purported to be concerned with physical disease itself. In Buddhism, bodily illness was one of the primary forms of suffering that enlightenment enables us, in some way, to overcome, and Hellenistic philosophy was no less preoccupied with the threat that physical illness was thought to pose to our well-being. However, neither tradition presented itself as offering an alternative to medical practice in the primary sense. In various ways, the value of this practice was affirmed. But it was tacitly assumed that medical practice has significant limitations and that physical disease is a more or less inevitable feature of human life. There is, perhaps, some incongruity in this stance, at least insofar as the assertion of the medical analogy may be interpreted as claiming an authority similar to that possessed by medical practice. Nonetheless, the aim of these traditions was not in any direct way to prevent or cure physical diseases, but to enable us to achieve a superior mental or psychological attitude with respect to these diseases (among other things). However, unlike medical practice, which cannot guarantee good physical health even when done well, these traditions claimed that their practices did guarantee psychological health when done well. In this respect, they claimed greater authority than could plausibly be claimed for medicine itself.

Both Buddhist thought and Hellenistic philosophy may be interpreted as defending philosophies of what it means to live a good human life or to live well (in Buddhism, this is nirvana as an enlightened condition in this life; in Hellenistic philosophy, it is *eudaimonia*, often translated as happiness). A striking common feature of these two traditions is that they believe that tranquillity is a necessary and important feature of living such a life. By tranquillity they meant, broadly speaking, a stable long-term psychological state that is characterized by the absence of many or all emotional oscillations and is brought about, not by what happens to a person, but by a person's achieving a proper orientation to the world through some form of wisdom. Hence, in their appeals to the medical analogy, these traditions interpreted living well as implying a form of psychological health characterized by tranquillity. By the same token, they understood living poorly as implying a form of mental disease characterized by various kinds of emotional turbulence such as fear, anxiety, distress, grief, anger, etc. They gave more attention to these negative states, but many positive emotional states such as delight and excitement were usually also regarded as incompatible with tranquillity. However, some states that appear to involve emotion, such as compassion for others or joy in one's virtue, were sometimes thought to be compatible with tranquillity. I will take anger as my central example of a disruption of tranquillity. Buddhism and the Hellenistic schools were united in maintaining that human well-being requires a tranquil life that is mostly or entirely free of emotions such as anger.

This leads to another complication in the medical analogy. For both traditions, a person's mental disease, understood as emotional turbulence, was thought to depend crucially upon beliefs of the person that were false or unwarranted, and psychological health, interpreted as implying tranquillity, was thought to depend on eliminating these beliefs and, at least sometimes, replacing them with true beliefs. Philosophy was important, at least in part, because it purported to be able to modify a person's beliefs so that he or she could overcome mental diseases and attain psychological health. For example, anger is a painful and agitated mental state that is commonly brought about by the belief that a person has wronged or harmed someone and is often accompanied by the belief that the wrongdoer should suffer some harm as proper desert for the wrongful action. If philosophy could show that these beliefs about wrongdoing and punishment were mistaken or without warrant, then philosophy might play a role in the elimination of anger and the attainment of tranquillity in this respect. It could eliminate the disease of anger and bring about the health of tranquillity. This exemplifies the core idea of philosophy as analogous to medical treatment. However, in medical practice in the primary sense, the removal of a patient's false or unwarranted beliefs is arguably much less central because physical diseases are less likely to be directly caused by, much less to consist in, beliefs—though this point was probably less obvious in the ancient medical practices than it is in modern Western medicine.[6]

Insofar as Buddhist thought and the Hellenistic schools maintained that philosophical argument could bring about tranquillity by changing the beliefs on which emotional turbulence depends,

[6] Insofar as the ancient practices took a religious or ethical approach, in contrast to an empirical one, they may well have supposed that a person's physical disease sometimes depended on the person's beliefs. In fact, the Buddhist doctrine of *karma* might an instance of this: it maintains that the moral quality of a person's actions affects his or her future well-being, where this includes physical disease and health. However, the tradition is ambiguous on this point. For discussion, see Lynken Ghose, '*Karma* and the Possibility of Purification: An Ethical and Psychological Analysis of the Doctrine of *Karma* in Buddhism,' *Journal of Religious Ethics* 35 (2007), pp. 259–90.

their approach may be said to be cognitive. However, in both traditions, techniques other than philosophical argument were often employed—in particular, an array of exercises involving, for example, direct efforts to calm the mind, close observation of mental states, modification of habits, anticipation, postponement, distraction, advice or consolation, invocation of role-models, self-examination and confession. Some forms of Buddhist meditation were manifestly non-cognitive in that they aimed to take us beyond 'applied and sustained thought' and even to 'the cessation of perception and feeling.'[7] Overall, with the exception of the Pyrrhonian Sceptics, both traditions purported to have a multifaceted expertise in bringing about psychological health in the form of tranquillity.

Medical Analogies in Buddhist and Hellenistic Thought

Let us now look more closely at the employment of the medical analogies in these traditions. In the Pāli Canon, there is a well-known story in which the Buddha is compared to a surgeon who removes a poison arrow from a man: just as the surgeon, in order to heal the wound, did not need to answer various questions concerning the person who shot the arrow, so the Buddha, in order to cure us of suffering, did not need to answer various speculative metaphysical questions.[8] The story has been interpreted in different ways, but on the most straightforward reading its point is simply to emphasize the practical purpose of the Buddha's teaching. He was interested in philosophical questions only insofar as they enabled us to overcome suffering. That is why, he said, he taught the Four Noble Truths and left answers to unrelated philosophical questions 'undeclared.'

In the standard formulation, these truths state that suffering is a pervasive feature of human life; the origin of suffering is craving; the cessation of suffering—nirvana—is brought about by the cessation of craving; and the way to achieve this is the Eightfold Path. Craving is said to be rooted in ignorance or delusion with respect to basic Buddhist philosophical teachings, specifically impermanence, dependent origination, no-self and (in the Mahāyāna tradition) emptiness. Nirvana is only briefly and elusively portrayed, but in one central sense it is a peaceful psychological

[7] Ñāṇamoli and Bodhi, *The Middle Length Discourses of the Buddha*, pp. 267–8 (I 174–5).

[8] See Ñāṇamoli and Bodhi, *The Middle Length Discourses of the Buddha*, pp. 533–6 (I 426–32).

condition.[9] Emotions such as anger are ordinarily considered incompatible with it.[10] However, the tranquillity of nirvana is said to co-exist with compassion and loving-kindness for all beings. These themes are emphasized in both the Theravāda and Mahāyāna traditions.

Buddhaghosa, an important Theravāda commentator, used a medical analogy (actually a simile) to explain the Four Noble Truths: 'The truth of suffering is like a disease, the truth of the origin is like the cause of the disease, the truth of cessation is like the cure of the disease, and the truth of the path is like the medicine.'[11] This draws attention to the fact that the Four Noble Truths employ a causal analysis to show us how to move from suffering to nirvana. The comparison with medical practice seems obvious. However, Buddhaghosa gave little attention to this comparison and made no reference to any specific features of Indian medical practice.[12]

In Indian Mahāyāna Buddhism—the Madhyamaka tradition in particular—there are frequent comparisons of medical practice and Buddhist practice. Major figures such as Nāgārjuna, Āryadeva, Candrakīrti and Śāntideva all employ some form of medical analogy. Sometimes they make the general point that Buddhist thought and practice is a medicine that brings the health of enlightenment—as in the passage from Śāntideva quoted at the beginning. But very often much more specific claims are made. A common theme is that, just as medicine is often painful or distasteful, so Buddhist practice is often unpleasant or difficult.[13] We are also

[9] See Ñāṇamoli and Bodhi, *The Middle Length Discourses of the Buddha*, pp. 536 and 540 (I 431 and 436).

[10] See Ñāṇamoli and Bodhi, *The Middle Length Discourses of the Buddha*, p. 100 (I 15–16).

[11] Bhadantācariya Buddhaghosa, *The Path of Purification (Visuddhimagga)*, Bhikkhu Ñāṇamoli, tr. (Seattle: Buddhist Publication Society Pariyatta Editions, 1999), p. 520 (XVI 87).

[12] There has been some scholarly discussion of the claim that the Four Noble Truths are based on a medical model. For a review of this literature, and scepticism concerning the claim, see Zysk, *Asceticism and Healing in Ancient India: Medicine in the Buddhist Monastery*, pp. 38 and 144–5 (n. 2).

[13] See Nāgārjuna, *Buddhist Advice for Living and Liberation: Nāgārjuna's* Precious Garland, Jeffrey Hopkins, tr. (Ithaca, New York: Snow Lion Publications, 1998), pp. 114, 143 and 144 (2.142, 4.372, and 4.376), and Śāntideva, *The Bodhicaryāvatāra*, pp. 69 and 101 (7.22 and 8.144).

urged to follow the advice of Buddhist teaching just as we should follow the advice of doctors.[14] In addition, we are told that Buddhist doctrines must be properly applied in the same way that medicine must be properly applied.[15] This last point relates to the central Mahāyāna theme of skillful means: that there are many different ways of bringing people to enlightenment and that Buddhist teaching must be interpreted in light of this principle. This theme appears in several of the comparisons. For example, we are told that different doctrines are taught for different illnesses.[16] In an important passage, Candrakīrti referred to the Buddhas' 'skill in prescribing medicine for their disciples.' Because they 'have superior abilities in the liberating methods of great compassion,' he said, they teach in a way that 'conforms to the nature of foolish people's understanding.' Specifically, they teach that 'the five aggregates are substantial things' even though, in ultimate truth, there are no substantial things.[17] The idea that Buddhist teaching is often conducted in terms of the conventional truth of everyday language—what is useful but ultimately false—is another common Mahāyāna theme.

Sometimes there are references to specific medical procedures. For instance, on occasion a feature of Buddhist practice is described as an antidote.[18] By far the most widely discussed comparison to a medical procedure is put forward in defense of the Madhyamaka claim, famously expressed by Nāgārjuna, that emptiness—the absence of inherent or substantial nature—is not a view, but the elimination of all views, and that anyone who thinks it is a view is incurable.[19] In the *Ratnakūta Sūtra* it is said that this is similar to a medicine that must not only cure an illness but, having done so, be expelled from

[14] See Śāntideva, *The Bodhicaryāvatāra*, pp. 18, 29 and 44 (2.55, 4.48 and 5.109).

[15] See Āryadeva, *Āryadeva's Catuḥśataka: On the Bodhisattva's Cultivation of Merit and Knowledge*, Karen C. Lang, tr. (Copenhagen: Akademisk Forlag, 1986), p. 85 (VIII 18).

[16] See Āryadeva, *Āryadeva's Catuḥśataka: On the Bodhisattva's Cultivation of Merit and Knowledge*, p. 85 (VIII 20).

[17] Candrakīrti, *Four Illusions: Candrakīrti's Advice for Travelers on the Bodhisattva Path*, Karen C. Lang, tr. (New York: Oxford University Press, 2003), p. 160 (7.237).

[18] See Āryadeva, *Āryadeva's Catuḥśataka: On the Bodhisattva's Cultivation of Merit and Knowledge*, p. 65 (VI 5) and Śāntideva, *The Bodhicaryāvatāra*, p. 41 (5.81).

[19] See Nāgārjuna, *The Fundamental Wisdom of the Middle Way: Nāgārjuna's* Mūlamadhyamakakārikā, Jay L. Garfield, tr. (New York: Oxford University Press, 1995), p. 36 (XIII 8).

the body. If the medicine remained, the patient would be in even worse shape than if the medicine were never taken.[20] Candrakīrti quotes this passage in his defense of Nāgārjuna's understanding of emptiness.[21] The point, it seems, is that the realization of emptiness, initially taken as a view by a person who assumes that views are necessary, would lead that person to the conclusion that he or she should have no views—but this conclusion should then be applied to emptiness itself: emptiness, taken as a view, should be expelled along with all other views. This is another application of skillful means. The purgative analogy is intended to alleviate the paradox of a view being used to eliminate all views, including itself. The point is quite specific, and whatever plausibility it has is largely independent of the general form of the medical analogy.

Let us now turn to the Hellenistic schools. Epicurus' central ethical claim was that happiness is a life of pleasure. However, for the most part, he thought pleasure should be understood negatively as the absence of bodily pain and psychic disturbance: 'when we say that pleasure is the goal,' he wrote, '[we mean] the lack of pain in the body and disturbance in the soul.'[22] Hence, tranquillity is an essential and important part of happiness. This was to be attained through an empirical understanding of nature that would undermine our fear of death and the gods and would show us that the pain of unsatisfied desire could be alleviated by restricting ourselves to easily fulfilled natural and necessary desires. Little is known about Epicurus' views on anger except that he probably condemned some but not all forms of it. However, his disciple Philodemus wrote a work

[20] In the Pāli canon, the Buddha's teaching is said to be a purgative that always succeeds; see F. L. Woodward, tr., *The Book of the Gradual Sayings (Anguttara-Nikāya)*, vol. 5, (London: Luzac & Company (for The Pāli Text Society), 1961), pp. 153–4 (10.108). However, in this text, the claim is that right view purges wrong view with no suggestion that right view then purges itself.

[21] See Candrakīrti, *Lucid Exposition of the Middle Way: The Essential Chapters from the Prasannapadā of Candrakīrti*, Mervyn Sprung, tr. (Boulder, CO: Prajñā Press, 1979), pp. 150–51 (248–9).

[22] Epicurus, 'Letter to Menoeceus,' in Brad Inwood and L. P. Gerson, eds. and trs., *Hellenistic Philosophy: Introductory Readings*, Second Edition (Indianapolis: Hackett Publishing Company, 1997), pp. 30–31 (131). Cf. Epicurus, 'Letter to Menoeceus,' pp. 30 and 31 (128 and 135); Lucretius, *On the Nature of Things*, Martin Ferguson Smith tr. (Indianapolis: Hackett Publishing Company, 2001), pp. 35–6 (2.18–19); and Cicero, *On Moral Ends*, Raphael Woolf, tr. (Cambridge: Cambridge University Press, 2001), p. 25 (1.71).

entitled *On Anger* in which he condemns most forms of anger as excessive and based on 'empty' beliefs (such as that retaliation is pleasant), but allows that there is a moderate form of anger, depicted as painful but natural, that cannot be eliminated.[23] Philodemus thought that the wise person punishes those who harm him because it is 'something most necessary,' even though 'what results is most unpleasant, as with drinking wormwood, and surgery.'[24] The idea is that insofar as the desire to punish is natural and necessary to protect against aggression, the wise person will punish. However, he will not go to much trouble to do it since 'nothing external is worth much.'[25] Lucretius also thought there were some limits to the extent to which philosophy could eliminate anger.[26]

The best-known Hellenistic formulation of a medical analogy is attributed to Epicurus: 'Empty are the words of that philosopher who offers therapy for no human suffering. For just as there is no use in medical expertise if it does not give therapy for bodily diseases, so too there is no use in philosophy if it does not expel the suffering of the soul.'[27] In another passage, Epicurus said we should study philosophy in order to attain happiness, depicted as 'the health of the soul.'[28] The medical analogies were perhaps even more prominent later in the Epicurean tradition. Philodemus called a brief formulation of the Epicurean method of attaining happiness 'the fourfold

[23] For discussion of Philodemus on anger, see Julia Annas, 'Epicurean Emotions,' *Greek, Roman and Byzantine Studies* 30 (1989), 145–64 and Richard Sorabji, *Emotion and Peace of Mind: From Stoic Agitation to Christian Temptation* (New York: Oxford University Press, 2000), pp. 26 and 201–3.

[24] Quoted in Annas, 'Epicurean Emotions,' p. 159.

[25] Quoted in Annas, 'Epicurean Emotions,' p. 158.

[26] See Lucretius, *On the Nature of Things*, pp. 75–6 (3.309–22). For a survey of Epicurean views on anger, see William V. Harris, *Restraining Rage: The Ideology of Anger Control in Classical Antiquity* (Cambridge, MA: Harvard University Press, 2001), pp. 99–104. See also Nussbaum, *The Therapy of Desire: Theory and Practice in Hellenistic Ethics*, Ch. 7.

[27] A. A. Long and D. N. Sedley, eds. and trs., *The Hellenistic Philosophers, vol. 1: Translations of the Principal Sources, with Philosophical Commentary*, (Cambridge: Cambridge University Press, 1987), p. 155 (25C). For discussion of the medical analogy in Epicureanism, see Nussbaum, *The Therapy of Desire: Theory and Practice in Hellenistic Ethics*, Ch. 4.

[28] Epicurus, 'Letter to Menoeceus,' p. 28 (122).

remedy.'[29] In addition, he made extensive use of various forms of the medical analogy in works such as On *Frank Criticism*.[30] Many of his comparisons are similar to those we have already seen in Buddhism. For example, he makes reference to the need for bitter medicine,[31] proper judgment in applying medicine,[32] and the adjustment of treatment to specific cases.[33] There are also references to purgatives[34] and to those who are incurable,[35] though the point of these comparisons is altogether different than in the Madhyamaka discussions. Lucretius wrote that, just as doctors promote the health of children by coating bitter medicine with honey, so he was presenting the 'somewhat off-putting' Epicurean philosophy 'in harmonious Pierian poetry' and 'the sweet honey of the Muses.'[36] Finally, Diogenes of Oenoanda described the sickness that Epicureanism was to treat as a 'plague,' spreading from one person to another, that required putting 'out in public for all the drugs that will save them.'[37]

The basic ethical claim of the Stoics was that we should live in accord with nature (also depicted as God and reason). This means acting rationally, and hence virtuously, with respect to our natural impulses for self-preservation, family, society, etc. The Stoics' distinctive contention was that virtue, so understood, is both necessary and sufficient for happiness. This implies that possession of 'externals' such as health or wealth is not necessary for happiness. Since the universe is governed by reason, whatever happens is for the best. Hence, whether one attains these externals or not should be accepted as for the best. Though we

[29] Long and Sedley, *The Hellenistic Philosophers, vol. 1: Translations of the Principal Sources, with Philosophical Commentary*, p. 156 (25J). The remedy says: 'God presents no fears, death no worries. And while good is readily available, evil is readily endurable.' Cf. Epicurus, 'Letter to Menoeceus,' p. 31 (133).

[30] For a summary of these, see the editors' 'Introduction' in Philodemus, *On Frank Criticism*, David Konstan, et al., eds. and trs. (Atlanta: Scholars Press, 1998), pp. 20–23.

[31] Philodemus, *On Frank Criticism*, pp. 95 and 117 (Cols. IIb and XVIIa).

[32] Philodemus, *On Frank Criticism*, p. 71 (Frs. 63–4).

[33] Philodemus, *On Frank Criticism*, pp. 31, 39 and 83 (Frs. 7-8, 20, and 79).

[34] Philodemus, *On Frank Criticism*, p. 71 (Frs. 63–4).

[35] Philodemus, *On Frank Criticism*, pp. 67 and 85 (Frs. 59 and 84N).

[36] Lucretius, *On the Nature of Things*, pp. 28–9 (1.937–950); repeated at p. 100–101 (4.10-25).

[37] Quoted in Nussbaum, *The Therapy of Desire: Theory and Practice in Hellenistic Ethics*, p. 137.

ordinarily have reason to pursue these externals, we should not fear or be distressed about their loss. All ordinary emotions such as fear, anger and grief are false judgments that mistakenly suppose that some external is good and its absence bad (or vice versa). Fully rational and virtuous persons would not make these mistakes and so would be without these emotions. They would live a tranquil life. This outlook is orthodox Stoicism but it is especially evident in the Roman Stoics. For example, Seneca wrote essays on the importance of tranquillity and the elimination of anger. He said that happiness is 'peace of mind, and lasting tranquillity.'[38] and that, 'instead of moderating our anger, we should eliminate it altogether.'[39]

The medical analogy was prominent among the earliest Stoics. Chrysippus spoke of a 'method for the diseased mind' that is analogous to the medical method for 'the diseased body.' He said that there is a 'doctor' who cures each of these, and that there is 'an analogy between the methods of cure for each.' It is evident that the diseases of the mind are emotions and that the doctor who is to cure them is the Stoic philosopher.[40] Medical analogies were also frequently employed by later Stoics such as Musonius Rufus, Epictetus and especially Seneca. Once again, there is considerable diversity in the points made, and some overlap with the medical analogies in Buddhism and Epicureanism. Often a general form of the analogy was put forward. For example, Musonius, echoing Epicurus, declared that 'just as medical argument is no use unless it brings human bodies to health,' so philosophical 'argument is no use, unless it conduces to the excellence of the human soul.'[41] There was much attention to applying general principles to particular cases. Epictetus said a philosopher needs to know when and how to apply doctrines just as a physician knows when and how to apply medicines.[42] Seneca wrote that there were

[38] Seneca, *Epistles* 66–92, Richard M. Gummere, tr. (Cambridge, MA: Harvard University Press, 1920), p. 449 (92.3).

[39] Seneca, 'On Anger,' in Seneca, *Moral and Political Essays*, John M. Cooper and J. F. Procopé, eds. and trs. (Cambridge: Cambridge University Press, 1995), p. 114 (3.42.1).

[40] See the passages on pp. 211–12 of Graver's edition of Cicero's *Tusculan Disputations*. For discussion of the medical analogy in Stoicism, see Nussbaum, *The Therapy of Desire: Theory and Practice in Hellenistic Ethics*, ch. 9.

[41] Quoted in Nussbaum, *The Therapy of Desire: Theory and Practice in Hellenistic Ethics*, p. 324.

[42] See Epictetus, *The Discourses of Epictetus*, Christopher Gill, ed., Robin Hard, tr. (London: J. M. Dent (Everyman), 1995), pp. 188–89 (3.21.18–20).

'cures for the soul' just as there were prescriptions for healing the eyes. The task of philosophers, he said, was 'to learn the method and the time of treatment.'[43] On occasion medical analogies were employed to make claims specific to Stoicism, and sometimes in polemics against competing philosophies. Since emotions were regularly described as diseases, Seneca could claim, in opposition to the Aristotelian view that we should moderate but not eliminate emotions, that he did 'not understand how any half-way disease can be either wholesome or helpful.'[44] Seneca also described vices as diseases: the diseases of the mind, he said, 'are hardened and chronic vices, such as greed and ambition.'[45] And he suggested that punishment should be regarded as a cure: chastisement 'is not a matter of doing harm, but of curing in the guise of doing harm.'[46]

As presented by Sextus Empiricus, Pyrrhonian Scepticism maintained that for every possible belief there is an equally sound argument for and against it and that, upon recognizing this, suspension of all beliefs follows and tranquillity ensues. Included among these beliefs are beliefs about whether something is good or bad. If we do not think anything is good or bad, then we will never be upset about missing what is good or obtaining what is bad. Hence, while maintaining suspension of all beliefs about the contentions of 'dogmatic' philosophers such as the Epicureans and Stoics, the Pyrrhonian Sceptics claimed to produce what these dogmatists only promised—a tranquil life (at least to the extent possible given that some feelings such as thirst cannot avoided). To the question of how we are to live if we suspend all beliefs, the Sceptics had a straightforward response: we follow 'everyday observances,' without regard for their truth, namely the guidance of nature, feelings, laws and customs, and various kinds of expertise.[47] According to Sextus, 'the aim of the Sceptic is tranquillity in matters of opinion and moderation of feeling in matters forced upon us.'[48] 'Tranquillity,' he says, 'is freedom from disturbance and calmness of soul.'[49] The Sceptics

[43] Seneca, *Epistles 1–65*, Richard M. Gummere, tr. (Cambridge, MA: Harvard University Press, 1917), p. 443 (64.8–9).

[44] Seneca, *Epistles 93–124*, Richard M. Gummere, tr. (Cambridge, MA: Harvard University Press, 1925), p. 333 (116.1).

[45] Seneca, *Epistles 66–92*, p. 143 (75.11).

[46] Seneca, 'On Anger,' p. 23 (1.6.1).

[47] See Sextus Empiricus, *Outlines of Scepticism*, Julia Annas and Jonathan Barnes, trs. (Cambridge: Cambridge University Press, 1994), p. 9 (1.23–4).

[48] Sextus Empiricus, *Outlines of Scepticism*, p. 10 (1.25).

[49] Sextus Empiricus, *Outlines of Scepticism*, p. 5 (1.10).

did not feature freedom from anger as an aspect of tranquillity, but insofar as anger depends on beliefs about what is good or bad, their position implies that a Sceptic would be free of anger.[50]

The Sceptics employed medical analogies with much less frequency than we find in the Epicureans and Stoics, and mostly for rather different and limited purposes. In one case, we are told that the Sceptics 'wish to cure by argument...the conceit and rashness of the Dogmatists.'[51] In this employment, the psychological diseases are construed as philosophical beliefs mistakenly regarded as justified, and psychological health is freedom from these beliefs. The diseases are not ordinary emotions such as anger and grief as such, though perhaps the assumption was that these emotions presuppose the philosophical beliefs. In the continuation of the analogy, we are told that, 'just as doctors for bodily afflictions have remedies which differ in potency...so Sceptics propound arguments which differ in strength.' According to Sextus, while some dogmatists require 'weighty arguments,' others are 'easily cured' and only require arguments with 'a milder degree of probability.'[52] This is an instance of paying attention to the particular features of patients, but it is the only such instance in Sextus, and it is a surprising point in that the variation is not in kinds or degrees of sophistication of arguments, but in how good the arguments are.

For the most part, the only other medical analogy in Sextus addresses the question about how the Sceptics, lacking beliefs, can put forward sceptical arguments, as they relentlessly do. According to Sextus, after sceptical arguments do their work, they are applied to themselves and disappear: 'arguments, like purgative drugs which evacuate themselves along with the matters present in the body, can actually cancel themselves along with the other arguments which are said to be probative.'[53] As has been widely and correctly noted, the purgative analogy in Pyrrhonian Scepticism bears some resemblance to the purgative analogy in Madhyamaka Buddhism. However, it is worth observing that in both cases the fact that the analogy is medical is somewhat incidental: a non-medical analogy, such as a drain cleaner that expels both the blockage and itself, would work just as well. Moreover, though the purgative analogy is

[50] See Nussbaum, *The Therapy of Desire: Theory and Practice in Hellenistic Ethics*, pp. 313–15 and Sorabji, *Emotion and Peace of Mind: From Stoic Agitation to Christian Temptation*, pp. 27–8 and 198–200.

[51] Sextus Empiricus, *Outlines of Scepticism*, p. 216 (3.280).

[52] Sextus Empiricus, *Outlines of Scepticism*, p. 216 (3.280–81).

[53] Sextus Empiricus, *Outlines of Scepticism*, p. 118 (2.188).

striking, it does nothing to alleviate philosophical worries about relying on beliefs and arguments to reach a stance in which no beliefs and arguments are maintained (as well as worries about the cogency of this stance).

Both the medical analogies employed by Sextus emphasize the instrumental role of argument in bringing about suspension of belief rather than the importance of argument as a means of attaining truth. This may not be unexpected for a sceptic. But it highlights the fact that the medical analogies in Pyrrhonian Scepticism bear only a limited resemblance to those in Epicureanism and Stoicism—and in much of Buddhism as well.

The Attractions of the Medical Analogy

Let us now consider why the medical analogy, in its general as well as it more specific forms, was so prominent in Buddhist and Hellenistic thought. One reason is that it is rather obvious. Medicine in the primary sense claims an expertise in producing physical health, something widely desired. But most people think there is more to living well than physical health: there is also well-being that is psychological (mental, emotional, spiritual, etc.). Any outlook that purports to be able to produce psychological well-being might naturally regard it as a kind of health (of the mind, soul, person, etc.) and to think of its activity in producing this health as a kind of medicine. In fact, other traditions have also been attracted to the analogy. Since the Buddhist and Hellenistic traditions claimed to be able to bring persons to a state of psychological well-being, it is not surprising that they found the medical analogy attractive.

There is, however, a more specific feature of these traditions that made the analogy especially appealing. As we have seen, though their conceptions of psychological well-being differed in various ways, Indian Buddhism and the Hellenistic schools agreed that tranquillity is a necessary and important part of psychological well-being. Moreover, they generally agreed that troublesome emotions such as fear, grief, and anger were paradigm cases of disruptions to tranquillity. Such emotions can easily be seen as psychological diseases analogous to physical diseases. For example: anger is generally painful, sometimes in ways that are abnormal, excessive or chronic; it can disrupt basic activities of life; and in some cases it can bring about premature death. If we think of such emotions as psychological diseases, then it is plausible to think of their absence—tranquillity—as psychological health. Hence, the emphasis in these traditions on tranquillity as a crucial feature of psychological well-being was probably a powerful impetus to employing the medical analogy in its general form.

In addition, the application of general knowledge to particular cases is an important feature of both medicine and the Buddhist and Hellenistic traditions. This theme is constantly stressed in the medical analogies. Beyond this, what is noteworthy is the many different forms the analogies take. There are references to drugs, antidotes, purgatives, surgery, instruments, etc. Appeals are made to bitter medicine, sugar-coated medicine, and medicine of different strengths. The diversity of forms of medical treatment was mirrored by the diversity of kinds of therapy in these traditions. In addition, medical analogies were sometimes used to make claims that were specific to a particular outlook: for example, in the purgative analogy in Madhyamaka Buddhism and Pyrrhonian Scepticism, and in Seneca's critique of Aristotelianism. In sum, comparisons with medicine were prominent because the medical motif was fruitful: it proved quite useful in asserting a wide variety of points.

The Limitations of the Medical Analogy

Though there are some good reasons why Buddhist and Hellenistic thinkers were attracted to the medical analogies, there are also significant respects in which these analogies, especially in the general form, are problematic. First, in the case of physical disease and health, there is fairly wide agreement about the referents of the terms. For example, people do not ordinarily need to be convinced that cancer is a disease and its absence a form of health. Nor do people need to be convinced that there is reason to try to avoid cancer. The same is true of many other conditions.[54] There may be less agreement within the medical domain about psychological health, but in any case what is striking about the Buddhist and Hellenistic outlooks is that they put forward an understanding of psychological health that is clearly at odds with what most people think. Though tranquillity as freedom from mental turmoil has obvious attractions, the interpretation of tranquillity as the complete or near complete absence of emotions such as anger, fear and grief renders it a controversial conception of psychological health. Though these emotions are painful, most people need to be convinced that human life would be better without them. Moreover, there are prima facie good reasons for this:

[54] In various ways, all of these outlooks maintained that physical disease was to be avoided.

on some occasions, these emotions appear to be insightful, appropriate and useful responses to the world. The case is even stronger for the value of positive emotions such as delight and excitement that are precluded by a conception of tranquillity as freedom from emotion. For most people, emotions are an important part of human life. In addition, these traditions believed that in various ways it was necessary to withdraw from ordinary life in order to achieve genuine tranquillity: this is most obvious in the case of Buddhist monasticism, but the Hellenistic schools also encouraged diverse forms of withdrawal, psychological and otherwise. That psychological health requires downgrading the importance of ordinary life is also controversial.

A related point is that medicine in the primary sense works within the constraints of our biological nature: any conception of physical health that is at all empirical needs to respect what is biologically necessary and possible. The general form of the medical analogy might be thought to suggest something similar for psychological health. In fact, however, in Buddhist and Hellenistic thought conceptions of psychological health are put forward that, to many persons, are beyond the limits of human capacity: we cannot realistically expect human beings to free themselves of emotions to the extent that these traditions imagined. A second related point is that many people are physically healthy throughout much of their lives with fairly little effort: in favourable conditions, physical health can be expected for many people. By contrast, for Buddhism and the Hellenistic schools, the state of psychological health envisioned requires extraordinary effort on the part of anyone, so much so that it is at best the exception rather than the rule that people attain this state. Except for Pyrrhonian Scepticism, all these traditions repeatedly acknowledged the great difficulty of achieving their goal.

A second set of issues arises from the question of whether there is more to living well than tranquillity. I have argued that, from one point of view, tranquillity is plausibly interpreted as psychological health and that philosophies that regard tranquillity as essential to living well have, in this respect, good reason to embrace the medical analogy. But if we think that living well also requires living virtuously, then the medical analogy is problematic. Virtue involves a set of dispositions to act in certain ways under various circumstances. However, being physically healthy is a condition that does not entail any dispositions to act in one way rather than another. There are characteristic ways in which a virtuous person lives, but there are no characteristic ways in which a physically healthy person lives. There are, of course, habits pertaining to diet and exercise that are instrumentally conducive to achieving and maintaining good health. But there are no actions that are characteristically expressive of being healthy. By contrast, there are actions that are characteristically expressive of being just, courageous, or compassionate. Hence, the medical analogy is not naturally suited to a philosophy that regards virtue as a necessary feature of living well.

To some extent, the significance of this disanalogy depends on the role assigned to virtue in an account of living well. The Pyrrhonian Sceptics did not assign it any role since they did not defend an account of living well.[55] They simply reported that they had no beliefs, followed the fourfold guide, and experienced tranquillity and moderate feeling. The disanalogy does not speak directly against this stance. The Epicureans believed that the virtues were justified only instrumentally as being conducive to a life free of physical pain and mental turmoil. Hence, the role of the virtues was analogous to the role of proper diet and exercise in promoting physical health. But being free of pain and turmoil is not itself a disposition to do anything. Once again, the disanalogy might not really matter.

However, both Buddhism and Stoicism supposed that there is a single enlightened state that involves both tranquillity and virtue. This suggests that the medical analogy is better suited to one part of their conception of living well than the other part. To a large extent, these traditions applied the medical analogy primarily to tranquillity rather than to virtue. But this was not always the case. For example, as we will see, both Śāntideva and Seneca sometimes suggested that wrongdoing on the part of those we are tempted to be angry with may be understood as an analogous to a physical disease—as a condition to be cured.

In fact, however, we cannot separate issues of tranquillity and virtue on any view. Though emotional turbulence such as anger may be viewed as a kind of psychological disease—a painful and disruptive condition we would like to be free of—in at least many of its forms it raises a normative question—'what is the proper response to the wrongdoing of others?'—to which any tranquillity philosophy implies an answer. Insofar as tranquillity as a condition mostly or entirely free from anger is regarded as necessary for living a good human life, some stance with respect to virtue has already been taken. One of the primary objections to tranquillity philosophies is that anger is a morally required response to serious wrongdoing on the part of others.[56] Both Buddhism and Stoicism directly reject

55 See Sextus Empiricus, *Outlines of Scepticism*, p. 7 (1.16–17).

56 For example, see Nussbaum, *The Therapy of Desire: Theory and Practice in Hellenistic Ethics*, p. 403, and Martha Nussbaum, *Upheavals of*

this: they maintain that the virtuous response to wrongdoing is free of anger. But Pyrrhonian Scepticism and Epicureanism implicitly reject this objection as well, at least insofar as they are committed to an ideal of tranquillity precluding all or most forms of anger. Since the normative question cannot be avoided, any tranquillity philosophy implies a position with respect to it, and regarding psychological well-being as analogous to physical well-being is not a helpful model for reflecting on this question.

This brings us to a final difficulty for the general form of the medical analogy. As noted earlier, all these traditions supposed that the emotional turbulence precluded by tranquillity depends on beliefs that are to be eliminated or replaced as false or unwarranted. To the extent that they gave arguments for belief modification (as all of them did), they may appear to be engaged in a familiar philosophical enterprise. But this enterprise bears little similarity to medical practice in the primary sense. Though beliefs of the patient can sometimes influence the prevention and cure of physical disease, this qualifies the more fundamental fact that most physical disease has a causal structure that, to a large extent, does not include and is not affected by beliefs of the patient—at least on any empirical approach to medicine. In physical medicine, it sometimes helps if patients have confidence in their doctors and have a positive attitude, but it is only doctors, and not patients, who need to go to medical school. In the Buddhist and Hellenistic traditions, for the most part, there is a sense in which we all must go to school because, as Cicero says, 'we should make every possible effort to become capable physicians for ourselves.'[57] In this case, a patient's psychological health requires modification of his or her beliefs, and this directly requires acquisition of the respective form of wisdom—even if it is only what is sometimes interpreted as the Madhyamaka or Pyrrhonian wisdom of no-belief.

What often appears to be assumed in these traditions is that the relevant beliefs are voluntary and responsive to reason—and also that we are responsible for these beliefs and may be praised or blamed for having them. Cicero explicitly endorses this understanding, and it appears to be at least tacitly assumed throughout much of Buddhist and Hellenistic thought. For example, in discussions of anger,

---

Thought: The Intelligence of Emotions, (Cambridge: Cambridge University Press, 2001), p. 394.

[57] Cicero, *Cicero and the Emotions: Tusculan Disputations 3 and 4*, p. 5 (3.6).

persons prone to anger are addressed as if their anger (or disposition to anger) depends on beliefs, and as if they are capable of abandoning or modifying these beliefs in response to what are presented as good reasons for doing so (for example, that anger has all sorts of harmful effects). The vocabulary of responsibility, and of praise and blame, is equally evident. Much of the discussion of anger in Śāntideva, Philodemus and Seneca conforms to this model. Insofar as this is true, there is a significant disanalogy with medicine in the primary sense, since physical disease, on empirical approaches, mostly does not depend on beliefs that are voluntary and responsive to reason.[58]

There is a related disanalogy. Physical health partly depends on good fortune. This is one reason why medical practice cannot guarantee health. But the psychological health promised by these traditions was thought to be mostly or entirely immune to fortune: attaining the proper mindset—wisdom—was thought to be sufficient for attaining tranquillity, which was understood precisely as a peaceful state of mind that is secure in the face of the vicissitudes of fortune. These traditions guaranteed psychological health in that they claimed that each of us, with the aid of instruction, had the capacity to bring about wisdom, and hence tranquillity, for ourselves and that once we had done this nothing could disrupt it.[59]

A common objection to this claim is that, to a large extent or in important respects, emotions such as anger are neither voluntary nor responsive to reason in the ways required by tranquillity philosophies. Hence, there is no prospect that philosophy, with its emphasis on rational argument, could bring about tranquillity as the absence of emotional turbulence. This is one source of Bernard Williams' critique of Hellenistic philosophy as a form of therapy.[60] For various reasons—Darwinian, Freudian, Strawsonian, neurophysiological and others—many people believe that emotions are so deeply and securely rooted in a non-rational or irrational part of us that, for the most part, they cannot be touched by philosophy. Earlier forms of this objection were widely debated in Greek and Roman philosophy, and the Epicureans and Stoics made only limited theoretical

[58] See note 6 above.

[59] There are some tendencies in Mahāyāna Buddhism to put less emphasis on our own capacity for enlightenment and more emphasis on the assistance of bodhisattvas. This does not change the fact that enlightenment brings tranquillity in the face of fortune.

[60] See Bernard Williams, 'Do Not Disturb,' review of Nussbaum, *The Therapy of Desire: Theory and Practice in Hellenistic Ethics, London Review of Books* 16 (October 20, 1994), pp. 25–26.

concessions to it. However, in both the Buddhist and Hellenistic traditions, the widespread employment of psychological or spiritual exercises having at best minimal dependence on philosophical theory is tacit testimony to the limited power of philosophy in this sense. The observation, on the occasion of anger, that 'in the past I have acted just as badly (as the person with whom I am now angry)' may or may not be helpful, but whatever efficacy it possesses owes little to philosophy.[61] One way that philosophy could be therapeutic is simply by borrowing from therapy in a familiar sense, but this would not address the question whether or not something recognizably philosophical, such as the rational analysis of rather abstract topics, could itself be therapeutic or play an essential role in therapy.

If emotions could be modified or eliminated, but not because they depend on beliefs that are voluntary and responsive to reason, then in this respect the medical analogy might be affirmed: in the psychological as well as physical realms, it might be said, whatever is causally efficacious in bringing about the state of health would have a claim to our attention. But this would mean that philosophy in the analogy would be assessed in terms of its causal efficacy in producing psychological health, not (necessarily) in terms of its ability to produce justified true beliefs (or even justified suspension of beliefs) on the basis of reason, the possession of which would ensure psychological health. There are some manifestations of this approach in these traditions. In his discussion of anger, Seneca said we should regard wrongdoers 'with the kindly gaze of a doctor viewing the sick.'[62] As we have seen, Seneca portrayed vice as a disease and punishment as a cure. If we took these suggestions seriously, we might be led to stop regarding wrongdoing as rooted in voluntary beliefs that could be modified by rational reflection and to suppose instead that whatever is causally efficacious in curing the disease of wrongdoing would be appropriate. According to Seneca, 'I must find for each man's illness the proper remedy—one person may be cured by a sense of shame, another by exile, a third by pain, another by poverty, another by the sword.'[63] There is a partial parallel to this in Śāntideva. When persons harm people we care about, he said, we should 'regard it as arising on the basis of conditioning factors and refrain from anger towards them.'[64] In fact,

[61] For example, see Śāntideva, *The Bodhicaryāvatāra*, p. 53 (6.42) and Seneca, 'On Anger,' pp. 65–6 (2.28).
[62] Seneca, 'On Anger,' p. 51 (2.10.7).
[63] Seneca, 'On Anger,' p. 34 (1.16.4).
[64] Śāntideva, *The Bodhicaryāvatāra*, p. 56 (6.65); cf. p. 53 (6.33).

'even if people are extremely malignant, all that is skilful should be done for them.'[65] Since wrongdoing is, like all things, causally conditioned (a standard Buddhist teaching), we should not be angry at wrongdoers but skillfully try to help them overcome wrongdoing. In view of Śāntideva's reliance on medical analogies, this might be taken as implying that whatever is causally efficacious in curing a person of wrongdoing should be undertaken. However, regarding persons who have wronged us as persons with a psychological disease requiring a cure is not the only, nor even the dominant, motif in either of these authors' discussion of anger. For the most part, in addressing persons prone to anger, the assumption is that they can be convinced to change their beliefs and actions through rational reflection.

Of course, rational philosophical argument might be employed, but valued only for being causally efficacious in bringing us to a tranquil mental state. The medical analogies in Sextus suggested this perspective and, in light of the Mahāyāna Buddhist idea of skillful means, Candrakīrti's use of the purgative analogy might be interpreted in this way as well. If skillful means were the fundamental criterion of Buddhist practice, then philosophical argument might sometimes be therapeutic. But this would provide us, not with an understanding of philosophy as therapy, but with an understanding of therapy that leaves room for a form of philosophy as a useful tool for some persons. Pyrrhonian scepticism does not speak of skillful means, but insofar as it takes the end to be tranquillity and moderate feeling, there would seem to be no obstacle to employing whatever is causally efficacious in bringing this about—perhaps philosophy for some and drugs for others.

These approaches might establish greater affinity with medicine in the primary sense, but only by regarding philosophy, not as an essential source of wisdom, but as one therapeutic technique among many others. However, what speaks against this, and what remains one of the primary difficulties with the general form of the medical analogy, is that in all these traditions great emphasis is placed on wisdom—on a proper understanding of the world—as the source of living a good, and hence tranquil, life (perhaps with the exception of the Pyrrhonian Sceptics, for whom the only wisdom could be realizing that we should suspend our beliefs). In whatever way wisdom is understood—and it is understood very differently in these diverse traditions—it does not look much like physical health. Though obviously some understanding of the world can be conducive to

[65] Śāntideva, *The Bodhicaryāvatāra*, p. 61 (6.120).

physical health, such understanding is not a constitutive feature of health any more than proper diet and exercise are. A physically healthy person, as such, has neither dispositions to act nor an outlook on the world.

In sum: though the general form of the medical analogy has obvious attractions for these tranquillity philosophies, it is limited for the reasons rehearsed: their extraordinary conceptions of psychological well-being, the fact that emotions such as anger pose inescapable normative questions about how to live, and the importance in their accounts of beliefs that are voluntary and responsive to reason—or at least of a proper cognitive orientation to the world. However, it is not evident that proponents of these traditions were generally unaware of these differences. For the most part, they probably just employed medical analogies, both in the general form and in more particular forms, for the limited value they realized they had.

Rationality as the Therapy of Self-Liberation in Spinoza's *Ethics*[1]

MICHAEL HAMPE

The Issue: Science and Happiness

A given statement may be plausible, well founded or true. An individual action may be judged courageous, useful or good. Human beings are judged as well, for statements or actions that invite such evaluations, though the terms used may be different: a person may be described as truthful and virtuous, clever and happy. Epistemology and ethics – the theories that justify theoretical and practical judgements – may address not only the criteria used to assess states of belief, assertions, knowledge and the like, actions, omissions and feelings, but also the *people* that give rise to them. Nowadays, the issue of when and how a *human being* becomes clever, truthful, good or happy is less a matter of philosophy and more a question for religion, psychology and pedagogy. This has not always been the case. There has been a perceptible shift in moral philosophy: in antiquity, inquiries as to when a *life* is to be classified as good or happy were prevalent; in the modern era, the focus is primarily on when an *individual action* is to be regarded as right or good, wrong or bad.

It has been argued[2] that the *absence* of an ideal of how human beings *should be* is a problem for modern philosophy, inasmuch as the latter is unable to rely on Aristotelian ideas of a happy life (which, it is claimed, are impossible to justify outside the framework

[1] An earlier version of this chapter appeared in German in A. Beckermann and D. Perler, *Klassiker der Philosophie heute* (Stuttgart: Reclam, 2005), pp. 230–250. Citations from the *Ethica Ordine Geometrico demonstrata* are given as follows: the first Roman numeral indicates the Part, the Arabic numeral the proposition, axiom or definition. Propositions are indicated by 'p', definitions by 'def', appendices to the Parts by 'app', prefaces by 'praef', notes to propositions by 'sch', and lemmata by 'l'. The abbreviation 'defaff' indicates affect definitions in Part III; 'dem' refers to the proof of a proposition.

[2] Alasdair MacIntyre, *After Virtue: A Study in Moral Theory* (London: Duckworth, 1981), p. 58.

doi:10.1017/S1358246109990233

of ancient Greek conventions), or indeed on the religious conceptions of humankind and models of happiness contained within Judaism, Christianity and Islam. Without a concrete idea of human development towards a goal that is deemed morally justified, the argument goes, it is impossible to distinguish between *manipulation* and *education*, between guiding people towards maturity and making arbitrary changes to their personality.

Spinoza is one of the fiercest critics of the teleological view of the world and of humankind. He rejects many of the convictions shared by most of his contemporaries: that nature was designed with a goal in view; that there is a purpose to God's creation; and that there are ideals of humanity that constitute the objectives of a development towards happiness and that are *wished* by nature or God and *imposed* on human beings (IappIVpraef). Yet he nevertheless continued to view philosophy as a kind of *deliverance from unhappiness*. For Spinoza, the rational argumentation that he conducts in his Ethics is part of an approach to life that leads towards happiness and a *doctrine of wisdom*, and is thus a therapeutic enterprise. In this sense the 17th-century thinker positions his philosophical project among its forebears in classical antiquity, such as that of the Stoics; however, he articulates an explicitly therapeutic modern philosophy that is presented as a scientific enterprise or reflection on the scientific method, rather than as a therapy of human life outside the domain of science.

Since this volume is devoted not to Spinoza but to therapeutic philosophy, a brief excursus on the life and work of this unusual modern philosopher may be of use before we go on to consider his philosophical therapy.

Spinoza was born in Amsterdam on 24 November 1632, the third child of Miguel Despinoza, a Portuguese merchant, and his second wife Deborah. The descendant of Jews forcibly converted in Spain and Portugal during the 15th century (known as *marranos*), he spoke Portuguese as his first language. The *marranos* attempted to maintain their faith under difficult conditions, but in so doing frequently alienated themselves from both Judaism and Christianity. This background has led Karl Löwith to assert that Spinoza's philosophy occupies a 'special place' in the thought of the modern era, having completely divorced itself from Jewish and Christian ideas.[3]

[3] Karl Löwith, 'Gott, Mensch und Welt in der Metaphysik von Descartes bis zu Nietzsche' (1967), in his *Sämtliche Schriften 9: Gott, Mensch und Welt – G.B. Vico – Paul Valery* (Stuttgart: Metzler, 1986), pp. 3–194; p. 155. On Spinoza as a *marrano* philosopher see also

Spinoza entered Talmud school in 1639. From 1650 onwards he began to distance himself from Judaism, and attended the Latin school of Jan van den Enden. It has been argued that van den Enden had already identified nature and God, anticipated Spinoza's 'deus sive natura' formula, and espoused political ideas that later emerged in Spinoza's *Theologico-Political Treatise*.[4] In 1656, the Jewish community denounced Spinoza for alleged heresy and excommunicated him. His education under van den Enden awakened in him an interest in Cartesian philosophy and the natural sciences. After an attempt to continue his father's business in collaboration with his brother, he worked as an independent scholar and constructor of telescopes and microscopes. His *Theologico-Political Treatise* was published in 1670 and banned by the Dutch state in 1674. A year before the ban, Spinoza had turned down an invitation from the University of Heidelberg because he was unsure that he would be able to avoid disrupting established religion, which was a condition of accepting the post (*Collected Works*, vol. 6, 206). In 1675 he abandoned an attempt to publish his principal work, *Ethics*. He died on 23 February 1677 of lung disease, probably contracted by inhaling glass dust while grinding the lenses of his optical instruments. His *Opera Posthuma* were published the same year, and banned in 1678. The problems Spinoza experienced with the religion he was born into and his enthusiasm for the then modern sciences are probably the main roots for his kind of rationalistic philosophical therapy, which make him a unique figure in the landscape of modern thought.

Spinoza, it has been said, was a critic of teleology and an advocate of the view that nature is a matrix of laws susceptible of scientific investigation from which human beings cannot exempt themselves, and that 'perfection and imperfection ... are merely modes of thinking' (IVpraef) that come about through conventional comparisons and contingent classifications. Yet *at the same time* he asserted that there is a philosophical path to happiness that can be elucidated through a strict process of argumentation. How could he square these apparently opposing views? How could he simultaneously regard humans as entirely part of a purposeless and deterministically perceived nature and as beings who could achieve happiness or

Yirmiyahn Yovel, *Spinoza and other Heretics: The Marrano of Reason* (Princeton: Princeton University Press, 1989), pp. 15–127.

[4] W. N. A. Klever, 'Spinoza's Life and Works', in Don Garrett (ed.), *The Cambridge Companion to Spinoza* (Cambridge: Cambridge University Press, 1996), pp. 13–60; p. 18.

salvation in the traditional sense by means of philosophical examination – and fail to achieve it without those means? How was he able to formulate his conception of human happiness in the language of religion, describing a person as happy when they understand that they are 'in God', yet regard the Christian idea of a creator with a personal identity transcending nature as a *fiction*? The two relevant statements that need to be reconciled come from the fourth and fifth parts of the *Ethics*. The first reads:

> It is impossible, that Man should not be part of Nature, or that he should be capable of undergoing no changes, save such as can be understood through his nature only as their adequate cause. (IVp4).

The second claims:

> Our mind, in so far as it knows itself and the body under the form of eternity (*sub aeternitatis specie cognoscit*), has to that extent necessarily a knowledge of God, and knows that it is in God, and is conceived through God. (Vp30).

Philosophical Therapy Between Technique and Practice

The minimalist conception of happiness that can be found in both naturalist ideas and those of Spinoza consists in the purely negative absence of *pain* and *suffering*. The mitigation of these discomforts is often viewed as a *technical* problem to be resolved by a form of medicine that is either somatic or directed towards the life of the soul. The analogy between the doctor and the wise man has been widespread since the ancient Greeks and Buddhists, and is also found in religion.[5] Nevertheless, a distinction must be made between technical and practical knowledge, or between a *technical* and *practical* approach to one's own life.

For Aristotle (EN VI,4,1140a), technical knowledge deals with the correct means of achieving a given objective. Practical knowledge is knowledge of ends as such. A technical approach to life will view an existence led without pain and suffering as the means to another end, such as the experience of states of desire. A practical approach to life, meanwhile, will seek to achieve an *existence that is an end in itself*, the realisation of a way of life in which action and experience need not be directed towards anything other than that life.

5 See Christopher Gowans, this volume.

Insofar as the modern era ever correlates knowledge and happiness, it is in the hope of *technical progress* as the result of advances in scientific understanding, leading for instance to the successful eradication of diseases and the formulation of a set of instructions for correct living in the shape of a non-conventional morality (as in Descartes). At the end of the *Ethics*, in a statement setting out the aim of his deliberations, Spinoza criticises the technical approach to life: 'Blessedness (*beatitudo*) is not the reward of virtue (*virtus*), but virtue itself; neither do we rejoice therein, because we control our lusts, but, contrariwise, because we rejoice therein, we are able to control our lusts (*libidines*).' (IVp42)

The word 'lusts' points to a fundamental issue in Spinoza's view of happiness: the *release from dependency*. That which induces lust provokes regret when it is *absent*, because it is *coveted* and yet is no longer available. Although, as we will see later, its presence enhances a being's power to act, as soon as its presence can no longer be taken for granted it leads to *dependence* on the external circumstances which make that presence more likely – a dependence that ultimately causes the affected being to become unhappy. In its absence, that which provokes lust gives rise to *hope* that it will return, and *fear* that it will not. But for Spinoza, fear and hope are feelings that lead to unhappiness because they reduce a being's power to act (IIIp18schII & IIIdefaff12 & 13).

Spinoza's recognition of this relationship, and his appreciation of the price exacted by lust for the temporary and ephemeral, constitute very important practical, indeed therapeutic insights.[6] In consequence, that which induces lust is immediately linked to the regret that may follow it, and thus ceases to appear attractive. Anyone who strives for these lust-inducing objects in the full knowledge that they will result in a sense of loss, longing, hope and fear, is *addicted*: they are in quest of a joy they know will be followed by pain, and will cause them to rue their action. Controlling lust is therefore not a method by which the ascetic is to be rewarded with greater happiness, but rather a manifestation of independence from external causes of lust; in other words, a sign of low 'susceptibility to addiction.' To understand this assertion, we need to examine the concept of *independence* or *freedom* within Spinoza's conception of happiness.

[6] The thought process bears similarities to the teachings of the Stoics; see Martha Nussbaum, *The Therapy of Desire: Theory and Practice in Hellenistic Ethics* (Princeton, NJ: Princeton University Press, 1994), pp. 316–401.

The reality (*realitas*) of every being, human or otherwise, and its real perfection (as opposed to that judged on the basis of arbitrary ideals) resides in the degree of its power for action (*potentia agendi*, IIdef6 & IVdef8). The more a being is active, the more virtuous it is and the less it suffers (Vp40). Acting freely means being oneself the cause of something in the world (cf. Idef7). It follows from this that the *technical* 'removal' of pain or suffering, by which something such as an analgesic or a surgeon acts on me, is a procedure that involves using suffering to relieve suffering: something – a healing substance or a doctor – acts on me in order to prevent something else – a poison or a tumour – from continuing to act on me. In cases such as this, where the solution is technical, it is not *my action* that frees me from suffering, but rather the action of something else on me – something on which I may become just as dependent as I might be on a source of lust that renders me an addict and on which, in the event of serious illness, I am also *de facto* dependent.

Consequently, Spinoza viewed freedom as having nothing to do with indeterminacy or the choice of a will located outside natural necessities. He maintains, with exemplary clarity: 'Therefore those who believe, that they speak or keep silence or act in any way from the free decision of their mind (*libero mentis decreto*), do but dream with their eyes open' (IIIp25). Rather, freedom is independence from circumstances that are temporarily favourable or unfavourable to me (fortuna) such that I may in my actions follow my own nature or law (*sui juris*, IVpraef). Spinoza makes a sharp distinction between the free realisation of one's own nature and the quest for imagined ideals. The development of a human being towards the status of an individual leading a happy life therefore consists *not* in the *transformation* or *perfection* of a person in accordance with a specific ideal but rather in the realisation of the possibilities that are inherent in a being by virtue of its nature, in which realisation, however, it is hindered by external circumstances, including the 'blind' belief that it is obliged to realise a particular pattern of existence. A fundamental condition of freedom is therefore an insight into one's own reality and the abandonment of errors that prevent that insight – in other words, *unprejudiced self-knowledge*.

Imagined Ideals, Shared Concepts, Associations and Conclusions

This process of thought requires the ability to distinguish between imagined ideals and erroneous self-judgements on the one hand,

and the 'true nature' of a being and true self-judgement on the other. How can this be achieved?

Different people experience what in modern parlance are termed different *conditioning histories*. In one culture, belching after a meal may be regarded as a sign of approval of the food consumed; in another, it may be viewed as an impertinence. Differences in upbringing will lead such behaviour to be linked to different affects based on associations of praise and blame. For Spinoza, therefore, writing in the third part of the *Ethics* (IIIp51), the result of such conditioning histories is that 'different men may be differently affected by the same object', and that 'the same man may be differently affected at different times by the same object' (IIIp51, cf. also IIIp15). Most things that we particularly love or hate, covet or fear, are perceived by us affectively in this way because of our conditioning history, which might just as easily have been different. Conditioning histories also give rise to ideals of things that are anchored in our imagination (*imaginatio*) and that, ultimately, constitute our view of what makes for a happy or unhappy life. States of joy and suffering come about primarily because people look for things that correspond to their preconditioned ideals, and avoid and fear things that do not correspond to them or that resemble negative ideals. Because conditioning histories are *contingent*, with praise or blame being attached to different circumstances, the imaginary ideals that result in objects being experienced as pleasant or unpleasant are also contingent.

For Spinoza, however, the human mind (*mens humana*) does not consist solely of fantasy or imagination and arbitrary networks of associations. Rather, it also contains 'common notions' (*notiones communes*) which relate to that which is shared by all human beings, and indeed all bodies (IIl2). The human mind need not remain trapped by associations, such as thinking of a pleasant taste when looking at a cake or of pain when hearing the sound of a dentist's drill. People are *different* because they have different conditioning histories, causing each to see the world in a slightly different way and judge things in their own manner. Yet all people also have something in *common*, sharing notions and conclusions arrived at through reason that are independent of their history (IIp18d).

To put it simply, the practice or therapy outlined by Spinoza consists firstly in deconditioning the human mind in a way that results in a *removal of contingent judgements of things* and ideals – a process that in some ways resembles psychoanalysis and is also to be found in the process of 'de-imaging' ('Entbildung' – the dismantling of established images).[7] In the second phase of Spinoza's philosophical therapy, the mind should *conclude* solely on the basis of *common notions*. Because that which can be understood by means of common notions necessarily relates to the *true nature* of a being, and since rational thought is an activity, those who conclude *solely* with the aid of true common notions can no longer suffer and necessarily realise their true nature.

Indeed, Spinoza himself considers his *Ethics* to be a work that operates solely with true common notions. It is constructed '*more geometrico*,' which is to say that the conclusions reached in it claim to be as strict as in the geometry of Euclid. This rational method, combined with the use of common notions, ensures that readers of the *Ethics* engage in an activity in which their mind cannot suffer. Moreover, because this activity contains instructions for the dismantling of contingent associations, the first and second steps to happiness are here indistinguishable: understanding one's own affective patterns on the basis of common notions is at once part of the process of deconditioning the mind and the realisation of true reason-nature. Rational conclusion is itself the practice adopted by the happy person: understanding the particular on the basis of true common notions.

This all sounds highly rationalistic, and indeed it is: a happy person is a reasonable person, one whose contingent life story has become irrelevant and who, reaching conclusions about the world solely with the aid of common notions, views it from the standpoint of eternity – as Spinoza puts it, '*sub specie aeternitatis*.'

The Practice of Transforming One's Own Mind and Body

Spinoza advocates what is termed a 'dual aspect theory' of the relationship between body and soul. According to this theory, mind and body are not two things related to each other, but rather one and the same thing that can be *described* in two different ways (IIp13). For everything that happens in the body there is an idea in the mind. A person's conditionings are both mental links and physical connections that are more or less transparent to the person

[7] Cf. with reference to knowledge of God: Meister Eckhart, *Deutsche Predigten und Traktate*, edited and translated by J. Quint (Munich: Hanser, 1963), pp. 352 ff.; Meister Eckharts Predigten, edited and translated by J. Quint, *Die deutschen und lateinischen Werke*, Sermons vol. 3 (Stuttgart: Verlag W. Kohlhammer, 1976), pp. 437 ff.

making the association: looking at a chocolate cake causes one's mouth to water. If we accept this psycho-physical parallelism, we can change in one of two ways: when in a bad mood caused by the prospect of an unpleasant situation, we may take a tablet that changes the state of our brain in such a way that the bad mood becomes impossible. This is the *technical* solution, in which we remain passive because we allow the pill to act on us. The other option is to *reflect on why* a situation leads to a bad mood and what association is responsible for it. Armed with this knowledge, we may then attempt to dismantle this association by, for example, repeatedly *thinking* of something pleasant while imagining the anticipated situation. This, then, amounts to 'combating' a negative affect that causes suffering by means of another that is positive.[8] This approach corresponds to the *active* strategy proposed in Spinoza's philosophical therapy. The ideal he pursues is to convert as many of the *contingently associative* relations in the human mind into ones that are *inferential*. Inferential relations are ones that use common notions to move from one idea to the next, without the imagination playing any role. In Spinoza's view, such a conversion is also a conversion of the body: 'Even as thoughts and the ideas of things are arranged and associated in the mind, so are the modifications of body ... arranged and associated in the body ...' (Vp1) The body, then, can be structured in a more or less 'rational' way, and this will determine the degree to which it is active and capable of survival. Spinoza also calls this 'skill' ('aptitude').

Moreover, there is no bodily state we cannot understand if we analyse it in sufficient detail (Vp4). Without employing precise physical or physiological analysis, which is of only limited relevance here (IIp13sch), we are able to modify our mind and body through reflection. Physical change comes about through an 'internal view' of our body when we consider what feelings or affects we have fallen prey to, and why.[9]

In the context of present-day discussions on the relationship between neurology and philosophy, Spinoza's psycho-physical

[8] The process of *reconditioning* is also familiar from psychoanalysis and neural connectionism; cf. in this regard Achim Stephan, 'Psychoanalyse und Konnektionismus', in *Ethik und Sozialwissenschaften* 4 (2001), pp. 543–554.

[9] cf. Michael Hampe, 'Der Körper von innen. Zur Wahrnehmung des Körpers in Spinozas Doppelaspekttheorie der Affekte,' in *Affekte und Ethik. Spinozas Lehre im Kontext*, ed. A. Engstler and R. Schnepf (Hildesheim: Georg Olms Verlag, 2002), pp. 129–148; p. 136.

parallelism and critique of the Cartesian concept of the mind as an independent substance capable of acting on the body have caused him to be seen as a precursor of materialistic naturalism. Even the hope that neuroscience can establish a neurologically-based method of controlling emotional problems has been traced back to Spinoza.[10] Yet this interpretation is based on a misunderstanding. It blurs the distinction between technique and practice, associates Spinoza too closely with the scientistic hopes of Descartes, and underestimates the concept of a philosophical *programme of self-deliverance*. The fact that, according to Spinoza, people change when something acts on their body just as they do when something acts on their mind – that they undergo psycho-physical modifications in both cases, and that all these changes are founded on natural laws – should not blind us to the truth that he favoured one particular form of change over all others: namely, that which is advanced by a *process of self-knowledge undertaken by the being who is changing*. For it is only in this process of acquiring knowledge that the changing being is active. Theoretically there is also the possibility of changing one's mind by changing one's body, e.g. by following some physical practices like learning to play an instrument. These practices are ways of being active as well. But they do not play any role in Spinoza's argument, as far as I see. Perhaps this is due to the unimportance this type of exercise has in the Jewish tradition. It is essential to understand this difference between changing oneself by being active and being changed by passively receiving something or even by suffering, in order to determine to what degree Spinoza's philosophical therapy differs from medical therapy in the modern sense, which is considered a *technique* rather than a *practice*.

In a technical development, humanity's *collective progress of knowledge* is of help to the individual when, for instance, their suffering is relieved by taking a tablet that is the product of pharmacological research. Spinoza, by contrast, favours the liberation from suffering that comes about through the process of increasing knowledge taking place within the suffering person herself. One may question whether he conclusively demonstrated that the process works.[11] There is, however, no doubt that he *believed* he was offering a practicable programme of self-knowledge that liberates from suffering, leads to happiness, and can be achieved independently of collective

[10] cf. Antonio Damasio, *Looking for Spinoza: Joy, Sorrow, and the Feeling Brain* (New York: Harcourt, 2003), passim.

[11] cf. Rüdiger Bittner, 'Spinozas Gedanke, dass Einsicht befreit,' in *Deutsche Zeitschrift für Philosophie* 42 (1994), pp. 963–971.

scientific progress. Spinoza's naturalism is not scientistic. It is not just the collective progress of knowledge in the natural sciences that offers true insight into the workings of nature. For Spinoza, the deterministic view of nature espoused by the modern natural sciences has above all a *negative function*: to free people from the illusions of transcendence that give rise to fear and hope, and help them to accept their own implication *in* and dependence on natural circumstances. Specifically, Spinoza transforms the knowledge of nature that each suffering being must acquire into a self-therapeutic *practice* that does not rely on the help of technology to liberate us from suffering.

Viewed against the backdrop of present-day psychological knowledge, Spinoza appears to have been overly optimistic about the possibility that we may direct our attention to our own feelings and pursue our own paths of association. As psychoanalytical processes in particular have demonstrated, true self-knowledge is impossible to obtain spontaneously. Yet it is perhaps superficial to believe that Spinoza's presentation *suggests* the desired deconditioning can simply happen and is available to all. The last words of the *Ethics* are: 'If the way which I have pointed out as leading [to blessedness or happiness] seems exceedingly hard, it may nevertheless be discovered. Needs must it be hard, since it is so seldom found. How would it be possible, if salvation (*salus*) were ready to our hand ... that it should be by almost all men neglected? But all things excellent are as difficult as they are rare' (Vp42sch).

The steps in this necessarily repeated process of deconditioning that Spinoza describes as the most important are, on the face of it, not difficult to perform: 1. *understanding* one's own affective status (answer to the question 'What am I feeling?'); 2. *detaching* one's attention from the emotionally judged object and directing it instead towards one's own body as the *prime cause* of the affect; 3. *understanding the instability* of the emotion that arises out of association and the stability and activity-enhancing character of those affects that come about by reasoned action; 4. *insight* into the multifarious causes of each affect, or the removal of belief in monocausality; and 5. *insight* into the fact that the plurality of causes can be penetrated by logical thought, and that one does not stand 'helpless' before it (Vp20sch). As our emotions, concepts and ways of reacting to the world are more or less deeply entrenched in our habits, a change by deconditioning these connections will not be a quick one, but one that resembles the continuous cleaning or polishing of one's state, to use a metaphor from the Buddhist literature.[12]

[12] Cf, e.g. *The Sūtra on the Merit of Bathing the Buddha*, trans. by Daniel Boucher in Donald Lopez, *Buddhism in Practice* (Princeton:

Spinoza does not merely develop these steps of change *in abstracto*, but offers a whole series of feelings as specific examples of how they are to be applied: how hatred of a person comes about because I view that person as the free and single cause of a state of suffering that I am experiencing, and how hatred can be removed by considering why I suffer on account of this person, and what makes me susceptible to being affected by them in this way. I can then perceive how unstable this feeling is, given that shortly before I might have felt benevolence or love towards that person. I can move on to consider the many causes that have led me to my harmful action towards that person, and to my own vulnerability. Finally, I should experience joy at this process of knowledge – a joy that replaces the hatred.

In Spinoza's eyes, an affect such as hatred is founded on inadequate knowledge; it is connected to untrue opinions about the object of that hatred. The person who hates views the object of their hatred as the free and sole cause of their suffering. Yet because this judgement fails to recognise that person's own causal implication as the hater, the internal causal complexity of their body, and the causal implication of the hated object in the matrix of nature, it is a *false* opinion.

The endeavour to understand the feeling of hatred and the conditions that lead to its creation and persistence immediately puts this false opinion in context. It has been asked whether, even if affects such as hatred that cause suffering are based on false opinions, a true knowledge of them is really possible.[13] Yet there is no reason why erroneous states of mind cannot be analysed through knowledge. Of course, this process involves a *change of emphasis*. In its efforts to recognise false belief as such, the mind shifts its focus from the object that is falsely understood towards the false understanding of that object. In his cognitive removal of emotions that cause suffering, Spinoza himself refrained from this change of emphasis. Those who try to understand hatred can no longer hate, because their mind is attempting to understand their own body and its causal complexity as well as the causal circumstances of the hated being. In the

---

Princeton University Press, 1995), pp. 59–68. Boucher's source for the translation is *Taisho shinshu daizokyo* (Tokyo, 1924–1934), 698, vol 16, pp. 799c–800c. He explains that the sūtra is 'a short text—a little over a page in the standard Chinese Buddhist canon—that was translated into Chinese, presumably from Sanskrit, by the famous monk and pilgrim Yijing (635–713 CE).'

[13] Thomas J. Cook, 'Affektive Erkenntnis und Erkenntnis der Affekte. Ein Problem der spinozistischen Ethik,' in *Affekte und Ethik*, ed. A. Engstler and R. Schnepf, pp. 164–181; p. 165.

process, the mind becomes active and ceases to suffer; and indeed, it is precisely this that constitutes the therapy of rationality.

For Spinoza, there is nothing transcendent and perfect beyond the endlessly complicated natural causal links. What transcends us, and what (to use Schleiermacher's formulation for religious feeling) we are *per se* dependent on, is nature in its endless complexity, and it is for this reason that Spinoza refers to it as God. Consequently, true knowledge of the causal complexity of nature is knowledge of God: 'The more we understand particular things, the more do we understand God' (Vp24).

For example, someone who tries to understand a particular feeling of hatred and perceives the causal complexity of the conditions that give rise to this state of suffering is in fact engaged in understanding God. Because human beings are part of nature and have something in common with all that is natural, they may make any aspect of nature the starting point of this knowledge – including the affects that cause suffering. And because such knowledge of nature is equivalent to knowledge of God and involves an endlessly advancing process of rational thought – i.e. endless mental activity – it is what Spinoza calls *happiness*. Self-knowledge, knowledge of God, and an inherently sensible knowledge of nature are here combined into a therapeutic practice that is a condition of happiness. Accordingly, there is a consistency between the propositions (IVp4 and Vp30) quoted at the end of the second section.

General Theories and Individual Life

The precondition for this rational therapy of our emotional dependence is the existence of concepts that are not dependent on arbitrary conditioning histories, and rational processes of conclusion that enable us to understand that 'true nature' of ourselves that can be grasped by those concepts. While not an anthropological ideal, this is *anthropological essentialism* of a kind that we no longer automatically take for granted.

Most people will instead tend to identify themselves with an arbitrary history that conditions their life and their view of things: it is that which distinguishes them from everyone else. Of course, it is indisputable that there must be something people have in common if they recognise each other as people. Knowledge undoubtedly has something to do with common notions. The problem of true self-knowledge as presented in Spinoza nevertheless appears to point to a *removal of all* arbitrary elements that make up a human being.

As long as a process of self-knowledge operates with common notions and yet remains tied to what has been termed the 'contingent conditioning history' of an individual, it undoubtedly remains the reflective process of an individual. For Spinoza, however, something more is at stake: the *removal* of conditioning, and of the judgements of things that arise from it. For Spinoza, therefore, the removal of conditioning also implies the removal of *contingency*. And yet, does this not mean that the ultimate goal of self-knowledge is the dismantling of the individual world-view that has arisen contingently? Does not the 'sub specie aeternitatis' perspective imply the abandonment of each person's individual understanding of the world, meaning that Spinoza's concept of happiness involves the abandonment of individuality? There is something in this interpretation. Indeed, it highlights the problematic relationship between science and happiness: science attempts to obtain findings that have *general* validity, while happiness is a matter of *individual* life. Can generally valid knowledge by itself ever promote individual happiness? Can there be a scientific therapy for human unhappiness? Does this not also require a more precise understanding of the individual – one that cannot be obtained through the generalities of science (concepts and nomological premises)? This question also ties in with the difficult issue of what precisely is the reality – if any – that Spinoza ascribes to the suffering individual, and whether such an individual, in need of therapy, is more than arbitrariness and error.

Because Spinoza conceived his *Ethics* as a way of leaving behind suffering and moving towards happiness, he must have acknowledged the suffering of individuals as genuine. Critics (such as Bayle and later Hegel,[14]) who deny that he acknowledged the reality of the individual are mistaken.[15] Because of its psycho-physical parallelism, every state of mind – including error – has a physical counterpart. The difficult question is whether individuality can be *more* than suffering, error, and the physical body's lack of skill or capacity for survival. Possibly not. Perhaps, for Spinoza, the abolition of contingent individuality is the price of happiness and the aim of therapy. In this sense his teaching may exhibit certain parallels with Buddhism.[16]

From a methodological perspective, the problem of self-knowledge in Spinoza is the same as that which has been posed since the 19th

[14] Cf. Löwith, 'Gott, Mensch und Welt in der Metaphysik von Descartes bis zu Nietzsche,' p. 180.

[15] Cf. Wolfgang Bartuschat, *Baruch de Spinoza* (Munich: C. H. Beck, 1996), p. 76.

[16] Cf. David Burton, this volume.

century: a contrast between disciplines that explain by reference to general laws (nomothetic) and those that describe individual lives (idiographic). Knowledge based on common notions that are not calibrated invariably remains knowledge of the general rather than the individual. One pear differs from another in that, although it *also* has a weight, it is a *different* one, that can be expressed in calibrated concepts using such figures as *so and so many* kilograms. To say anything more about the difference between the pears, we must record the story of their genesis. In turn, in order to do this we need more than common notions: we must identify places and points in time by *names*. Spinoza's conception of self-knowledge contains neither calibrated common notions – numbers – nor nameable times and places. It remains at the level of a relatively concrete doctrine of affects – but one that deals with affects that we can *all* have against the backdrop of a general theory. Spinoza *understands* these difficulties inasmuch as he differentiates *de facto* between as many affects as there are individuals (IIIp57), but he does not resolve them theoretically. This dilemma – that of describing the individual person using common notions, indeed desiring to *help* that person therapeutically by means of a general theory – places Spinoza's concept in the same boat as all the psychoanalytic and psychotherapeutic methodologies that identify individual life stories using the resources of a general conceptual scheme with a view to improving them, but without taking into account the significance of narratives of individual life stories. The fraught relationship between science and wisdom that clearly emerges here – one that is characteristic of modern thought, and perhaps of the entirety of modern culture – appears also to be a constituent part of Spinoza's conception of philosophy. Indeed, this tension remains unresolved to this day. Spinoza was possibly the last modern philosopher to tolerate it within his work, before it was subsumed in a kind of 'division of labour' between religion, psychotherapies, literature and science.

English translation by Rafael Newman, Zurich

Two Pedagogies for Happiness: Healing Goals and Healing Methods in the *Summa Theologiae* of Thomas Aquinas and The *Śrī Bhāṣya* of Rāmānuja

MARTIN GANERI

Introduction

The scholastic mode of intellectual enquiry has been looked down upon in Western philosophical circles over the last few centuries, not least because of the central role of authorities shaping the reasoning that takes place and because of the fine distinctions and disputational mode of discourse it employs. The scholastic approach is, however, a prime example of philosophy as *therapeia*, of intellectual inquiry and reflection concerned with the healing transformation of human life, with what kind of knowledge and behaviour brings about human happiness. The scholastic approach is motivated and determined by consideration of what the final human goal might be and what are the means to achieve it. Authorities are important because they tell us about the goal and means. Distinctions and disputation are important because they help us learn in a way that transforms our minds and actions.

'Scholasticism' as a term has its origins of course in the medieval Latin West. Nonetheless it has come to be recognised as a useful analytical category to describe a type of intellectual enquiry found in a number of different religious traditions. An example of this is the collection of studies brought together by José Ignacio Cabezón.[1] For his part Cabezón uses the term in the context of his own study of Indo-Tibetan Buddhism. And it is from this he draws out a set of eight characteristics for the scholastic approach in

[1] José Ignacio Cabezón, *Scholasticism: Cross-cultural and Comparative Perspectives*, (Albany, New York: State University of New York Press, 1998).

doi:10.1017/S1358246109990245

general.[2] Of these the sixth characteristic is especially relevant for a consideration of scholasticism as *therapeia*: a commitment to systematicity, which is the attempt at recapitulating in the written word the basic orderliness found in the world. As Cabezón explains:

> Scholastics strive to reproduce in their writings the basic orderliness they believe to be found in the world. Their philosophical literature often evinces a complex structure that divides and subdivides the subject matter under discussion to insure: *a.* a logical flow to the 'narrative,' seen as essential to pedagogy, *b.* consistency between former and latter points, and *c.* completeness (that nothing has been omitted).[3]

What follows is an example of such cross-cultural study of scholasticism, one which will consider the *Summa Theologiae* of the great medieval Christian and Dominican thinker Thomas Aquinas (1224/25-74 C.E.) and the *Śrī Bhāṣya* of an equally great medieval Hindu and Vedāntic thinker, Rāmānuja (c. 1017-1137 C.E.). Both Aquinas and Rāmānuja identify the final goal of human life as being the knowledge or vision of the first cause, God for Aquinas and *Brahman* for Rāmānuja. This knowledge brings with it happiness, or more precisely, beatitude (*beatitudo*) in the case of Aquinas, and bliss (*ānanda*) in the case of Rāmānuja.

Both the *Summa* and the *Bhāṣya* might also be called 'pedagogies' for this happiness. To call them 'pedagogies' is to suggest they should be approached in a different manner to the way they have often been treated. Both *Summa* and *Bhāṣya* have often been seen simply as resources for constructing an account of what is called 'the philosophy of Aquinas' or 'the philosophy of Rāmānuja,'

[2] At the end of the book, he summarises these as follows: '(1) a strong sense of tradition, (2) a concern with language (with scripture, and with language generally as a medium of expression), (3) proliferativity, by which I mean the tendency to include rather than exclude (texts, categories, lists, etc.), (4) completeness (the tendency of the tradition to conceive of itself as overlooking nothing that is religiously essential), (5) the belief that the universe is epistemologically accessible, (6) a commitment to systematicity, which is the attempt at recapitulating in the written word the basic orderliness found in the world, (7) rationalism, a commitment to reasoned argument and the avoidance of contradiction, (8) self-reflexivity, the tendency to objectify and then subject to critical scrutiny first-order practices such as exegesis and argumentation, yielding second-order forms of discourse such as hermeneutics and logic, respectively' (p. 237).

[3] Cabezón, *Scholasticism: Cross-cultural and Comparative Perspectives*, p. 6.

rather than as texts that have to be read through as they stand. In recent years there has, however, been a greater interest in exploring the pedagogical function of both Western and Vedāntic scholastic texts.[4] Speaking about the *Summa*, Mark Jordan states that, 'To enter a pedagogy is to lend one's lived time to the retelling of the text's narrative, to the re-enactment of its teaching.'[5] Both *Summa* and *Bhāṣya* invite us to lend our 'lived time to the retelling of the text's narrative, to the re-enactment of its teaching.' In each case the text leads the reader step-by step in a process of learning that transforms him or her.

Aquinas and the Summa Theologiae: The Healing Work of Teaching

That Aquinas' type of scholasticism might be therapeutic in character is suggested by Vivian Boland, who calls it 'the healing work of teaching.'[6] He refers here to the phrase often used to describe Aquinas' teaching, *sana doctrina*, which is routinely translated as 'sound teaching,' but which, he suggests, would be better translated as 'healthy teaching.' That Aquinas does conceive of teaching as about human health is manifest in his discussion of human teaching in general and the particular work of the *Summa*. As Boland points out, Aquinas himself makes use of the medical analogy for teaching:

> The analogy with the medical doctor is Aquinas' favourite way of explaining what is involved in teaching. One can imagine Socrates nodding in approval, and one might also think of Wittgensteinian understandings of philosophy as therapeutic. A human being may properly be said to teach another, Aquinas says, and even to be his master, *magister*, in the same way as a

[4] Two recent studies, to which this chapter will make frequent reference, are: on Aquinas by Mark Jordan, *Rewritten Theology: Aquinas after His Readers* (Oxford: Blackwell Publishing, 2007), and on the Vedānta by Francis Clooney, *Theology After Vedānta* (Albany, New York: State University of New York Press, 1993).

[5] Mark Jordan, *Rewritten Theology*, p. 31.

[6] Vivian Boland O. P., 'The Healing Work of Teaching: Thomas Aquinas and Education,' in Gabrielle Kelly O. P. and Kevin Saunders O. P. eds *Towards the Intelligent Use of Liberty: Dominican Approaches in Education* (Adelaide: ATF Press, 2007), pp. 32–41.

> doctor may be said to heal a sick person, by assisting natural processes.[7]

For Aquinas this analogy serves to make clear the proper relationship between teacher and learner. In the healing art the primary agent is the sick person himself or herself. It is his or her natural capacity to become well and to be healthy that medicine is meant to help and foster. In like manner, in the work of teaching it is the learner who is the primary *agent*, and it is his or her capacity for learning that teaching is meant to nurture and bring to fruition.[8]

In the *Summa*, Aquinas places his discussion of human teaching in the wider context of God's government of the created world. Teaching thus becomes a way in which human beings share in the divine government, through bringing others to a greater understanding of God and his created world, including the place of human beings within it. By extension, human teaching is a sharing in the healing work of Jesus of Nazareth, regarded by Aquinas as the most excellent of teachers, bringing freedom and life through his teaching as well as curing the sick of their bodily ailments.[9]

Aquinas starts the *Summa Theologiae* as a whole with a discussion of a particular sort of teaching: sacred teaching (*sacra doctrina*) and its necessity for human beings, its nature and extent.[10] Aquinas argues that sacred teaching is necessary *ad humanam salutem*.[11] Again the standard translation of this phrase as 'human salvation' misses the therapeutic character of such teaching and the richness of what Aquinas intends by *salus* is better expressed by 'human health,' in the widest sense of human flourishing.[12]

Sacred teaching is necessary for human health, Aquinas argues, because human health comes through the knowledge of God, which

[7] Vivian Boland O. P., *St. Thomas Aquinas* (London: Continuum, 2007), p. 48.

[8] For instance *Summa Theologiae* 1.117, 1.

[9] On Aquinas on Christ's teaching: ST 3.42, 1–4. For an extended discussion of Christ as the most excellent of teachers see Boland, *St. Thomas Aquinas*, pp. 97–103.

[10] ST 1.1

[11] ST 1.1.1

[12] As Victor White O. P. puts it: '"Salus" is not just "salvation" in the sense of pie-in-the-sky: it must be given its full significance of "health," "weal", "well-being," "total integration";' *Holy Teaching: The Idea of Theology According to St Thomas Aquinas* (London: Blackfriars Publications, 1958), p. 10.

constitutes final happiness for human beings.[13] And, in the first place, sacred teaching means the revealed knowledge of God that exceeds the natural capacity of the human intellect to learn unaided and which is necessary for us if we are to make any progress towards God. In a wider sense sacred teaching is intellectual reflection on this revealed knowledge, such as that is found in the *Summa* itself. Revelation teaches us about the goal of human life and the means to it, while intellectual reflection clarifies its meaning and works out how human thoughts and actions are to be directed in conformity with it.

Sacred teaching in whatever form is, then, a healing work directed to a healing end, human happiness. In the case of sacred teaching, the work of medicine and the work of teaching are no longer analogues but a single unified reality, since God is the ultimate source of both human healing and human teaching.[14]

Aquinas and the Summa Theologiae: The Summa as a Pedagogy of Happiness

That the *Summa* is intended to be a pedagogy is indicated at the very beginning of the work. Aquinas states that the *Summa* is intended 'to instruct beginners' (*incipientes erudire*). Moreover, it is a new type of account, meant to overcome shortcomings in the teaching methods of existing works:

> For we have considered that newcomers to this teaching are very much hindered by those things that are written by various people, partly indeed on account of the multiplication of useless questions, articles and arguments, partly also because those things which they must know are not handed over according to the order of instruction, but according as the commentary on books requires or according as the occasion of disputation allows, partly indeed because the frequent repetition of the same things causes boredom and confusion in the minds of hearers. To avoid these and other such things, we will try, trusting in divine help, to pursue those things that relate to sacred teaching as concisely and clearly as the matter allows.[15]

The *Summa*, then, is intended to 'hand over what belongs to Christian religion in that manner which befits the instruction of

13 ST 1.12,1
14 ST 1.117, 1 ad 1.
15 ST Prologue.

beginners,' suited to their capacities and one that will lead them step-by-step to knowledge.

The basic building blocks of this ordered account are the series of micro-debates, the articles, that form the *Summa* from beginning to end. Each of these micro-debates replicates textually the oral disputations held in the medieval schools, the houses of study and learning. Each one focuses on a particular topic, considers one set of views (the objections), then a counter view, then sets forth the considered opinion of the teacher, and finally answers the earlier views put forward in the light of this opinion. As they carry the teaching forward the micro-debates of the articles are grouped together into the larger units of the questions and then again into the larger topics and sections that go to make up the *Summa* as a whole.

And the smaller and greater units refer the learner back and point him or her forward as the discussion carries on. The introductions to the larger units map out the learning territory, indicate the steps by which the discussion will proceed and locate it within the wider context of the text. In other words, they reproduce the system that Cabezón depicts as one of the characteristics of scholasticism, the 'basic orderliness they believe to be found in the world' through 'a logical flow to the 'narrative,' seen as essential to pedagogy.'[16] The chief aim of sacred teaching, Aquinas says, is to hand over 'knowledge of God, and not only as he is in himself, but also as he is the beginning of things and their end, especially of the rational creature,' and so the *Summa* has three major parts dealing, he says, 'first, of God; secondly, of the movement of the rational creature to God; thirdly, of Christ, who as man is our way of getting to God' (Intro to 1.2). And the ordered account of the *Summa* is meant to be worked through as it stands, in the order of its presentation and in its entirely.

At the same time, the heart of the *Summa* is really the massive second part, which deals with the moral life. One influential view of the historical context in which Aquinas chose to compose the *Summa* put forward by Leonard Boyle is that the *Summa* was the product of Aquinas' own concerns as a teacher, responsible for setting up a new house of studies in the Dominican priory of Santa Sabina in Rome.[17] The *Summa* was composed as a teaching manual to train Dominican students for their pastoral commission to teach the Christian faith and hear confessions. They were 'the beginners' Aquinas is thinking

[16] Cabezón, *Scholasticism: Cross-cultural and Comparative Perspectives*, p. 6.

[17] Leonard Boyle O. P., *The Setting of the Summa Theologiae of Saint Thomas* (Pontifical Institute of Medieval Studies: Toronto: 1982).

about in the prologue. And following Boyle's suggestion, Mark Jordan argues that the *Summa* should be understood as addressing the need to set the moral life within the wider context of the Christian faith: the doctrines of God, Trinity, creation and Incarnation.[18] The new account of the *Summa* is intended, he argues, 'to incorporate moral and pastoral topics within the pattern of the great Christian creeds.'[19] For Jordan the *Summa* is thus a pedagogy in the moral life:

> [The *Summa*] is the pattern for an ideal pedagogy, a pedagogy for middle learners in a vowed community of Christian pastors. When enriched by adaptation to a particular classroom, the pedagogy teaches the place of moral theology within theology in the only way anyone can (on Thomas' account of teaching). Learners are invited to study morals though a clarifying reminder of arguments about God as creator and governor; they are habituated into moral knowledge not only through practice with its disputative elements, but through dialectical narration of patterns for lived virtues and ways of life; and they are then shown, in the great disclosure at the turn from the second part to the third, that the power moving their inquiry back to God has been the power of their incarnate Lord.

The teaching is to be a single, continuous solicitation to acquire and exercise the habit of theology in all its parts.[20]

It is here that the focus on happiness becomes evident. At the very beginning of the second part, Aquinas comes back to consider the final goal of human life as the end to which the whole of the moral life has to be directed and this turns into an extended discussion of human happiness as that goal, which then extends into the whole discussion of human actions and the virtues. Mark Jordan sees the location of this discussion as itself a deliberate act of pedagogy:

> Within *Summa* 1-2...the reader begins with the end, with the goal towards which human life tends...The entire structural unit moves forward in response to the pull of the highest human end. Its sequence of articles is dictated as a series of steps approaching the end, beginning with the primary possibility of choice and ending with the uniquely efficacious gift of grace (1-2.6).[21]

[18] Mark Jordan, *Rewritten Theology*, especially Chapter 6, 'The *Summa of Theology* as Moral Formation.'
[19] Jordan, *Rewritten Theology*, p. 7.
[20] Jordan, *Rewritten Theology*, p. 120.
[21] Jordan, *Rewritten Theology*, p.139.

Human happiness is, then, the starting point for the whole discussion of the moral life, which is itself the central focus of the *Summa*'s teaching. As Fergus Kerr argues, human happiness or beatitude can be seen as the key to understanding both Aquinas' account of ethics and the *Summa* as a whole, the connection that links together the doctrine of God, theological ethics and the Christology.[22] As he puts it:

> The exposition of virtue ethics is, thus, focused on the divine beatitude which is shared by the blessed but already able to be anticipated in the moral life here and now. Ethics, for Thomas, is not so much founded on reason, or law, as motivated by anticipated happiness.[23]

As a pedagogy structured around the search for human happiness, the *Summa* begins with the question of sacred teaching's necessity for the human health that is happiness. In the first part it commences its section on the unity of God with an affirmation that the knowledge of God is necessary for human happiness (ST 1.12) and it ends the account of the unity of God with a discussion of the happiness of God himself (ST 1.26). It starts the second part on the moral life with a discussion of happiness as the final goal of human life, the end that orders the whole of moral theology (ST 1-2. 1-5). And it starts the third part on the Incarnation of Christ with the statement that Christ is the 'one who shows' human beings through his humanity the way to 'attain the happiness of eternal life' (ST 3, Prologue), a happiness that Christ enjoys himself (ST 3.10).[24]

Rāmānuja and the *Śrī Bhāṣya*: The Healing Tonic of Vedāntic Teaching

Within the different schools of the Indian tradition of the Vedānta the principal work through which teaching is conveyed is the *Brahma Sūtra Bhāṣya*. A Vedāntic *bhāṣya* is a commentary on the *Brahma Sūtras*, the aphoristic text that is held to give the foundational teaching of the Vedāntic tradition, centred on the revelation contained in the Upaniṣads, which are taken by Vedānta to reveal knowledge of *Brahman*, the ground of being, knowledge of the true nature of the finite self (*ātman*) and of the relationship between them. The

[22] Fergus Kerr O.P., *After Aquinas: Versions of Thomism* (Oxford: Blackwell, 2002), pp. 114–133.
[23] Kerr, *After Aquinas*, p. 130.
[24] Kerr, *After Aquinas*, p. 131.

realisation of this knowledge brings with it release (*mokṣa*) from the cycle or rebirth (*saṃsāra*). A *bhāṣya* constructs a systematic account out of the various statements found in the Upaniṣads as being the correct interpretation of the terse *sūtras*, which stand in need of further explanation. A *bhāṣya* thus offers a counterpart to the ordered account of the *Summa*. Of the different schools of Vedānta the one best known in the West remains that of Advaita (Non-dualism) and the *Bhāṣya* of Śaṅkara (788-820 CE); but equally important is the *Śrī Bhāṣya* of Rāmānuja, whose own system came to be known as Viśiṣṭādvaita (Non-dualism of the differentiated).

As with the *Summa*, so the Vedāntic *bhāṣya* has often been treated as a mine from which ideas might be extracted, without concern for the particular way the *bhāṣya* presents its teaching. A corrective to this in recent Western scholarship has come with renewed emphasis on the Vedānta as *Uttara Mīmāṃsā*, the Later Exegesis (its traditional name in the Indian tradition) and a recognition that, as the Later Exegesis, Vedānta is centred on proper exegesis of the Upaniṣads and on the practice of correct meditation on these texts. Its primarily concern is with the formation of Vedāntic learners, so that they can actually pursue knowledge of *Brahman* as the final goal of human life.[25]

For Rāmānuja the *Sūtras* gives what we might call a healing tonic for the self, languishing in *saṃsāra*. In his introduction to the *Śrī Bhāṣya* and subsequent commentary on the first four *Sūtras* (1.1.1-4) Rāmānuja develops his own account of what the sacred teaching of the Vedānta is for and how it brings this about, its necessity and scope:

> The nectar of the words of Parāsara's son, which was collected up from the middle of the milk-ocean of the Upaniṣads, which restores to life the self whose strength of life has departed because of the blazing fire of *saṃsāra*, which was well guarded by earlier teachers, [but] put out of reach through many contradictory opinions, which is made accessible by my own words, may those who well-minded earth-dwellers drink it in daily.[26]

[25] An important example of this approach is to be found in the work of Francis Clooney, such as *Theology After Vedānta* (Albany, New York: State University of New York Press, 1993); see also his 'Binding the text: Vedānta as Philosophy and Commentary' in *Texts in Context: Traditional Hermeneutics in South Asia* (Albany, New York: State University of New York Press, 1992), pp. 47-68.

[26] Ś.Bh.1.1.1, translated from *Śrī Bhāṣyam Bhagavad-Rāmānuja-viracitam Śārīrakamīmāṃsābhāṣyam*, the critical edition (The Academy of Sanskrit Research, Melkoṭe) Vol. 1 (1985), pp. 1-2.

It is the nectar-like teaching of the Upaniṣads which 'restores to life the self whose strength of life has departed because of the blazing fire of *saṃsāra*' that the *Bhāṣya* explains and communicates.

And as the first *Sūtra* indicates, the Later Exegesis that comprises both the *Sūtras* and *Bhāṣya* is concerned with satisfying the *brahmajijñāsā*, the 'desire to know *Brahman*,' a desire that arises when it is realised that the knowledge taught in the Upaniṣads alone can bring release from the 'blazing fire of *saṃsāra*.' Moreover, as Rāmānuja goes on to argue, the sacred teaching of the Upaniṣads, interpreted by the Later Exegesis, is necessary for this since the knowledge of *Brahman* is beyond the reach of other instruments of human knowledge.[27]

The *Sūtras* guide us in the right exegesis of the Upaniṣads and they make *Brahman* known. But they also guide us in terms of how to practice meditation. For Rāmanuja, meditation (*dhyāna or upāsana*) is said to be a kind of *bhakti* (devotion). It has the form of 'steady remembrance' (*druvānusmṛti*), which comes to have the same form as vision of *Brahman*, thus moving the Vedāntic learner on to the final goal of unrestricted vision of *Brahman* in the released state:

> Meditation has the form of continuous remembrance unbroken like a stream of oil, because of the revelation that steady remembrance is the means of final release [in the passage], 'The remembrance is steady; in the attainment of remembrance there is freedom from all knots (Ch.U. 7.26.2). And that remembrance has the same form as seeing.[28]

In itself the *Bhāṣya* and the learning it offers are intended for those who are qualified by birth and ritual status to study the Vedas, those who belong to the three higher castes. Later Śrī Vaiṣṇava tradition calls this path *bhakti-yoga* (discipline of devotion), distinguishing it from the easier alternative path of *prapatti* (surrender) open to all.[29] Those who undertake *bhakti-yoga* are committed to a rigorous and life-long programme of devotional meditation along with the performance of ritual and other actions proper to their status and the practice of yogic discipline conducive to the arising of the knowledge sought. The 'steady remembrance' of *Brahman* is something that comes about only gradually within the individual practitioner.[30]

[27] Ś.Bh. 1.1.3.

[28] Ś.Bh.1.1.1 (Melkoṭe) vol. 1, p. 17.

[29] S. M. Srinivasa Chari, *Vaiṣṇaivism: its Philosophy, Theology and Religious Discipline* (Delhi: Motilal Banarsidass, 1994), pp. 99–120.

[30] Ś. Bh. 1.1.1 (Melkoṭe) vol.1, pp. 20-24; for an account of this see Robert Lester, *Rāmānuja on the Yoga* (Madras: Adyar Library, 1976).

For his part Rāmānuja does not use the medical analogy as such either to analyse the human condition or to explain what is involved in teaching and learning. However, the medical analogy as Aquinas uses it, and indeed his understanding of the healing work of sacred teaching, could appropriately be extended to Rāmānuja's understanding of Vedāntic teaching. For Rāmānuja the Vedāntic teaching is also a healing means to a healing goal, a healing tonic for the self languishing in the bondage of *saṃsāra*. Moreover, the teaching is there to enable the learner to go through a process of learning for himself. The primary focus and the primary agent in the learning process is the one who 'desires knowledge of *Brahman*.'

Rāmānuja and the Śrī Bhāṣya: Bhāṣya as a Pedagogy for Happiness

It is precisely as Later Exegesis that the pedagogical character of a Vedāntic *bhāṣya* can be seen. Francis Clooney describes Vedānta as constructing a 'Text' from the Upaniṣads, the *Sūtra* and *bhāṣyas*. The Vedāntic learner is one who has to learn how to read this Text properly. As he comments on Advaita Vedānta:

> I wish to emphasise that the Text, composed entirely of adhikaraṇas [sections] is *the* privileged vehicle of our entrance into the realm of Advaita, and thereafter into the acquisition of its fruit: refined, discriminate knowledge of *Brahman*. One goes through the Text, one is changed by it; one cannot go outside it, or around it.[31]

To understand Advaita properly is to hear it, listen to it, submit to it, engage in it, practice it – that is, to 'read' it properly, to become its approved 'reader.'[32]

The pedagogical character of any Vedāntic *bhāṣya* becomes clear when we consider the way the *Bhāṣya* groups the sūtras together and gives shape to the *Sūtra* text as a whole. As in the *Summa*, the *Bhāṣya* is constructed as a series of micro-debates which themselves reflect textually the kind of oral instruction carried out in the Vedāntic schools. The *Bhāṣya* takes one or a number of *sūtras* to form the framework around which this micro-debate is formed (*adhikaraṇa*), with a subject of discussion, an initial doubt about the answer, then a first view, then replies and counter views, before a

31 *Theology After Vedānta*, p. 55.
32 *Theology After Vedānta*, p. 37.

final conclusion resolving is made. The *adhikaraṇas* are then grouped into larger units and the *sūtras* as a whole are divided up into four major sections (*adhyāya*): the first showing that the Upaniṣads teach *Brahman* and what they teach about *Brahman*, the second refuting the objections made by other traditions of thought and refuting those traditions themselves, the third dealing with meditation as the means to release and the forth setting out the released state itself.

As he organises the *sūtras* into these greater units, Rāmānuja makes the pedagogy explicit. At each major break he indicates what the *sūtras* are doing, summarising what has been learned so far and what is now about to be taught. The one who 'desires to know *Brahman*' is meant to work through the *Bhāṣya* in the order it is written, follow it through step-by-step, to be informed and transformed by it so as to engage in meditation properly and fruitfully. He is to follow the discussion of each *adhikaraṇa* as it is given, see how they refer forward or back to other *sūtras*, see how they are linked together one after the other, see how they are grouped together into the larger units.

The Vedāntic learner, like the student of the *Summa*, is called to give his 'lived time to the retelling of the narrative.' To know *Brahman* through Vedānta requires that the *Bhāṣya* itself is read through and worked through, as it employs various different strategies to link the *sūtras* and the *adhikaraṇas* together. Clooney characterises Vedāntic reading as a practical and performative activity, meaning a process of working through the text that requires the reader to engage with and be transformed by the text.[33]

Moreover, just as the *Summa*'s central focus within its own pedagogy is on the practical, in the form of the moral life, so at the centre of the *Sūtra* text and hence of the *Bhāṣya* is the third major section dealing with the practicalities of meditation.[34] Already at the beginning of the *Bhāṣya* Rāmānuja has stated that meditation is the means to get knowledge of *Brahman* and indicated what form it takes. In his introduction to the third major section he first looks back over the last two major sections, saying that their main purpose was to establish that the Upaniṣads do teach that *Brahman* is the object of mediation. He looks forward to the third section as teaching the nature of meditation which the means to obtain *Brahman*:

[33] Clooney, *Theology After Vedānta*, 'Binding the text', 'Scholasticisms in Encounter'; e.g. *Theology After Vedānta*, pp. 34-35.
[34] Clooney *Theology After Vedānta*, p. 64.

> By means of the previous two *adhyāyas* it is established that the Vedānta texts teach *Brahman* as the sole cause of all the world, the one from whom even the suggestion of any fault is excluded, the unbounded ocean of noble qualities, since it has to be meditated on by those who wish liberation.....now by means of the latter [two *adhyāyas*] the intention is to consider what obtaining *Brahman* is like (*prāpti prakāra*) with the means of obtaining *Brahman*. This being the case, in the third *adhyāya* [there will be a] consideration of meditation which is the means.[35]

And then at the beginning of the fourth major section he states that its theme is the fruits of the meditation that has been taught. The practical business of meditation, then, is at the heart of the pedagogy of his *Bhāṣya*.

One distinctive feature and strategy of Rāmānuja's *Śrī Bhāṣya* is his exploitation of the very fabric of the pedagogy itself in order to vindicate his teaching about *Brahman* and *Brahman*'s relationship with the world. Rāmānuja's Śrī *Bhāṣya* not a new type of teaching work but continues an established history of Vedāntic commentary on *Brahma Sūtras*, and his task is to show that it is the authentic interpretation of the *Sūtra*. And at certain points in the *Bhāṣya* he introduces what we might call a 'complex coherence' into the commentary that only succeeds because he makes use of what counts as a single unit of discussion within the *Bhāṣya*. In certain *adhikaraṇas* (the smallest unit of discussion) he first advances one view of the relationship between *Brahman* and the world in order to affirm the established interpretation of the *Sūtra*, but then advances a somewhat different one later on in the same *adhikaraṇa*, which gives his own final teaching.[36] If such statements were extracted from the *adhikaraṇa* frame, Rāmānuja's account would seem incoherent, as has often been alleged. But kept within the same *adhikaraṇa* it becomes clear that they have to be read together, that the reader has to go through the unit of discussion to the end before he can understand what Rāmānuja is doing. In such a way the need to work through the *Bhāṣya* as it stands is manifest.

And this is an example of what Francis Clooney has called the 'performative' character of Indian scholasticism in general.[37] By this he means that the 'systematic or ordered composition' they produce, to

[35] Ś.Bh. 3.1.1, (Melkoṭe) vol. IV, p. 2.

[36] Especially, Ś.Bh.1.4.23-29, 2.1.4-12.

[37] Francis X. Clooney S. J., 'Scholasticisms in Encounter: Working through a Hindu Example,' in Cabezón, *Scholasticism: Cross-cultural and Comparative Perspectives*, pp. 177-200.

go back to Cabezon's description of scholasticism, is meant for the formation of members of an existing community in how to think and act:

> Mīmāṃsā, Vedānta, and Śrīvaiṣṇavism are best thought of as *performative* scholasticisms. Despite their commitments to rationality and the world-encompassing and systematic nature of their self-presentations, they are primarily concerned with the formation of proper persons within a community sharing key values where the presentation of arguments in a reasonable form is aimed not so much at gaining the assent of (all) reasoning persons, but at confirming the community in its account of itself and corresponding practices.[38]

In the case of Rāmānuja, the *Śrī Bhāṣya* works within the values of Vedānta, its revealed texts, its *Sūtra* text, its established norms for correct exegesis, and aims to show members of that community how his account is the authentic teaching of the Vedānta.

Finally, then, is the *Śrī Bhāṣya* a pedagogy for happiness? We have seen that the motivating force that drives someone to undertake the Later Exegesis is the 'desire to know *Brahman*,' a desire which arises from the recognition that knowledge of *Brahman* brings release from the limitations and frustrations of rebirth. Yet the knowledge of *Brahman* brings more than just release as such; it also brings bliss (*ānanda*) and the promise of this bliss is an important theme running through the account. For Rāmānuja bliss is just the pleasing aspect of knowledge and to be a knower is to be one who experiences bliss (*Ś.Bh*.1.1.1).[39] The self languishing in *saṃsāra* is denied the bliss it might have because its knowledge is restricted by its association with embodiment. The motivation for meditation is grounded in the unsatisfactory nature of the embodied self's life and awareness of the transcendent blissful perfection of *Brahman* (*Ś.Bh*.3.1-2). Bliss is one of central essential qualities of *Brahman* which is to be included in all meditations (Ś.Bh.3.3.11-17, cp 1.1.13). As the self comes to know *Brahman* it comes to share in the attributes that *Brahman* itself has, its essential qualities, including its bliss. In the state of release the finite self realises its own true nature *qua self* as being knowledge and bliss, free from the constraints placed by its various embodiments (*Ś.Bh*.4.4.17). Thus the desire for bliss is always there in the 'desire to know *Brahman*.'[40]

[38] Clooney, 'Scholasticisms in Encounter,' p. 187.

[39] Ś.Bh. 1.1.1 (Melkoṭe), vol. 1, p. 134.

[40] Stephen Clark, this volume, touches on related themes in his discussion of the original meaning of 'therapeia' as loving and serving the lord.

Conclusion: Scholastic Therapeia for The Contemporary Philosopher

These two scholastic accounts, then, are pedagogies for happiness and both represent philosophy as *therapeia*. As such they suggest that the scholastic manner of intellectual enquiry may have something, after all, to contribute to our doing philosophy today in our modern academic institutions. In the collection of studies of scholasticism edited by Cabezón, Paul Griffiths argues that the root metaphor for scholastic intellectual practice is that of reading. The scholastic is one who is dominated by the text he studies, transformed by the text, and the scholastic institution is best described as a 'house of reading.' In contrast to this, Griffiths argues, the root metaphor for contemporary academia is that of writing. The contemporary academic is concerned with the production of texts, with getting things out in print, with being cited and getting academic credit for his or her compositions. The university becomes a 'house of production' rather than a house of reading.[41]

If we accept that philosophy as *therapeia* is a good and worthwhile pursuit and if we accept that the scholastic mode of intellectual enquiry is itself philosophy as *therapeia*, then maybe the scholastic approach does serve as a useful corrective, or at least complement, to the way we do academic work today. The scholastic approach challenges us to retrieve the idea of philosophy as transformative and pedagogical reading and to retrieve the idea of philosophical institutions as houses of this reading, so that they can also be houses of healing, houses for happiness.

[41] Paul Griffiths, 'Scholasticism: The Possible Recovery of an Intellectual Practice,' in Cabezón, *Scholasticism: Cross-cultural and Comparative Perspectives*, pp. 201-235.

The Thinker and The Draughtsman: Wittgenstein, Perspicuous Relations, and 'Working on Oneself'

GARRY L. HAGBERG

In 1931, in the remarks collected as *Culture and Value*, Wittgenstein writes: 'A thinker is very much like a draughtsman whose aim it is to represent all the interrelations between things.'[1] At a glance it is clear that this analogy might contribute significantly to a full description of the autobiographical thinker as well. And this conjunction of relations between things and the work of the draughtsman immediately and strongly suggests that the grasping of relations is in a sense visual, or that networks or constellations of relations are the kinds of things (to continue the ocular metaphor) brought into focus by *seeing* in the right way.

This should not come as a surprise: emphasis on the visual constitutes a leitmotif running throughout Wittgenstein's writings from the earliest to the latest, and we know that for him one way of making progress in philosophy is to loosen, and then—when philosophical problems have been dissolved—finally escape from the grip of simplifying 'pictures' or conceptual templates that attempt to generalize beyond their contextually specific sphere of applicability. And that escape constitutes, and is the measure of, philosophical-therapeutic progress. Indeed, also in 1931 he wrote, in response to people saying that philosophy does not generally progress and that we are still working with, and on, the problems bequeathed to us from the ancients, that those who level this complaint do not grasp why 'this has to be so.'[2] 'It is,' he writes, 'because our language has remained the same and keeps seducing us into asking the same questions.' And by seduction, he means the ensnaring grammatical 'look' of language: "the verb 'to be' ... looks as if it functions in the same way as 'to eat' and 'to drink.'" And we speak of 'a river of time' and 'an expanse of space,' and we have the *adjectives* 'identical,' 'true,' 'false,' 'possible,' and so forth (as though we are attributing generic or Platonic properties to the particulars before us, thus giving rise

[1] Ludwig Wittgenstein, *Culture and Value*, ed. G. H. von Wright and Heikki Nyman, trans. Peter Winch (Oxford: Basil Blackwell, 1980), p. 12.
[2] *Culture and Value*, p. 15.

doi:10.1017/S1358246109990257

to metaphysical questions concerning the nature not of the particular but of the Platonic quality it allegedly exemplifies or in which it participates). The achievement of conceptual clarity, of perspicuity, is also a result of the kinds of philosophical therapy Wittgenstein has shown us throughout his investigations. Indeed that achieved perspicuity is very often described by Wittgenstein as a perspicuous *overview* (*'übersicht'*). Without such a clarification (itself of course initially an ocular term), 'people will keep stumbling over the same puzzling difficulties and find themselves staring at something which no explanation seems capable of clearing up.'[3]

The distinct kind of Wittgensteinian therapy being discussed here has, since the writings of John Wisdom, been likened to psychoanalysis, and this analogy has proven enlightening in a number of ways. But in characterizing Wittgenstein's work one should bear in mind that this is after all an *analogy*, and so it has its limits, can be taken too far, and can insinuate misleading expectations. This distinctive kind of therapeutic work, for example, can be taken as excessively personal (to the point that it loses force or value beyond the individual psychology within with this work takes place) and so be only of correspondingly limited value to the discipline of philosophy. This, to put it bluntly, is utterly false. Rush Rhees writes:

> Philosophy as therapy: as though the philosopher's interest were in the personal disabilities of the perplexed: and as though he were not perplexed himself – as though philosophy were not discussion. Some remarks which Wittgenstein himself made are partly responsible for this. But he was suggesting an analogy with therapy; and he was doing this in an attempt to bring out certain features in the method of philosophy: to show the difference between what you have to do here and what you would do in solving a problem in mathematics or in science. It was not a suggestion about what it is that philosophy is interested in. If Wittgenstein spoke of 'treatment', it is the problem, or the question, that is treated – not the person raising it. It is not the personal malaise of the 'patient' which makes the perplexity or question important. What has led me to this perplexity is not my personal stupidity. Rather it is a tendency in the language which could lead *anyone* there, and keeps leading people there.[4]

[3] *Culture and Value*, p. 15.

[4] In 'Assessments of the Man and the Philosopher', in K. T. Fann, ed., *Ludwig Wittgenstein: The Man and His Philosophy* (New York: Dell, 1967), pp. 77–78. This passage is helpfully discussed in Ronald Suter, *Interpreting*

At the same time, one wants to bear in mind that it is a philosophical or conceptual problem expressed in words, where those are the words of a particular person with a particular sensibility and experiential background as spoken or written in a particular context—all in such a way that the meaning of the words is inflected by those occasion-specific particularities. One can thus go too far in the direction Rhees is pointing out here as well and render the matter in what would then be insufficiently personal terms. The balance—fitting to a nuanced awareness of the multiform determinants of linguistic meaning—is and should be a delicate and in a sense bi-focal one.

So this affords, as we say, a glimpse of some of the content of Wittgenstein's remark about the similarity between the thinker and the draughtsman, but one needs to say more to show why and how the recognition of this similarity can prove helpful. As one part of the task of clarifying relations, the thinker assembles cases in which terms such as 'identical,' 'true,' 'false,' 'possible'—and many other philosophically seductive words such as 'intentional,' 'willed,' 'caused,' 'planned', 'preconceived,' 'remembered,' 'recollected,' 'inner,' 'content', and 'reflected upon'—actually function, and these uses, seen in particularized contexts, often show one of two things. They show either (1) that the uses of such terms in context are very remote from the philosophical or metaphysical use of the term in which the general or Platonic question concerning the nature of the thing (willing, causing, preconceiving, remembering, etc.) is asked, to such an extent that we come to doubt our grasp of the very meaning of the term in the metaphysical sense; or (2) that a wide range of intermediate cases *connects* the seductively puzzling case before us to related unproblematic cases, cases in which the criteria for the use, for the meaning, for the intelligible comprehension of the term or concept in question are given. This kind of 'connective analysis,' as it has been called, reveals the 'interrelations between things,' to return to Wittgenstein's words concerning the similarities between the thinker and the draughtsman. And both (1) the sense of disorientation to the language in which the general philosophical question is expressed, and (2) the gradually-dawning awareness that the criteria that emerge for particularized usages of these philosophically-troublesome words do not (legitimately) carry over to the generalized philosophical case, are themselves also measures of therapeutic progress.

Wittgenstein: A Cloud of Philosophy, a Drop of Grammar (Philadelphia: Temple University Press, 1989), p. 48.

A good draughtsman will clarify the relations between all the various parts in such a way that the drawing itself constitutes a perspicuous overview of the building—and incidentally here we see one philosophical motivation for architectural modernism (of precisely the kind practiced by Wittgenstein in his house for his sister in Vienna), in that the relations will be clearer in a design that is not obscured by ornamentation. But note that, for Wittgenstein as for the draughtsman, not everything visual, or visually 'plotted', is by virtue of that fact good, i.e. conducive to perspicuity, be it philosophical or architectural. We have just seen above that the 'look' of words, the parallelisms on their grammatical surfaces, can deeply mislead. Phraseology that for the user unwittingly insinuates metaphysical 'pictures,' in Wittgenstein's sense, is a bewitchment of our intelligence by language that is itself pictorial, as in the phrase 'the river of time.' The visual, or our way of seeing, can be clarified, and it can also be profoundly clouded or confused. A good thinker articulates, in Wittgenstein's phrase, 'all the interrelations between things,' as does the good draughtsman. If a bad one, then, obscures them, we might think, as an extreme example, of a draughtsman who generates drawings like those of M. C. Escher in depicting impossible or internally contradictory states of affairs and yet who does not realize he is doing so. (Imagine a construction company working from Escher's drawings—'slab', 'pillar', 'beam,' and perhaps 'what?!').[5] The 'painting' of a false self-portrait in autobiographical writing, or creating what becomes a verbally-encrusted, deceptive self-definition (where, to put it one way, the 'dots' of a life narrative are falsely or misleadingly connected), would constitute the parallel unrecognized anti-therapeutic failing in self-understanding.

Of the interrelations that the draughtsman perspicuously represents, some would be the formal elements within the design (say of an architectural façade). The strength, and the significance, of a vertical line is determined in part by its interaction with the other

[5] I am referring here to Wittgenstein's imagined microcosm of linguistic usage, the 'builders' language'; see Ludwig Wittgenstein, *Philosophical Investigations*, 3rd ed., trans. G. E. M. Anscombe (Basil Blackwell, 1958), §§ 1–38. See Also Rush Rhees, 'Wittgenstein's Builders,' in *Discussions of Wittgenstein* (London: Routledge and Kegan Paul, 1970), pp. 71–84; Warren Goldfarb, 'I want you to bring me a slab. Remarks on the opening sections of the *Philosophical Investigations*,' *Synthese* 56 (1983), pp. 265–282; and Norman Malcolm, 'Language Game (2),' in his *Wittgensteinan Themes: Essays 1978–1989* (Ithaca: Cornell University Press, 1995), pp. 172–181.

verticals in the composition, its role in relation to horizontals, its placement within the illusory third dimension or the receding space of the image, and so forth. This makes the rendering deeply analogous to a language-game, to a circumscribed context or conversational microcosm within which certain verbal 'moves' get their interrelations to other moves, to previously-said things, to things left unsaid, to what was implied, and so forth. Here the analogy is indeed deep, and it is perhaps no accident that Wittgenstein begins his discussion of language-games in *Philosophical Investigations* with the builder's language. And recall that he said there that '[i]t disperses the fog to study the phenomena of language in primitive kinds of application in which one can command a clear view of the aim and functioning of the words...' (*PI*, §5). Simplicity here functions (as the removal of decoration does in an exactly parallel way in modernist architecture) as that which allows the important elements—elements that, like language, get their *point* within the context of their 'utterance'—to be seen. Thus to grasp the larger context of the line, the vertical beam, the horizontal slab, is not an *addition* to the fundamental perception of that particular element—no, the context rather is an ineliminable prerequisite for seeing the beam or slab for what it is in the most elemental sense. The context, within which the architectural element, or 'gesture,' makes sense or takes its point—or has its 'interconnections'—is just like the language-game within which the word, the phrase, the utterance, gets its point and, indeed, shows its meaning-determining 'interconnections.' And to understand that word, or more likely the group of words used collectively, to see it within its meaning-determining web of interconnections, is precisely to make the therapeutic progress described just above, i.e. to see both (1) the remoteness of this actual usage from the linguistically-disoriented generalized question and (2) the illicit or linguistically-deceptive borrowing of criterial legitimacy that can give those clouded expressions their appearance of sense, their Escher-like false plausibility.

This relation between the work that the thinker does clarifying language and dispelling confusions and the work of the draughtsman or architect who clarifies the design and its network of interrelations, surfaces time and again throughout Wittgenstein's writings. We see it in the 1930 draft of the 'Foreword' to *Philosophical Remarks*, where—of his work there in the philosophy of language—he writes: 'I am not interested in constructing a building, so much as in having a perspicuous view of the foundations of possible buildings.'[6]

6 *Culture and Value*, p. 7.

Judith Genova[7] offers a very helpful elucidation of what is meant by the important phrase 'a perspicuous view.' She begins[8] with Wittgenstein's already quoted remark from *Philosophical Investigations*, § 5: 'It disperses the fog to study the phenomena of language in primitive kinds of applications in which one can command a clear view of the aim and functioning of the words.'[9] Genova writes: 'Clarity's main virtue is that it reveals the connections between things and thus provides a view of the whole...' (p. 28). Here there emerges a link (also helpfully explained by Genova) between the later Wittgensteinian notion of perspicuity and the early work of the *Tractatus*: in *Tractatus* 6.45 Wittgenstein wrote 'To view the world *sub specie aeternitatis* is to view it as a whole—a limited whole. Feeling the world as a limited whole—it is this that is mystical.'[10] The modernist gaze, as one might call it, could be succinctly described in just these terms. To see all of the connections between elements perspicuously would be to see that architectural microcosm as a limited whole. And if god is, indeed, in the details, we need to keep these in sharp focus. In *Philosophical Investigations*, §51, Wittgenstein wrote 'In order to see more clearly, here as in countless similar cases, we must focus on the details of what goes on; must look at them *from close to*.' This passage is also discussed in Genova (p. 41), who articulates well the need for a 'double perspective,' one that both moves in for fine detail and moves back for an overview. It is worth recalling in this connection that in 1938 Wittgenstein wrote the entry quoting Longfellow: 'In the elder days of art,/ Builders wrought with greatest care/Each minute and unseen part,/For the gods are everywhere,' adding to it the parenthetical note to himself '(This could serve me as a motto).'[11] Also in the early 1930s he writes: 'Remember the impression one gets from good architecture, that it expresses a thought. It makes one want to respond with a gesture.'[12] And in 1942 he writes, further cementing the analogy between a purposive and meaningful human gesture made within a context that is in ineliminable part constitutive of its

[7] In *Wittgenstein: A Way of Seeing* (London: Routledge, 1995).

[8] In her Chapter 1, 'Commanding a Clear View,' pp. 27–54.

[9] This itself, I would suggest, is deeply analogous to the methodological imperatives of modernism in architecture: to strip away ornamentation, where this is understood as a form of concealment, in order to reveal the aim and functioning of the elements of the structure.

[10] Discussed in Genova, p. 29.

[11] *Culture and Value*, p. 34.

[12] *Culture and Value*, p. 22.

meaning and a 'move' or gesture made within architecture: 'Architecture is a *gesture*. Not every purposive movement of the human body is a gesture. And no more is every building designed for a purpose architecture.'[13]

For Wittgenstein, when philosophers are misled by the tricks (although this word should not for a moment suggest that they are simple or superficial)[14] of language, they use (or misuse) words in ways severed from the particularized context that ensures their

[13] *Culture and Value*, p. 42.

[14] On this point see Wittgenstein's observation in *Philosophical Remarks*, trans. Raymond Hargreaves and Roger White (New York: Harper and Row, 1975), pt. 1, sec. 2: 'Why is philosophy so complicated? It ought, after all, to be *completely* simple. –Philosophy unties the knots in our thinking, which we have tangled up in an absurd way; but to do that, it must make movements which are just as complicated as the knots. Although the *result* of philosophy is simple its methods for arriving there cannot be so. The complexity of philosophy is not in its matter, but in our tangled understanding.' Applied to the issue of self-understanding (of the kind that is the result of the autobiographical or self-directed therapeutic conceptual work being examined presently), this rightly suggests that the tracing of the etiology of conceptual confusion standing in the way of self-knowledge may well be no less complex and intricate than the life of a human being, but the end result may be a state of clarity that, in contrast to the complexity of the autobiographical labour that led to it, seems liberatingly simple. A deeply absorbing example of this process as it traces layered complexity and multiple resonances across and through a life, but then emerging in moments of perspicuous clarity, is shown in Bela Szabados, *In Light of Chaos* (Saskatoon: Thistledown Press, 1990). In the final passages of this autobiographical novel Szabados articulates the nature of the labour he has actually undertaken from the first page. In referring back to his reading of Popper and Marx with a group of young students and the impulse to not only understand the world but to change it, he writes: 'Yes, change it, but for the better, and this can not be done in terms of rigid schemes and systems, where the voice is privileged, univocal, and the source of violence. Perhaps the real revolutionary is he who revolutionises himself. I incline toward clarification, the dispelling of myth and confusion in the personal life and in the world – my conception is that of a cognitive therapist where the therapist is himself always the therapee, as well' (p. 124). This book also shows the considerable value, the meaning-determining significance, of the most fine-grained particularities in experience as they uniquely allow the kind of 'tracing' mentioned just above; Szabados closes the book with the line 'I resolve always to stay close enough to see the terrain clearly, never to lose sight of the terrain' (p. 125). His epigraph is Wittgenstein's remark: 'The lover of wisdom has to descend into primeval chaos and feel at home there.'

intelligibility and gives them a point. And as suggested above, the criteria that make this so much as possible reside within those contexts; they are not brought in with the individual words, item-by-item. If aestheticians ask of the nature of beauty itself, as at once an abstraction and a substantive, in such a way that no particular case is really relevant to the question, they severe the word from its criteria in just this way. In such circumstances of conceptual vertigo, *no* answer will seem satisfying. And the real problem, as we can be quick or slow to see, lies with just what this therapeutic approach addresses, i.e. the question and what it presupposes, and not the answer. Language, like architecture, imposes a certain discipline, of a kind that was brought into particularly sharp focus in the generation of J. L. Austin: not just *any* utterances constitute language, and not just any drawings constitute architecture. Wittgenstein wrote, in 1931:

> Philosophers often behave like little children who scribble some marks on a piece of paper at random and then ask the grown-up 'What's that?'— It happened like this: the grown-up had drawn pictures for the child several times and said: 'this is a man,' 'this is a house,' etc. And then the child makes some marks too and asks: what's this then?

The 'then' here is, for present purposes, especially interesting: the presumption on the part of the child is that *anything* can follow the intelligible drawings and be a drawing. Just as one might believe that, if we have a string of four or five sentences, then *any* combination of words following that would be a sentence, would be coherent, as well. But of course, the discipline intrinsic to language-games, be they linguistic or stylistic,[15] demands much more. The 'interconnections' that both the thinker and the draughtsman make lucid need to be present, and they may be in the foreground or in the background. If in the foreground, they can be the formally evident relations between horizontals and verticals within the plane of the façade, or the connecting thematic sinews between the episodes of an evolving conversation or narrative of any kind. But if in the background, they become in a sense even more interesting.

Wittgenstein had long been interested in the inexpressible, the unsayable, and in his early philosophical work in the *Tractatus* this

[15] I offer a discussion of the relations between linguistic and stylistic language-games in *Meaning and Interpretation: Wittgenstein, Henry James and Literary Knowledge* (Ithaca: Cornell University Press, 1994); see esp. Chapter 1, 'Language-Games and Artistic Styles.'

concept played a central role. In another remark, also published in *Culture and Value*, we see that by 1931, although he is clearly still interested in the concept, he is now thinking of it in a different way, with a different inflection, or with a different web of meaning-determining interrelations. He writes: 'Perhaps what is inexpressible (what I find mysterious and am not able to express) is the background against which whatever I could express has its meaning.'[16] It is thus not now a distinctive kind of content that evades propositional encapsulation or expression, but rather the background against which what is expressed functions—and we can take this in linguistic or in artistic and architectural form. The word 'mysterious' here plays an interesting role: we sense the presence of, or our reliance upon, that unspoken background—the evolved context of the expressive speech, gesture, or work of art or architecture—but it would prove exceptionally difficult to capture in any particular case everything, or even an approximation of everything, in the background that is, again, in good measure constitutive of the meaning of the expression. And what is 'mysterious' is thus *in a sense* a kind of ghostly presence; without it our expressions would not possess the significance they do. It is as though both the thinker and the draughtsman are able to bring to mind some parts of that background, making some strands of a very complex weave explicit, perhaps particularly the elements of the background that resonate importantly with the expression at hand. Thus the literary critic shows how Dante would not have been possible without Virgil, who in turn would not have been possible without Homer. The architectural historian shows how Le Corbusier's villa would not have been possible without Palladio. The musical analyst shows how the possibilities realized in Mozart's *Six Quartets Dedicated to Haydn* would not have been possible without Haydn and yet not foreseeable by him either. The art historian shows how early analytical cubism would not have developed without late Cezanne. But each of these quick examples, as will be evident, are far too brief to really capture the point—and that is the point. To genuinely grasp the deeper significance of the great steps taken by Dante, Corbusier, Mozart, and Braque and Picasso, we need to *articulate* a great deal more. And of that vast background content—content that is expressible, but not presently wholly recollectable—what is and what is not necessary to articulate will be context-dependent. One particular line of inquiry will make one strand emerge in higher relief; another inquiry will bring out another, and there will not be a point at which this

[16] *Culture and Value*, p. 16.

process is complete (which, incidentally, would explain one way in which works of art are inexhaustible). The presence of the past within the present works in precisely this way, and it gives a sense of what Wittgenstein meant by the word 'spirits' in his remark of 1930: 'The early culture will become a heap of rubble and finally a heap of ashes, but spirits will hover over the ashes.'[17] A *sense* of that surrounding constellation of interrelations that led to, that made possible, what is now rubble and ashes, will persist. That we perceive a work of art or architecture within such a network of relations is implicit in another of Wittgenstein's remarks from 1930, and it reminds us of how important it is, in aesthetic contexts, to be aware of acts of restraint, to be aware of what was possible, but *not* done – where what was possible but not done constitutes in a seemingly paradoxical way (seeming, because acts of omission are nevertheless acts) part of the content of the work. We of course understand persons, including ourselves, with similar layered combinations of commission and omission. 'Today' he writes, 'the difference between a good and a poor architect is that the poor architect succumbs to every temptation and the good one resists it.'[18] A language-game, be it linguistic or stylistic, opens many avenues of development, opens many possibilities. Understanding that game is, in large part, a matter of grasping those possibilities, seeing the artist within that expanding network, and seeing what he or she did do within that surrounding dense weave of what was left out, what was not done or, for the speaker, what was left unsaid. This too is not uniform: in some cases we will consider what an artist chose not to do (i.e. did not commit a crime of ornamentation within a context where a value on the perspicuous clarification of designed interrelations is paramount); in other cases, critically, we will see a possibility opened that the artist missed, one of which he or she was unaware in an aesthetically blameworthy sense, i.e. it will be something that *should* have been seen, or was seen by another artist with—as we metaphorically say—greater vision. This stands in direct analogy with the fact that we may criticize a person, a speaker of language, for having failed to say what should have been

[17] *Culture and Value*, p. 3.

[18] *Culture and Value*, p. 3. Good architecture is thus, in a sense, a moral matter (in that there is a prescriptive sense of what ought, and particularly ought *not*, to be done). Conversely, Wittgenstein describes (some) moral issues in architectural terms: in 1937, he writes, 'The *edifice of your pride* has to be dismantled. And that is terribly hard work.' *Culture and Value*, p. 26.

said. Indeed Wittgenstein, in 1940, criticizes himself in just these terms, saying that in his house for his sister he was working with a quite full awareness of the kinds of interrelations and possibilities within the stylistic game I have been discussing, but that a more romantic power is lacking in the building. He wrote: '...the house I built for Gretl is the product of a decidedly sensitive ear and *good* manners, an expression of great *understanding* (of a culture, etc.). But *primordial* life, wild life striving to erupt into the open—that is lacking.'[19] And if we have some difficulty imagining how the architectural expression of primordial striving might have been incorporated into that cool temple[20] of modernist consistency, internally generated, then that itself gives a sense of the way in which possibilities are circumscribed as well as opened within a stylistic language-game.

Be that as it may, everything I have said so far in this excursus into the interrelations between philosophy and architecture is, in the sense of Wittgenstein's use of 'background,' its own background for what is I think of fundamental importance here in terms of elucidating a notion of therapeutic philosophical work and the kind of progress it affords. He wrote, in 1931, this remark: 'Working in philosophy—like work in architecture in many respects—is really more a working on oneself. On one's way of seeing things. (And what one expects of them.)'[21] The phrase 'really more a working on oneself' itself invites a changed way of seeing work in philosophy. Working on oneself can mean any kind of autobiographical—in the broadest sense—inquiry, where one works toward a more capacious grasp not only of what one has done, and why one has done it, but also how one has come to hold the views one does, how pressures on one's thoughts have manifested themselves in various beliefs and actions, how what one said was opened—as a possibility—by earlier things one said, how one has understood the trajectories of one's own life projects, and so forth. And of course such autobiographical subjects can easily take a more explicitly philosophical turn: they can turn to how one pictures the act of introspection, how one pictures meaning in language (and often, by extension, how one pictures

[19] *Culture and Value*, p. 38. Also in 1934 Wittgenstein had written 'In my artistic activities I really have nothing but *good manners*.' (p. 25).

[20] Wittgenstein described his philosophical work in these terms, further underscoring the commonalities between architectural and philosophical work. See *Culture and Value*, p. 2: 'My ideal is a certain coolness. A temple providing a setting for the passions without meddling with them.'

[21] *Culture and Value*, p. 16.

meaning in the arts),[22] and indeed how one conceives of, pictures, a human being.

But more precisely with regard to all of the foregoing as background for a point to be made presently, an autobiographical project can—and very often does—take the form of 'representing all the interrelations between things,' like the work of the thinker and of the draughtsman. Or at least, as we have seen, representing *some* of those relations: the interrelations in the web of one's background will stretch beyond any particular autobiographical iteration. And various strands of that life, various collections of past experiences, will be brought into self-interpretative play with, will be enlivened by, a present or recent event whose meaning is in significant part constituted by those past resonances or whose content is in significant part determined by those sinews of association.

Similarly, like the progress-measuring escape from simplifying 'pictures' that would govern our thought and preclude the patient achievement of conceptual clarity, simple or truncated narratives of a life, or an episode in a life, will in a parallel way blind us to the contextually-specific particularities that not merely add to the experience, but indeed make it what it is. The draughtsman elucidates the complex interconnections; viewing the self's past for its significance in the present, for our present self-understanding, is much like experiencing art in three dimensions, for example viewing architecture or sculpture, precisely because, in moving around and through it, we constantly change our vantage point, which in turn changes what does and does not come into focus, what does and does not take a foreground or background position. Of doing philosophy, Wittgenstein wrote in 1937: 'I find it important in philosophizing to keep changing my posture, not to stand for too long on one leg, so as not to get stiff',[23] which is a nice way of embodying the point concerning the conceptual need for shifting vantage points and assembling a larger mosaic of initially separate perspectival positions; 'stiffness' in our present case would thus constitute the hardening of

[22] I offer a study of various ways in which preconceptions concerning linguistic meaning powerfully shape conceptions of artistic meaning in *Art as Language: Wittgenstein, Meaning and Aesthetic Theory*, (Ithaca: Cornell University Press, 1995). Of such connections Wittgenstein notes: 'Phenomena akin to language in music or architecture. Significant irregularity—in Gothic for instance (I am thinking too of the towers of St. Basil's Cathedral). Bach's music is more like language than Mozart's or Hayden's....' *Culture and Value*, p. 34.

[23] *Culture and Value*, p. 27.

one set of presently-perceived relations into what we mistakenly take as the final, settled, definitive, and complete life-narrative.

Also similarly, Wittgenstein claims that what we *need* in philosophy is a perspicuous overview, where this, as we have seen, is not meant in the sense of a generalized, Platonic concept to which no particular case is genuinely relevant, but rather where that overview is the *result* of patiently considering cases under that concept, seeing how it functions *in situ*. If we desire a fuller understanding of our own courage or cowardice, or pride or prejudice, we need an overview of the self's words and deeds *in that sense*. This constitutes a kind of connective analysis of the self's past, of one's intellectual genealogy.

We can also be misled by the surface appearance of a person's actions—or in the case of self-knowledge, our own actions—just as we can be misled, as Wittgenstein has shown, by the surface appearance of words. Both the thinker and the draughtsman (if good) clear up these confusions, and the author of a *Bildungsroman* takes both of these roles as he or she contemplates the design, the building, the construction of a life and the thinking, the pressures on thought, that shaped the construction. And again, the good *Bildungsroman* author makes these interrelations clear.[24] Some retrospective constructions of a life's story, its purpose, its developmental trajectory, will, like Escher's drawings, seem initially plausible and yet in the end fail genuinely to cohere, however good they may look on the level of surface design. If ultimately acceptable, we will—as a project that is at once philosophical therapy and autobiographical 'work on oneself'—see the connections between the equivalents in experience to a series of verticals, a strong horizontal, a set receding planes, a reiterated angle, a niche, a stylobate, and so forth. And coming to understand what we did do, what we did not, what was possible that we did see, and what was possible that we did not, are all ways of earning self-understanding. These are, in a distinctly architectural sense, language-games of the self, and we come to comprehend the range of possible moves within a person's character in a way strikingly parallel to language, to language-games. And here as well, grasping the larger context, the relevant sections of a person's experiential background, is not an *addition* to understanding the

[24] Such progressive interrelational clarifications are precisely what a reader sees while closely following the development of the eponymous protagonist in Goethe's great (and arguably first and most influential of the genre) *Bildungsroman, Wilhelm Meister's Apprenticeship*, ed. and trans. Eric A. Blackall in cooperation with Victor Lange (Princeton: Princeton University Press, 1995).

action in question, for it is within that relational matrix that the interconnections that make the action what it is become visible. When we speculate about how we ourselves, or another, might have been different, we imagine a different *set* of experiences, or 'interconnections,' grafted by contingency onto what we think of as the foundations of that person's character. This is, I think, more than merely incidentally reminiscent of Wittgenstein's metaphorical remark concerning his philosophical work that he is interested, not in constructing a building, but in gaining a perspicuous view of the foundations of possible buildings. And like the child's doodle after the grown-up's drawings, not just any string of words makes sense, nor does any construction constitute architecture. For deeply parallel reasons, not every undisciplined interpretative suggestion about a person, or about, reflexively, the self, constitute insight or self-therapeutic progress.[25] The radical relativist's undisciplined speculations, or the extreme post-modernist's 'any description goes as well as any other' ethos, turned loose on questions of self-interpretation, are in the realm of human understanding all too like the child's scribbles.

Much of our language of self-understanding and self-description is ocular, and this, as we have now glimpsed, is in differing ways, in

[25] Richard Wollheim offers a helpful discussion of some of the constraints under which such an interpretation may proceed in *The Thread of Life* (Cambridge, Mass.: Harvard University Press, 1984), pp. 171–177. He writes: 'That interpretation, properly understood, has something to tell us about the structure of the mind derives from the constraints under which it operates. In all domains interpretation is possible only under constraints – constraints imposed upon the interpreter, and specifying conditions that interpretation of one and the same text, or one and the same legal system, or one and the same person, must satisfy' (p. 171). But lest this be misunderstood, a special virtue of Wollheim's discussion is that he does not import a false (because radically oversimplified) model of belief-consistent rationality as the primary governing constraint in the interpretation of persons; rather, he rightly (and realistically) suggests that 'Instead of trying to devise in the abstract constraints upon interpretation intended to capture rationality, what we should do is to examine the actual processes by which persons do regulate, or try to regulate, their beliefs and desires, and then argue back to the constraints. It is to such processes, which are in turn part of leading the life of a person, and not to some idealized rationality, that the constraints upon interpretation must ultimately answer'(p. 173). Wollheim does not say so here, but this suggests why the close and exacting philosophical study of literature, i.e. particularized and highly detailed descriptions of the nuanced moral psychology of characters that show at a reflective distance what it actually is to lead the life of a person, is of irreplaceable value.

differing contexts, either conceptually incarcerating or therapeutically liberating. But it does in any event seem helpful to find a way to speak of what Wittgenstein called—in his later sense of the term—the 'mysterious,' the background against which our gestures, verbal or artistic, make sense. That expansive and unbounded network of relations gives our person-defining experience the character, the resonance, and indeed even the identity, it has. And yet it lies beyond the reach of the fully sayable at *any one* time, in any single context. Our way of seeing, with regard to our interpretation of ourselves and of others, can change according to which parts of that relational fabric we focus upon, which parts we make—like the work of the thinker and the draughtsman—particularly clear, which parts we render perspicuously. And what we expect, hope for, or demand of others and of ourselves is just a function of such relationally-interweaving inquiry. Sceptics, aware of the limitless nature of this background, might leap to embrace a blanket doubt concerning the very possibility of our knowledge of the self as well as of another. But while a full and final comprehensive articulation of the content of that background may not fall within the bounds of possibility, we need not for that reason embrace scepticism. Through the conjunction considered here of the work of therapeutically-inflected philosophy and the work of architecture, we can at least begin to see that the projects of self-knowledge and of other-knowledge, are—although they may not have fixed end-points—possible within our language-games of human understanding. Like works of art—and for parallel reasons—the project may be inexhaustible (and that is itself a wondrous thing). But then Wittgenstein also wrote, in 1938, 'In philosophy the winner of the race is the one ... who gets there last.'[26]

Wittgenstein's work on the house in Vienna for his sister was unquestionably architectural work—just as it was philosophical work, if in an extended sense we've only started to elucidate here.[27] And where these converged, where the labours of thinker and of the draughtsman came together, it became a distinctive kind of autobiographical work, or 'work on oneself', as well. Such work is driven by the desire for hard-won therapeutically liberating inter-relational clarification.

26 *Culture and Value*, p. 34.

27 I offer a fuller discussion in *Describing Ourselves: Wittgenstein and Autobiographical Consciousness* (Oxford: Clarendon Press, 2008).

Therapy and Theory Reconstructed: Plato and his Successors

STEPHEN R. L. CLARK

Theorein and Therapeuein

When we speak of philosophy and therapy, or of philosophy as therapy, the usual intent is to suggest that 'philosophizing' is or should be a way to clarify the mind or purify the soul. While there may be little point in arguing with psychoses or deeply-embedded neuroses our more ordinary misjudgements, biases and obsessions may be alleviated, at least, by trying to 'see things clearly and to see them whole', by carefully identifying premises and seeing what they – rationally – support, and by seeking to eliminate the residual influence of premises that we have long since, rationally, dismissed. I don't intend to argue with this account – though of course it may be as well to remember that 'philosophizing' may have more dangerous effects. It is not obvious that philosophical argument will always help us 'see things straight', and the Athenian democracy was not altogether wrong to think that some of Socrates' followers or pupils learnt quite the wrong things from him.

My goal here is rather to reconsider what it was that 'therapy' once meant. I shall begin from Aristotle's declaration, at the end of the *Eudemian Ethics*, that our task is '*ton theon therapeuein kai theorein*'[1]. Standard modern interpretations of Aristotelian ethics either ignore this and similar injunctions or interpret them solely as requiring us to be 'rational', without much effort to say what 'rationality' amounts to. Older, and especially Platonic, interpretations are more demanding. Perhaps the phrase can be translated differently, more shockingly? *Theoria*, 'contemplation', after all, is not mere, neutral *noticing*: it carries the clear suggestion that what we are drawn to 'contemplate' we must admire, or love. So Aristotle is, in effect, concluding his meditations on right action, character and 'happiness' with the simple injunction 'to love and serve the Lord'! What God is it that Aristotle suggests we should love (*theorein*) and serve (*therapeuein*), and what does 'service', in this context, mean?

1 *Eudemian Ethics* 8.1249b20.

doi:10.1017/S1358246109990269

By Aristotle's account elsewhere God actually is *theoria*, and in living thus 'theoretically' we live by what is most divine in us, and at the same time what is most really human. 'We must not follow those who advise us, being men, to think of human things, and, being mortal, of mortal things, but must, so far as we can, make ourselves immortal, and strain every nerve to live in accordance with the best thing in us; for even if it be small in bulk, much more does it in power and worth surpass everything.'[2] So 'contemplating God' is the same as 'contemplating contemplation': 'knowing God' is the same as 'God's knowing.'[3] And what is it that God knows? According to Aristotle's analysis, Himself.[4]

This notion was criticised very early. According to the author of the pseudo-Aristotelian *Magna Moralia*[5] 'whoever is preoccupied with himself is counted as insensible: a god like that would be absurd.' But later Platonic and Aristotelian tradition lived happily with the supposed absurdity, recognizing that God's knowledge, if it is to be incontrovertible, must somehow *contain* its objects. God is not, as we are, merely externally related to the things He knows, for if He were He could not Himself be sure that reality was as it was represented, even to Him. 'If intellect (*nous*) were not the same as what it intuited (*ta noeta*), there will be no truth; for the one who is trying to possess realities will possess an impression different from the realities, and this is not truth.'[6] God's thinking, the divine thinking, is one with what is thought.[7]

But this is not merely the conclusion of an abstract argument. As I remarked over thirty years ago,[8] this description of 'divine intelligence' is strikingly like Buddhist (and other mystagogic) accounts of enlightenment. It is a 'knowing without touching things: that is, without making things into objects in one's consciousness'[9]. '*Śūnyatā* ['emptiness'] is experienced only when it is both subject and object... 'Knowing and seeing' *śūnyatā* is *śūnyatā* knowing and

[2] *Nicomachean Ethics* 10.1177b30ff.

[3] *Metaphysics* 1.983a5.

[4] *Metaphysics* 12.1072b18ff.

[5] *Magna Moralia* 1213b4ff.

[6] *Ennead* V.3 [49].5, 23ff; see my 'A Plotinian Account of Intellect,' *American Catholic Philosophical Quarterly* 71 (1997), pp. 421–32.

[7] *Metaphysics* 12.1075a4.

[8] Stephen R. L. Clark, *Aristotle's Man: Speculations upon Aristotelian Anthropology* (Oxford: Clarendon Press, 1975), pp. 174-90.

[9] H. Dumoulin, *History of Zen Buddhism*, tr. Paul Peachey (London: Faber, 1963), p.165, paraphrasing Dogen.

seeing itself'.[10] And as Aristotle also said, 'on such a principle depend the heavens and the world of nature. And it is a life such as the best that we enjoy, and enjoy for but a short time... So that life and *aion* continuous and eternal belong to the god, for this is what the god is.'[11] God is Eternity – as Boethius also said some centuries later: 'the entire and perfect possession of endless life at a single instant.'[12]

It follows that we 'know' God when we experience the life that identically is God, when God lives us. Or remembering for a moment that other parallel to which I gestured: 'God is love; and he that dwelleth in love dwelleth in God, and God in him.'[13].'*Theorein ton theon*' is not to reason one's way to a conviction that there is a god, an ultimate authority or good, but to experience, to live, a certain sort of life, the sort to which all other lives aspire, and which does not depend for its existence on *our* experiencing it – since it is experienced, exactly, as something that is forever. And what is forever, for Plotinus as well as for St. John, is love: the One, Plotinus says, is at once beloved, lover and the love between (*erasmion kai eros ho autos kai autou eros*).[14]

Strangely, despite our modern respect for 'reason', we are usually less respectful than the ancients, and too easily suppose that 'reasoning' is in the end a tool or set of tools for achieving other goals. 'Reason is and ought to be the slave of the passions', according to Hume. But that is not what the ancients—or at least the Platonists and Stoics—thought. Reason, on Plotinus' account, is not to be valued because we can, with its help, perform socially useful actions, nor yet because we can, with its help, win more food, water, sex or shelter than less 'clever' creatures. It is to be valued because it is the presence in us of beauty. '*Nous* is our king. But we too are kings when we are in accord with it; we can be in accord with it in two ways, either by having something like its writing written in us like laws, or by being as if filled with it and able to see it and be aware of it as present.'[15] *Nous*, remember, is yet another name for God.

[10] D. T. Suzuki, *Zen Buddhism*, ed. William Barrett (New York: Doubleday, 1956), pp. 261–3.

[11] Aristotle, *Metaphysics* 12.1072b13f.

[12] *Consolation of Philosophy* 5.6.

[13] *I John* 4.16.

[14] *Enneads* VI.8 [39].15.

[15] *Ennead* V.3.3, 46ff.

How are we to come to 'see it and be aware of it'? And what sort of laws might be written in our hearts to make us accord with it? There is a – relatively – clear answer in the Hebrew Scriptures:

> And now, Israel, what doth the Lord thy God require of thee, but to fear the Lord thy God, to walk in all his ways, and to love him, and to serve the Lord thy God with all thy heart and with all thy soul, to keep the commandments of the Lord, and his statutes, which I command thee this day for thy good? Behold, the heaven and the heaven of heavens is the Lord's thy God, the earth also, with all that therein is. Only the Lord had a delight in thy fathers to love them, and he chose their seed after them, even you above all people, as it is this day. Circumcise therefore the foreskin of your heart, and be no more stiffnecked. For the Lord your God is God of gods, and Lord of Lords, a great God, a mighty, and a terrible, which regardeth not persons, nor taketh reward: He doth execute the judgment of the fatherless and widow, and loveth the stranger, in giving him food and raiment. Love ye therefore the stranger: for ye were strangers in the land of Egypt. Thou shalt fear the Lord thy God; him shalt thou serve, and to him shalt thou cleave, and swear by his name.[16]

The Hebrews were reckoned 'a nation of philosophers' because they were dedicated to love and serve the Lord in something like the way that a Platonic or Aristotelian philosopher would wish. But the Hebrew rules, it may well seem, were rather different from the Hellenistic. The justice that they embody is for the benefit of the fatherless, the widow and the homeless stranger. And it seems that their God is a lot more active in *enforcing* justice (in the end) than the God of the Philosophers could be, and more concerned about the details of ordinary life.

So what did the Greek philosophers have in mind? Where are we to look for God, and what are we to do?

> It does no good at all to say 'Look to God', unless one also teaches how one is to look. ... In reality it is virtue which goes before us to the goal and, when it comes to exist in the soul along with wisdom, shows God; but God, if you talk about him without true virtue, is only a name. Again, despising the universe and

[16] *Deuteronomy* 10.12–20. The rather gruesome imagery (for the average male especially) about 'circumcising the foreskin of your heart' has been discussed by Gillian Clark 'In the Foreskin of Your Flesh: The Pure Male Body in Late Antiquity', in *Roman Bodies*, ed. A. Hopkins and M. Wyke (Rome: British School at Rome, 2005), 43–54.

> the gods in it and the other noble things is certainly not becoming good. ...For anyone who feels affection for anything at all shows kindness to all that is akin to the object of his affection, and to the children of the father that he loves. But every soul is a child of That Father[17].

How are we to 'serve' God? After all, we can hardly do Him good, nor does He need our help to see things clearly! 'If I were hungry, I would not tell you, for the world and all that is in it is mine!'[18] The God of the Hebrews requires us to be thankful – and to keep our vows. Above all He requires us to treat others well, not to steal or slander. Can we suppose that the God of the Greeks had a similar requirement? To serve God is to obey His commands, and to love His offspring.

Divine Commands

One of the earliest lessons that first year philosophy students learn, as they suppose, is that Plato refuted the idea that the moral law could be derived from the command of any god. Why *ought* we to obey the commands of God unless it were true that He commanded only what was already right? If His commands weren't right we would be obeying only from fear. Oddly, in other contexts modern moralists don't seem to mind that we obey from fear: proper behaviour, they often seem to suppose, is only the best way of avoiding all the dreadful consequences of vice, cruelty and injustice. What difference does it make that it is the laws of nature rather than the laws of God that guarantee a dreadful end? Even more oddly, it is likely to be to the traditional 'God-fearers' who find fault with this. As G. K. Chesterton remarked, warnings about the perils of this or that activity 'only affect that small minority which will accept any virtue as long as we do not ask them for the virtue of courage. Most healthy people dismiss these moral dangers as they dismiss the possibility of bombs or microbes.'[19] The *proper* and far more reliable motivation

17 *Ennead* II.9 [33].15, 33–16.10. Compare *James* 2.15ff: 'What use is it for a man to say he has faith when he does nothing to show it? Can that faith save him? Suppose a brother or a sister is in rags with not enough food for the day, and one of you says, 'Good luck to you, keep yourselves warm, and have plenty to eat', but does nothing to supply their bodily needs, what is the good of that? So with faith; if it does not lead to action it is in itself a lifeless thing.'

18 *Psalm* 50.12.

19 G. K. Chesterton *Heretics* (New York: John Lane, 1905), p. 30.

for virtuous conduct is not fear but love – the love, specifically, of what is *good.* Acting out of reverence is not the same as acting out of fear, even if – as Socrates proposes – 'he who has a feeling of reverence and shame about the commission of any action, fears and is afraid of an ill reputation.'[20]

Those first-year students are misled. They are generally taught that a dilemma faces all those who found their conduct on the 'will of God': either what God commands is right in any case (and would still be right even if He changed His mind), or else His commands are 'arbitrary' and imaginably changeable, and the only motive to obey Him an immoral one. This gesture towards an absolute moral demand or absolute objective good is usually forgotten by their second year, when they will be told that some moralists are Kantians and others consequentialists (usually of some utilitarian kind), but that there is no real 'fact of the matter' to concern them. They will be told that the end of moral action is to do what can be supposed to be required and enacted universally, or else that it is some summated advantage of a kind that only an omniscient, disinterested and universally benevolent judge could be sure to see: 'the greatest good of the greatest number'. How either of these maxims differs from the original claim, that what is right is what would be (and maybe is) required by God, is very rarely explained. If the rightness of an action just is its being what would be required of us by an omniscient and impartial judge, why is it not right to do what is required by such a One?

The argument that Socrates had with Euthyphro, in any case, is not what commentators now suppose.[21] The question is posed 'whether the pious or holy is beloved by the gods because it is holy, or holy because it is beloved of the gods.'[22] Commentators almost always equate 'the pious or holy' with 'the morally right', go on to offer the specious dichotomy that I mentioned a moment ago, and conclude that the gods can only bear witness to moral truth, and not create it. But that is not how Socrates conducts the argument. Instead, he poses a weird dilemma: is that conduct and character loved by the gods because it is loved, or loved because they love it? The likeliest inference is that it is loved because they love it, just as

[20] Plato, *Euthyphro* 12c (tr.Benjamin Jowett). Fear for one's reputation, Socrates would certainly acknowledge, may easily work against a proper reverence, in a corrupt society.

[21] As Richard Joyce points out in 'Theistic Ethics and the Euthyphro Dilemma', *Journal of Religious Ethics* 30 (2002), pp. 49–75.

[22] *Euthyphro* 10a.

something is being carried because someone is carrying it. It is agency, after all, that is, precisely, active: passivity, precisely, is being acted on. Euthyphro concedes, without argument, that things are loved by the gods (*theophiles*) because the gods love them, but that they love them because those things are 'holy' (*hosion*). So being holy and being loved by the gods, so Socrates suggests, are different attributes, even if they belong to the same things.[23]

Actually, Euthyphro need not have conceded so much – and Socrates, as usual, only suggests that *some* error has occurred, without saying what. Maybe the gods have natural sentiments (so to speak) as much as we: why need there be any other way of characterising what they love than – simply – as what they love? We in our turn may wish or choose to please them by trying to be and do appropriate things – because we love them, just as any lover will seek to do what pleases his beloved, for no other reason than that it does. The underlying thought, of course, is that there should be some consistency in what is loved, that we cannot endure an irresoluble conflict of the sort depicted in Greek tragedy. There must be some way of resolving discord, perhaps by seeking to see some *one* thing that we all desire. But if there is, what can we say to *prove* that it is the thing we all desire, except that we all desire it? What could it even mean to ask whether we *should* desire it? Such questions can only be answered if there is something else that we desire more.

Euthyphro is disturbed that his father left a dependant of his who killed a household slave in a drunken brawl to die, tied up and untended, in a ditch, and is desperate to see the wrong avenged, and his family and father, thereby, cleansed.[24] This duty, he supposes, he owes to 'the gods'. Whatever overt dissension there may be amongst the Olympian gods – as Socrates concedes – none of them will approve of murder. Benjamin Jowett was strangely confident that Euthyphro's 'wrong-headedness, one-sidedness, narrowness, positiveness, are characteristic of his priestly office' – a judgement that owes more to Victorian anti-clericalism than a clear reading of the text! Quite why he is so sure that Euthyphro stands for 'the narrow and unenlightened conscience', and that the father was only 'accidentally guilty of homicide' (which is not, I suspect, how any modern court would judge the case), I don't know.

[23] *Euthyphro* 11a.

[24] The episode occurred a few years before, when the family was farming in Naxos. We may suspect that they have only recently returned to Athens, and Athens has only recently returned to proper civil life.

Perhaps there is a question whether 'a servant who is guilty of murder, and is put in chains by the master of the dead man, and dies because he is put in chains before he who bound him can learn from the expositors of religious law what he ought to do with him, is killed unjustly; and that on behalf of such an one a son ought to proceed against his father and accuse him of murder'[25]. Maybe so: but it is difficult to see how a question that can only be settled, if at all, by juridical decision, will be settled without proceeding to the court!

Euthyphro, as depicted, is clearly not a bigot.[26] He knows very well, and admires, the sort of conversation that Socrates enjoys. Meletus's charge against him, he says, is striking at the very heart of Athens.[27] He is himself ready to submit to Socrates' interrogation, even at an awkward, or even painful, moment of his life. That Socrates traps him into saying things he probably doesn't mean hardly makes him unique! Even his bragging remarks about his own abilities are openly ironical, as he also concedes that the Athenians don't listen.[28] If Socrates is allowed his humour, why not Euthyphro? Certainly, by the end he seems impatient, and eager to hurry off about his business, but perhaps with justice!

Piety is giving the gods their due, our service. But what service can we do the gods? We can't do them good. As the Hebrew prophets said, what do they, He, need from us? 'Is not attention always designed for the good or benefit of that to which the attention is given? As in the case of horses, you may observe that when attended to by the horseman's art they are benefited and improved, are they not?'[29] Euthyphro can only repeat what he has said before: 'Let me

[25] Plato *Euthyphro* 9a (tr. Benjamin Jowett). Note that it is not at all clear that the servant *is* guilty of murder: there was a drunken fight and the man himself was hurt. If the father is as readily excusable as Jowett supposed, why not the servant?

[26] See Mark J. Edwards 'In Defense of Euthyphro', *American Journal of Philology* 121 (2000), pp. 213–224.

[27] *Euthyphro* 3a.

[28] Talk of his 'monumental conceit and stupidity', Homeric fundamentalism, obtuseness and 'outlandish prosecution of his father' (as by Mark McPherran in 'Piety, Justice, and the Unity of Virtue'. *Journal of the History of Philosophy* 38 (2000), pp. 299–328) seems to me to be quite extraordinary. The tendency of commentators to *assume* that Euthyphro's concerns are ritualistic, selfish or 'superstitious' tells us more about them than about either Euthyphro or Plato.

[29] *Euthyphro* 13b (tr. Benjamin Jowett). For this reason the term '*therapeia*' is replaced by '*hyperetike*', but this is only a technical convenience.

simply say that piety or holiness is learning how to please the gods in word and deed, by prayers and sacrifices'[30] – which is very much what the Athenian Stranger tells us in *The Laws* – but the very context of the dialogue makes it clear that these 'prayers and sacrifices' include attempts to purify, to set things right.[31] They are not merely ceremonial. We don't do the gods any good—but we can please them, can be what they wish us to be. And what they wish is our cooperation in making 'many and fair things', things they love.[32]

As so often in the Socratic dialogues, it is what *isn't* said that is most significant. This is enough to excuse, though not to justify, the standard use made of 'the Euthyphro Dilemma.' But we need to read with care. Socrates, though he expresses shock and surprise that Euthyphro should think it so obvious that he should bring a case against his father, is himself depicted—in the *Gorgias*—as arguing, exactly, that it is our duty to bring a prosecution even against our friends, if they've done wrong.

> Rhetoric is of no use to us in helping a man to excuse his own injustice, or that of his parents or friends, or children or country; but may be of use to anyone who holds that instead of excusing he ought to accuse - himself above all, and in the next degree his family or any of his friends who may be doing wrong; he should bring to light the iniquity and not conceal it, that so the wrong-doer may suffer and be made whole; he should force himself and others not to shrink, but with closed eyes like brave men to let the physician operate with knife or searing iron, not regarding the pain, in the hope of attaining the good and the honourable; let him who has done things worthy of stripes, allow himself to be scourged, if of bonds, to be bound, if of a fine, to be fined, if of exile, to be exiled, if of death, to die, himself being the first to accuse himself and his own relations, and using rhetoric to this end, that his and their unjust actions may be made manifest, and that they themselves may be delivered from injustice, which is the greatest evil.[33]

Certainly this is a shocking thought, especially as regards the relations of sons and fathers. Whitlock has pointed to the analogous dispute in

[30] *Euthyphro* 14b (tr. Benjamin Jowett).

[31] A point not noticed by Frederick Rosen even in what is an unusually sympathetic treatment of Euthyphro, in 'Piety and Justice: Plato's *Euthyphro*', *Philosophy* 43 (1968), pp. 105–16.

[32] *Euthyphro* 14a.

[33] *Plato Gorgias* 480bff (tr. Benjamin Jowett).

Confucian ethics, and the significance for Chinese and Greek alike of *filial* piety.[34] The Athenian Stranger of *The Laws* endorses laws prescribing filial obedience, and in *The Republic* Plato openly rejects the stories of Zeus and Kronos, Kronos and Ouranos, to which Euthyphro appeals,[35] saying that even if they were true, the young should not be told them—but perhaps this is indeed one point on which the historical Socrates was widely reckoned to disagree![36] And even in *The Laws* there is a set procedure for Euthyphro's dilemma:

> [If a son wants to file a charge,] this is the law the son must observe. First of all he must go to the eldest Guardians of the laws and explain his father's misfortune, and they, after due investigation, must advise him whether to bring the charge or not. If they advise that he should, they must come forward as witnesses for the prosecution and plead on his behalf. [37]

Which is very much what Euthyphro is actually doing.

And despite the modern philosopher's opinion that Socrates is somehow subverting 'Divine Command Morality' he has himself no doubt that he should obey the gods, and that what they require of him is Justice, to do his job, and not desert his post (or escape from gaol). Would these things still be forbidden or required if the

[34] Greg Whitlock 'Concealing the misconduct of one's own father: Confucius and Plato on a question of filial piety': *Journal of Chinese Philosophy* 21 (1994), pp. 113–137. Whitlock too considers Euthyphro to be small-minded and censorious, but does not say why. See also Rui Zhu 'What if the Father Commits a Crime?', *Journal of the History of Ideas* 63 (2002), pp. 1–17.

[35] In *Cratylus* 396d Euthyphro is, by implication, said to have offered much the same sort of allegorized interpretation of these stories as were later endorsed by Plotinus and others: Kronos is the pure mind, created by 'looking up' to the heavens. Socrates declares himself inspired by this, though he also hopes, perhaps, to be purged of the idea!

[36] *Republic* 2 38. Rosen op.cit., suggests that part of Plato's purpose in the *Euthyphro* was to defuse the suggestion of Aristophanes' *Clouds* that Socrates approved of the stereotypical Greek crime of father-beating!

[37] Laws 11.929e. Zhu op.cit. accurately summarizes Plato's judgement by saying that 'if his filial piety clashes with his religious piety, the latter should always be given the upper hand. Doing otherwise is not only wrong but also useless, for justice always wins against a crime by a mortal. For this reason, the Confucian idea of covering up for a family member is categorically ruled out by both morals and wisdom.' Oddly, Zhu supposes that *Socrates* is so radical as to disapprove of this, and so to side with the Confucian ethic in which filial affection displaces civic duty.

gods thought otherwise? Why is that any more threatening than the question whether things would still be right or wrong if the facts of the matter changed? It is not 'analytically' true that, for example, the enjoyment of another's agony is wrong: are we to be alarmed at the thought that there is a 'possible world' where it's right? If that is alarming, should we not be glad that the eternal being of God makes such a world *impossible*? The *necessity* of God's being applies as well to His supreme commands as to His other 'attributes'. But of course there might be variations in the lesser, derivative commands, and we need not be alarmed by this. How should God or the gods make it right to do another job, or to commit self-murder? Why not simply by requiring this of us? The question should rather be: how would they let us know? And the answer, compatibly with everything that Socrates (or Plato) says, is that they would grant us a different talent, or let it be known that it was time to leave. 'My job', as Plato identifies it, is what I do best (implicitly, of the things needed to sustain my city or community): the gods can alter my job by altering my talents. 'My station' is assigned by the laws – both civil and natural–under which I find myself.

Why should the gods, and the laws they make for us, be readily obeyed? Might we not have reason to disobey? We may imagine that we could answer this by appealing to an independent good, our good or the good of those we care about: but if it is the gods who have *made* us as we are, and granted us the attachments appropriate to our sort of being, how exactly are these independent criteria? (The same problem, incidentally, afflicts those neo-Darwinians who urge us to defy the tyranny of 'the selfish genes' which have, supposedly, created us: even if we could somehow find some accidental motive for so doing, we know, on the very theory they profess, that we will fail. Out of the muddle of motives and inhibitions only those will last that have a reproductive edge. 'Human behavior—like the deepest capacities for emotional response which drive and guide it—is the circuitous technique by which human genetic material has been and will be kept intact. Morality has no other demonstrable function.'[38] Only if there were really a world beyond *this* world, and values not reducible to the genetic, does it make sense to try and defy the makers. God-fearers have less to fear from argument than evolutionary theorists of E. O. Wilson's sort!)

Plato's later story, in the *Timaeus*, is that the imaginable Creator (for it is not clear whether he is telling a story he believes, or only

[38] E. O. Wilson, *On Human Nature* (Cambridge, Mass.: Harvard University Press, 1978), p. 167.

offering a thought experiment), in devising the physical universe, was looking toward the eternal Forms of beauty. Later Platonist developments made two things clear: the world He made or makes is guided toward those Forms, seeking to embody them, as far as this is possible within a temporal and spatial setting; and the Forms are nothing other than the very thoughts of God. What the world is imitating, struggling ceaselessly to reflect, is God, conceived as a union of Thought and Thinker. All of us–that is to say, all creatures–are aiming at the only life that is eternal, the divine. The undivided intellect itself, it came to seem, exists in contemplation of the Good, beyond all reasoning and being. Our task, remember, is to reconnect with *Nous*, with the eternal, undivided intellect – which we do, in part, by looking toward the One, the origin of value and existence. The circle that Socrates presents to Euthyphro is real: the holy is loved by God because it's holy; it's holy because He loves it.

> Wherefore we ought to fly away from earth to heaven as quickly as we can; and to fly away means to become like God, as far as this is possible; and to become like him, means to become holy, just, and wise.[39]

How can we bring these metaphysical speculations a little closer to the practical? What is it, exactly, that we are being urged to do and think? And how did it ever happen that we have an option? What God or the gods love is the best of all things – which is to say they love themselves. And to do and be what the gods love is to be the gods, to live with the life they value. The service they require of us is to be like them:

> Then what life is agreeable to God, and becoming in His followers? One only, expressed once for all in the old saying that 'like agrees with like, with measure measure', but things which have no measure agree neither with themselves nor with the things which have. Now God ought to be to us the measure of all things, and not man, as men commonly say: the words are far more true of Him. And he who would be dear to God must, as far as is possible, be like Him and such as He is. Wherefore the temperate man is the friend of God, for he is like Him; and the intemperate or unjust man is unlike Him, and different from Him. And the same applies to other things; and this is the conclusion, which is also the noblest and truest of all sayings, that for the good man to offer sacrifice to the Gods, and hold

[39] *Theaetetus* 176b.

> converse with them by means of prayers and offerings and every kind of service, is the noblest and best of all things, and also the most conducive to a happy life, and very fit and meet. But with the bad man, the opposite of this is true: for the bad man has an impure soul, whereas the good is pure; and from one who is polluted, neither a good man nor God can without impropriety receive gifts. Wherefore the unholy do only waste their much service upon the Gods, but when offered by any holy man, such service is most acceptable to them.[40]

Ceremonial, Civil and Purificatory Service

The most widespread form of divine service is now poorly understood by post-Copernican urbanites like ourselves. 'In this city [of the world] virtue is honoured and vice has its appropriate dishonour, and not merely the images of gods but *gods themselves* look down on us from above.'[41] Serving the visible gods, the stars of heaven, is sharing in the complex dance that they perform above and around us, and so sharing in a simulacrum of eternity.[42] The same movements are endlessly repeated, but neither the stars nor those embedded in the ritual year need remember the merely linear, endless process. Seed-time and harvest, Christmas and Easter and 'the passionless Sundays after Trinity, neither feast-day nor fast'[43] are permanent realities. Nothing serious is ever really lost, since circular motion is unending without being infinite. Obviously, post-Copernicans look out on an entirely different sidereal universe, and even if we manage to believe the speculative cosmologists who imagine an infinity of worlds or aeons we know that our own personal and terrestrial history passes irrevocably from a far beginning to a distant end. Urbanites expect strawberries at any time of the year, and only play at the repeating seasons. We are, notoriously, in some danger of forgetting that 'More! More! Is the cry of a mistaken soul'.[44]

40 *Laws* 4.716cff (tr. Benjamin Jowett).

41 *Ennead* II.9 [33].9, 19ff.

42 *Ennead* IV.4 [28]. 8.

43 John Meade Falkner 'After Trinity' (1910): *Collected Poems* (Kings Newton: John Meade Falkner Society, 2008).

44 William Blake, 'There is no Natural Religion' (1788), section 5, in *Complete Writings*, ed. G. Keynes (Oxford: Oxford University Press, 1966), p. 97.

Plato, Plotinus and other Platonists were both a little closer to the ceremonial year, and readier to acknowledge the presence of the visible gods, the stars, and the periods they ruled:

> General opinion makes the Hours goddesses and the Month a god, and their worship has been handed on to us: we say also that the Day and the Night are deities, and the gods themselves have taught us how to call upon them.[45]

But they were also ready, as it were, to allegorize that ancient sidereal religion, and we too can glimpse what they saw in it. 'By contemplating the equivalence of the future and the past we pierce through time right to eternity'.[46] As *souls*, or as fallen souls, we only see things from particular angles, at particular moments, and are easily persuaded that the world as we see it is all the world there is. But even materialists know better: there are no privileged places, moments or timescales, and the *real* world is the one discovered, if at all, through reason, as the complete, well-ordered content of the Intellect. Learning to detach ourselves from sensory illusions, to live in the understanding that each of us is a *version* of reality, an entity wholly dependent on its membership of that real world and without any special status, is both an epistemological and a moral exercise. We serve the gods by pleasing them. We please them by sharing, sometimes, in their life, and dismissing the charms that bind us to our sensual, solitary delusions. Which is why Mark McPherran was not entirely mistaken in suspecting that the moral of the *Euthyphro* is that it is Socrates who does God service[47]—though I think he was wrong in supposing that this is simply by exposing human ignorance, and debunking radical claims to know what is required by justice.

No-one, so Plotinus said, would really prefer the *appearance* of the beloved to the real thing.[48] This is as much as to say that it is not our *feelings* that matter most to us, but our engagement with the real. 'Beautifulness is reality.'[49] Engaging with the astronomical,

[45] Proclus, *In Timaeum* 248d: quoted by Franz Cumont, *Astrology and Religion among the Greeks and Romans* (New York: Dover, 1960; 1st published 1912), p. 61.

[46] Simone Weil, *Intimations of Christianity*, tr. E. C. Geissbuhler (London: Routledge & Kegan, 1957), p. 96.

[47] See Mark L. McPherran, 'Socratic Piety in the *Euthyphro*', *Journal of the History of Philosophy* 23 (1985), pp. 283–309.

[48] *Ennead* VI.7 [38].26, 21f

[49] *Ennead* I.6 [1].6, 21

agricultural or ceremonial year is one way of remembering that there is a real world, that we are a part of it. But even without these aids—of which Plotinus availed himself rather little—it is possible to understand ourselves as elements in a larger, real world. *Civil* virtue requires us to prefer those public duties to our lesser, personal attachments.

In performing these duties we may also 'serve the gods', or at least the gods of our cities. But there are at least three reasons to reckon that even this service is not entirely what Plato, Aristotle, Plotinus and the rest preferred. First of all, such service is parochial: however glorious our city, however well-deserving of our love, it is not the only one, nor the City Herself of which it is a copy. Its service may even be corrupting. And secondly, all 'moral action' is inferior, dependent on the existence of evils that no truly virtuous persons could desire to exist, and all too likely to multiply those evils. All action is subject to the enchantments of the flesh.[50] If there are indeed this-worldly evils to be remedied, the virtuous do not wish this to be so. A truly courageous person (say) would not actually want to display courage—since that depends on there being wrongs to resist or even wars to fight 'as if a physician were to wish that nobody needed his skill'.[51] 'Pity would be no more, if we did not make somebody poor'[52]—unless pity (or better, liberality) is the name of something better than its practical performance. And thirdly, all action is uncertain—in the sense that we can never be sure of its outcome. It is not the *outcome* but the intent, the mode of thought, that matters.

So Aristotle chose to identify the higher, detached, contemplative life as that of the resident alien, not the citizen.[53] If we are to live the life of gods this cannot be the actively 'moral' life: that's not how they live.[54] One of Plotinus's converts, Rogatianus, 'gave up all his property, dismissed all his servants, resigned his rank … and only ate every other day'.[55] What exactly did he do to practice a superior virtue?

> For what can true self-control (*sophrosune*) be except not keeping company with bodily pleasures, but avoiding them as impure and belonging to something impure? Courage, too, is not being afraid of death. And death is the separation of body

[50] *Ennead* IV.4 [28].44

[51] *Ennead* VI.8 [39].5, 13–21.

[52] William Blake, 'The Human Abstract' (*Songs of Experience*), in *Complete Writings*, p. 217.

[53] Aristotle, *Politics* 7.1324a13ff.

[54] Aristotle, *Nicomachean Ethics* 10.1178b7ff.

[55] Porphyry, *Life of Plotinus* 7, Armstrong op.cit., vol. 1, p. 27.

> and soul; and a man does not fear this if he welcomes the prospect of being alone (*monos genesthai*). Again, greatness of soul is despising the things here: and wisdom (*phronesis*) is an intellectual activity which turns away from the things below and leads the soul to those above.[56]

The lesser, 'civic', virtues may be a necessary stage on the way upward, but they are not themselves the virtue that Plotinus wishes. True virtue lies in gathering up the energies we have invested in the outward, sensual world. We may or even must begin from beautiful sights, then beautiful ways of life, 'beautiful works, not those which the arts produce, but the works of men who have a name for goodness, then look at the souls of the people who produce the beautiful works'.[57] But the goal is to go back into yourself and see. 'Never stop working on your statue till the divine glory of virtue shines out on you, till you see 'self-mastery [*sophrosune*] enthroned upon its holy seat'.'[58]

This work is purification, a waking up from inappropriate images.[59] And Plotinus is not alone in advocating it. According to Nicholas Lash,

> The ancient traditions of devotion and reflection, of worship and enquiry, have seen themselves as *schools*. Christianity and Vedāntic Hinduism, Judaism and Buddhism and Islam are schools… whose pedagogy has the twofold purpose – however differently conceived and executed in the different traditions – of weaning us from our idolatry and purifying our desire.[60]

By the Platonic analysis of Soul, this is as much as to say that we need to separate ourselves from both lower souls, from the desirous and the spirited parts alike.

> There are different levels in the soul, only a bit of us is real and knows truth, the rest is fantasy, anxiety, resentment, envy, all

[56] *Ennead* I.6 [1].6, 7–13; see also I.2 [19].5, 6ff. *Monos genesthai* is better translated 'becoming pure'.

[57] *Ennead* I.6 [1].9, 4ff.

[58] *Ennead* I.6 [1].9, 13ff, after Plato *Phaedrus* 254b7.

[59] *Enneads* III.6 [26].5, 23ff.

[60] Nicholas Lash, *The Beginning and the End of 'Religion'* (Cambridge: Cambridge University Press, 1996), p. 21. See also Moses Maimonides, *The Guide of the Perplexed*, tr. Chaim Rabin, ed. Julius Guttman (Hackett: Indianapolis, 1995; original version 1190), Bk.3, ch.29: p. 178: 'the first purpose of the whole law is to remove idolatry and to wipe out its traces and all that belongs to it, even in memory'.

> selfish tricks – *you* know. We live in a dream, we're wrapped up in a dark veil, we think we're omnipotent magicians, we don't believe anything *exists* except ourselves.[61]

The motives and opinions of our sensual and social selves can be put aside, as no more than distorted images of our *real* life, the life we are to share with gods, the truth:

> The man who belongs to this world may be handsome and tall and rich and the ruler of all mankind (since he is essentially of this region), and we ought not to envy him for things like these, by which he is beguiled. The wise man will perhaps not have them at all, and if he has them will himself reduce them, if he cares for his true self. He will reduce and gradually extinguish his bodily advantages by neglect, and will put away authority and office. He will take care of his bodily health, but will not wish to be altogether without experience of illness, nor indeed also of pain.[62]
>
> And if you are wronged, what is there dreadful in that to an immortal?[63]

To serve the gods, which is to say, to live as the gods prefer, is to be stripped of lesser goods:

> The attainment [of the good] is for those who go up to that higher world and are converted and strip off what we put on in our descent; (just as for those who go up to the celebrations of sacred rites there are purifications and strippings off of the clothes they wore before, and going up naked) until passing in the ascent all that is alien to the God, one sees with one's self alone.[64]

According to one strand of the tradition, this will not be possible until we're dead:

[61] Iris Murdoch, *Acastos* (Harmondsworth: Penguin, 1987), p. 101 ('Plato' speaks).

[62] *Ennead* I.4 [46].14, 14ff.

[63] *Ennead* II.9 [33].9, 15f.

[64] *Ennead*, I.6 [1].7. I have examined something of the history and significance of this metaphor in 'Going Naked into the Shrine: Herbert, Plotinus and the Constructive Metaphor', in D. Hedley & S. Hutton, eds., *Platonism at the Origins of Modernity* (Dordrecht: Springer, 2008), pp. 45–61.

> It seems, to judge from the argument, that the wisdom which we desire and upon which we profess to have set our hearts will be attainable only when we are dead, and not in our lifetime. If no pure knowledge is possible in the company of the body, then either it is totally impossible to acquire knowledge, or it is only possible after death, because it is only then that the soul will be separate and independent of the body. It seems that so long as we are alive, we shall continue closest to knowledge if we avoid as much as we can all contact and association with the body, except when they are absolutely necessary, and instead of allowing ourselves to become infected with its nature purify ourselves from it until God himself gives us deliverance. In this way, by keeping ourselves uncontaminated by the follies of the body, we shall probably reach the company of others like ourselves and gain direct knowledge of all that is pure and uncontaminated–that is, presumably, of truth. For one who is not pure himself to attain to the realm of purity would no doubt be a breach of universal justice.[65]

No doubt Plato meant this fairly literally: that we shall be able to live as the gods live only when we are immortal gods (again). But there is an immediate *phenomenological* interpretation of his words. To know the truth, to live the life of God, we have to put ourselves aside, to silence that vulgar, chattering goblin who poses as our ego. Speaking scandalously of the god of love, for example, is impious.[66] We have to submit to correction:

> Refutation is the greatest and chiefest of purifications, and he who has not been refuted, though he be the Great King himself, is in an awful state of impurity; he is uninstructed and deformed in those things in which he would be truly blessed ought to be fairest and purest.[67]

Coming Down from the Mountain

Philosophizing may have some 'therapeutic' value, in the more familiar sense, to calm us down or reconcile us to our condition. But it

65 *Phaedo* 66bff.

66 *Phaedrus* 263b-c.

67 *Sophist* 227c, 228a-d, 230d; on the further history of this trope, see Marjorie O'Rourke Boyle, 'Pure of Heart: From Ancient Rites to Renaissance Plato', *Journal of the History of Ideas* 63 (2002), pp. 41–62.

may be that we need the gods' assistance to achieve the real goal: the gods must come to us, rather than we to them—which is why Plotinus declined to accompany his student Amelius on a temple-crawl.[68] Porphyry said that that 'it seems that the gods often set him straight when he was going on a crooked course 'sending down a solid shaft of light'.'[69] And so he came at last, so Porphyry interpreted the Delphic Oracle to say, to join 'the company of heaven, where affection rules, and desire, and joy and love kindled by God'.[70]

That is an enormous hope. The best that most of us can manage will be civil virtue, obedience to the laws that let us live together in a sort of peace. Those laws, we are told, had better come from God.

> [The] Cretans believe, as Homer says, that Minos went every ninth year to converse with his Olympian sire, and gave [them] laws which he brought from him.[71]
>
> These Cretan laws are with reason famous among the Hellenes; for they fulfil the object of laws, which is to make those who use them happy; and they confer every sort of good. Now goods are of two kinds: there are human and there are divine goods, and the human hang upon the divine; and the state which attains the greater, at the same time acquires the less, or, not having the greater, has neither. Of the lesser goods the first is health, the second beauty, the third strength, including swiftness in running and bodily agility generally, and the fourth is wealth, not the blind god [Plutus], but one who is keen of sight, if only he has wisdom for his companion. For wisdom is chief and leader of the divine class of goods, and next follows temperance; and from the union of these two with courage springs justice, and fourth in the scale of virtue is courage. All these naturally take precedence of the other goods, and this is the order in which the legislator must place them, and after them he will enjoin the rest of his ordinances on the citizens with a view to these, the human looking to the divine, and the divine looking to their leader, mind.[72]

The primary purpose of these laws, so Plato tells us, is to encourage *virtue*, of the sort I sketched before: the precise rules of marriage, property and the rest may be the best that can be managed nowadays,

68 Porphyry, *Live of Plotinus* ch.10.
69 Porphyry, *Life of Plotinus* ch.23, 18f.
70 Ibid., 30.
71 Plato, *Laws* 1.624; see Plotinus, *Ennead* VI.9 [9].7.
72 Plato, *Laws* 1.631b.

however wistfully we look back on the age of Cronos when no laws were needed, or look aloft to the heavens where obedience is by nature.

For Platonists the world of our present experience is 'fallen' and 'imperfect'. 'If all things are well done, can the doers act unjustly or err? And how can we assert that some things are according to nature, but others against nature, if all things that happen and are done are according to nature?'[73] And yet there is no need nor prospect of a 'better' world[74] in which to do our jobs. That job is to join with the gods, as Euthyphro suggested, in the making or remaking of many and noble things. 'Providence ought not to exist in such a way as to make us nothing. If everything was providence and nothing but providence, then providence would not exist; for what would it have to provide for?'[75]

But the point of that making or that attempt at making is in the end to allow the sight of beauty, or reality, the awakening and purification that the schools of philosophy promise. Sensual and civil success is not what Platonists promise, any more than prophets. It is enough to love and serve the Lord, to be awake.

[73] *Ennead* III.2 [47].16, 3ff.

[74] *Ennead* II.9 [33].5, 24f.

[75] *Ennead* III.2 [47].9, 1ff. Or as Nicolo Machiavelli put it, 'God is not willing to do everything, and thus take away our free will and that share of glory which belongs to us', *The Prince* [1513], tr. Paul Halsall; ch.26.

The Teacher as Mother or Midwife? A Comparison of Brahmanical and Socratic Methods of Education

KATE WHARTON

Socrates famously compares himself to a midwife in Plato's *Theaetetus*. Much less well known is the developed metaphor of pregnancy at the centre of the initiation ritual that begins Brahmanical education.[1] In this ritual, called *Upanayana*, the teacher is presented as becoming pregnant with the student. The *Arthavaveda* states:

> The teacher leads the student towards himself, makes him an embryo within; he bears him in his belly three nights.[2]

[1] For the purposes of this chapter we will define Brahmanical education as purely concerning the memorisation of the sacred inherited verses – the Vedas – that were recited during the *śrauta* ritual. The term 'Brahmanical' refers to the experts (*brahmins*) who wrote the *Brāhmaṇas* and formalised and expanded the śrauta ritual. The definition of Brahmanical culture used here is not purely historical, but represents an over-arching cultural paradigm that extends from the composition of the *Brāhmaṇas* in 800–600 BCE to the era of the *Dharmaśāstras* 100 BCE–200 CE. We use the term 'Brahmanical ritual' rather than 'Vedic ritual' to draw a distinction between the early/middle Vedic culture and the late Vedic (Brahmanical) era. In the early/middle Vedic period the sacred hymns of the *Vedas* were composed by a large population of antagonistic tribes, and the sacrificial rite was a festal gathering not yet formalised, however, in the late Vedic (or Brahmanical) era, when the *Brāhmaṇas* were composed, the rite became a highly elaborate and controlled event. It is this later more developed ritual culture that is of interest to us here. This chapter does not intend to provide a historical outline of the full variety of educational methods in ancient India but to illustrate one predominant strand that can be seen as core to the educational system. For a more detailed discussion of the historical context of the strand that this chapter isolates refer to the introduction and first chapter of my thesis, *Philosophy as a Practice of Freedom in Ancient India and Ancient Greece* (SOAS, University of London, 2008).

[2] Arthavaveda (*Śaunaka Recension*) 11.5.3, Meiko Kajihara, *The Brahmacārin in the Veda: The Evolution of the 'Vedic Student' and the Dynamics of Texts, Ritual and Society in Ancient India* (Harvard University Thesis, 2002), p. 136.

doi:10.1017/S1358246109990270

In this ritual action, the teacher becomes the mother of the pupil.

What is the difference between a mother and a midwife? The essential difference between these roles is that the mother gives birth and the midwife does not. In the *Upanayana*, the teacher becomes pregnant; in the Socratic analogy it is the student, not the teacher, who becomes pregnant: knowledge is presented as originating within him. Both these metaphors compare education to gestation, labour and birth, but the way they set out the teacher–pupil relationship is completely opposite. In the *Upanayana*, the mother directly generates and forms the student. The pregnant teacher is presented as the sole source of knowledge. In the Socratic analogy the midwife watches over the student and aids him as *he* gives birth.

In the *Theaetetus*, Socrates argues that the educational process must be centred around the potential of the student, so that they initiate their own growth and give birth to their own truth. Socrates claims that knowledge cannot be passed down directly from teacher to pupil. He observes that growth in wisdom is only authentic if a pupil's 'progress is amazing both to other people and to themselves.' Socrates is adamant that this progress is never due to anything his students have learned from him: instead 'they discover within themselves a multitude of beautiful things, which they bring forth into the light.'[3] In the Socratic model, the teacher stands to one side, like a doctor, and helps the student to critically examine his pregnancy to see whether it will come to full term.

In the *Upanayana* ritual there is absolutely no distance, no boundary, between teacher and pupil. The student bonds with his teacher as a child held in the womb. To understand the contrast between the pedagogical ideals of the teacher as a mother and the teacher as a midwife let us look in more detail at the *Upanayana* ritual and its function within ancient and medieval Indian education. The *Dharmaśāstras* (100 BCE–200 CE) state that *Upanayana* was mandatory, automatically undergone by all the higher castes in accordance with the laws of Manu. There was no choice involved: every male child of the higher castes would undergo *Upanayana* between the ages of five and eight. The Brahmin's whole childhood was dedicated to the imitation of his teacher as he recited Vedic mantra. When he is reborn in the *Upanayana* ritual the student is consecrated, like his teacher before him, to be a vessel for the Vedas, the sacred verses. The

[3] *Theaetetus* 150e. John Cooper, *Plato: Complete Works* (Indianapolis/Cambridge: Hackett, 1997), p. 167.

image of pregnancy in the *Upanayana* is a metaphor for how knowledge is inherited, shared and passed between teacher and pupil: through and in the transmission of the Vedas, they identify with each other, becoming as if one body—and one mind.

The *Upanayana* ritual also dramatises the student's commitment to tradition. The womb from which the student is reborn is not the womb of any particular individual, but the womb of the Vedas themselves; the teacher gives the student over completely to the possession of the Vedas. The *Upanayana* dramatises the pupil's memorisation of his first sacred *mantra* and it ensures that the student relates to the truth of the Vedas as to his mother who created and bore him. The *Laws of Manu* refer to the *Upanayana* as 'birth from the Veda'.[4] It says that the Vedic mantra is the 'mother' of the student.[5] Laurie Patton has observed that in one Vedic hymn related to pregnancy, there is great anxiety over miscarriage, or the loss of an embryo, because it is seen as the loss not just of a child but 'more importantly [of] a Brahmin who knows verses.'[6] According to Patton, this hymn suggests that each embryo has value only in that it is a 'storehouse for sacrificial knowledge.'[7] In the *Upanayana* the student is consecrated to be such a storehouse; in imitation of his teacher he will memorise, preserve and pass down the entire corpus of verses.

The memorisation of the Vedas was an immense task. A student in a Ṛg Vedic school would have had to learn firstly, the *Ṛg Veda* (about 10580 verses), then the *pada*, *krama* and/or *jaṭā* texts (the same length), the *Aitreya Brāhmaṇa and Āraṇyaka*, and the six *Vedāṅgas* (which include the 4000 sūtras of Pāṇini's grammar).[8] The amount of information to be memorised, and the amount of time required, meant that there was no space within the educational period for anything except replication.

[4] *Manu Smṛti* 2.170; trans. Patrick Olivelle, *Laws of Manu* (Oxford: Oxford University Press, 2004).

[5] *Manu Smṛti* 2.171.

[6] Laurie Patton, ed., *Jewels of Authority: Women and Text in the Hindu Tradition* (New York: Oxford University Press 2002), p. 59.

[7] Patton, *Jewels of Authority*, p. 53.

[8] The *Gopatha Brāhmaṇa* states that the period of study for memorising one such Veda is twelve years (GB 2.5, CU 6.1.2.) Kane mentions various alternatives to this time found in the Law books, ranging from 3 to 18 years for each Veda, but twelve years seems to be the average. P.V. Kane, *History of Dharmaśāstra*, (Poona: Bhandarkar Oriental Research Institute, 1975), pp. 348, 352.

The essential educational method is demonstrated in the initiation itself. At the core of the *Upanayana* is the learning of the first mantra.[9] The *Brāhmaṇas* describe this as follows:

> As they sit facing each other west of the fire, the teacher, who is facing east, makes the student repeat the 'resonating' syllable OM, the 'great utterances' *bhūr, bhuvah, svah* and the *sāvitrī* verse.[10]

In one text, *Śatapatha Brāhmana* 11.5.4.13, this moment is seen as an act of impregnation. The text states that the *mantra* must be pronounced with the teacher and pupil sitting in correct position, face to face; otherwise 'if someone were then to say "he begat him perversely," it would be so.'[11] That the learning of the *mantra* is the basic reproductive technology of the womb of the teacher is stated explicitly in *ŚB* 11.5.4.17:

> Twofold indeed are these progeny, divine and human. Those human progeny are born from the vagina. The divine progeny are the meters – [the teacher] generates them from the mouth, and from there he generates the (student).[12]

The student is more than human after he has been reborn through the memorisation of the Vedas. He is no longer human progeny; instead he is divine progeny, born of the scriptures themselves.

We have seen that one Vedic hymn suggests that the Brahmanical student's life is valued only in so much as he is a vessel for the Vedas. We have seen that ritual rebirth is mandatory. This invites the question: Is the student freed or enslaved by his commitment to the Vedas? Born of the Vedas, born of the mouth of his teacher, does he become more than human, or is he rendered less than human, sub-human? Who is the rightful owner of his identity—the student himself or the tradition that has laboured over him and given him birth?

If we turn to more of the detail of the *Upanayana* ritual, we may be able to begin to answer these questions. The *Upanayana* begins with a series of gestures that represent joining, binding and enveloping. The student is wrapped in garments which are compared to

9 Timothy Lubin, *Consecration and Ascetical Regimen: A History of Hindu Vrāta, Dikṣā, Upanayana and Brahmacārya* (Columbia University Thesis, 1994), p. 191.

10 Lubin, *Consecration and Ascetical Regimen*, p. 191.

11 Lubin, *Consecration and Ascetical Regimen*, p. 136.

12 Lubin, *Consecration and Ascetical Regimen*, p. 136.

womb-layers.[13] Other ritual garments, such as the *mekhalā* belt,[14] are tied round the student to represent his commitment to his teacher. The extent of the student's union with the teacher is seen in this statement, which the teacher makes in this case to a group of initiates:

> We bend together your thoughts, your wills, your intentions; we make those of you there who are discordant bend (your wills) together.
>
> I grasp (your) minds with (my) mind; follow my thought with your thoughts; I put your hearts in my powers; go and follow along my course.[15]

In another version of the ritual, the teacher touches the heart of one student and says: 'I place your heart under my rule. Let your thought follow my thought. Take delight in my word wholeheartedly. Let Bṛhaspati join you to me.'[16] Bṛhaspati is the 'custodian of *brahman*' or revealed Vedic speech.[17]

The extent to which the student's mind and body is given over to the replication of the Vedas is revealed in Frits Staal's study of present day practices in Kerala, where the ancient tradition of Vedic memorisation is still active. Staal observes that the pupil's conditioning is rigorously controlled through a system of gesture, the student imitating not just his teacher's pitch and accent but also his head movements. Staal observes:

> The head is kept straight when the phrase is medium pitch, is bent down when it is low pitched and for the high pitched it is bent to the right side... There are *mūdras* (hand gestures) which accompany the vowels and consonants of the ṚV recitation.[18]
>
> And the students also count out the *vargas* with the fingers of their left hand and the half stanzas with the fingers of the right, again in imitation of their teacher.[19]

13 Kajihara, *The Brahmacārin in the Veda*, p. 21.
14 Lubin, *Consecration and Ascetical Regimen*, p. 183.
15 Lubin, *Consecration and Ascetical Regimen*, p. 189.
16 Lubin, *Consecration and Ascetical Regimen*, p. 189.
17 Lubin, *Consecration and Ascetical Regimen*, p. 182.
18 Frits Staal, *Nambudiri Veda Recitation* (S'Gravenhage: Mouton and Co, 1961), p. 41.
19 Frits Staal, *Agni: the Ritual of the Fire Altar* (Berkeley: University of California Press, 1982), pp. 359–379.

The historian Harmut Scharfe observes that this 'motoric memory' probably reinforced the retention of memorised sounds.[20]

It might indeed be argued that the student is completely controlled, that he is dominated, by the discipline of memorisation. Strict rules that define the student regimen are set out at the end of the *Upanayana*. These ensure that the student has no autonomy. He must beg for food and eat what he is given—so he has no control over his diet. He must wake and sleep according to the teacher's rhythm. He must be celibate and isolated from all social interaction. He must tend the fires daily and perform other servile tasks for his teacher such as washing, massaging and dressing. The student was brought up by his teacher with his every action directed by rule.

The combined effect of all these practices of self-denial, however, is to allow the student to become detached from any thoughts or inclinations that might distract him from the memorisation of the Vedas. The student regimen ensured that the student had no influence over any aspect of his daily routine—he never made a decision for himself or was allowed to pursue and gratify a desire. While he lived in his teacher's house he was treated like an embryo in the womb; he was trained to be passive and to exercise no agency. This meant that the quality of the student's attention was extremely pure—his focus was unwavering as he recited the Vedas. The student regimen removed the student far from all the variety of life, and his powers of concentration could develop to their utmost. The student was trained to be a perfect vessel for the Vedas: his ascetic regimen eradicated his inner life, so he became highly receptive, he could imitate and store the Vedas with perfect accuracy, and he was taught to live in a state of constant absorption, both absorbed in and absorbing the sacred verses.

The Law Books describe the ideal student as he listens to his teacher: 'Focusing his eyes and mind on the teacher, the pupil should touch his vital organs with *durbha* grass [and] control his breath three times for fifteen more each.' He must stand with joined palms looking at his teacher's face with 'his body, speech, organs of perception and mind under control.' The ideal student 'feels neither elation nor revulsion at hearing, touching, seeing, eating or smelling anything.' He must be completely absorbed in the practice of memorisation itself.

The development of the student's concentration—beginning remember, between the age of five and eight—can be seen in the

[20] Harmut Scharfe, *Education in Ancient India* (Leiden: Brill, 2002), p. 241.

practice exercises referred to as the *pada, krama* and *jaṭāpāṭha* versions of the Vedas.[21] These texts grammatically alter or re-order the words of the original hymns as a kind of memory test, so that the student knows the Vedas both forwards and backwards. The easiest test is the *padapāṭha*, which removes the normal rules for combining the letters at the beginning and ending of words (*saṃdhi*), and also separates words that are normally in a compound.[22] Another exercise, the *kramapāṭha*, offers a more complex challenge. It combines the original hymns with the *padapāṭha* in pairs of words that weave back and forth between the two forms: a-b, b-c, d-e, etc., with one word in *pada* form and the other in the original hymn (*saṃhita*) form. A further level of testing occurs in the *jaṭāpāṭha* form, when the original words of the hymn are completely rearranged. For instance if a *ṛg* verse ends with words a, b, c and d, it will be practiced as: a b, b a, a b c, c b a, a b c, b c, c b, b c d, d c b, b c d; etc.[23] These exercises suggest that what is being communicated in the transmission of the Vedic hymns is a method for developing concentration—the content of the hymns is not the object of study, but rather the whole effort of studying is aimed at a certain quality of absorption in the hymns.

Jan Gonda states that 'the high goal, the mastery of the holy text called for the application of the whole person, of the whole life, of all energy.'[24] When the student was involved in mnemonic practices there was simply no energy left for alternative patterns of thought, for self-centred reflection or analysis. Scharfe observes that during the educational process questions were discouraged and must absolutely 'not involve the meaning of the text.'[25] The student learnt a form, and the communication between teacher and pupil was always formatted: 'There [were] no explanations… only precise repetition [was] demanded.'[26] In the Law Books it is stated that the teacher is to the pupil 'the man who drills his ears with truth.'[27]

21 www.vedchant.com presents recordings and accounts of a variety of mnemonic practice chants.

22 Harry Falk, 'The Galits in the Ṛg Veda *Padapāṭha*: On the Origins of the *Samhitapāṭha* and the *Padapāṭha*,' in Axel Micheals, ed., *The Pandit* (Delhi: Manohar, 2001), p. 181.

23 Staal, *Nambudiri Veda Recitation*, p. 47.

24 Jan Gonda, *Change and Continuity in Indian Religions* (The Hague: Mouton, 1965), p. 295.

25 Scharfe, *Education in Ancient India*, p. 244.

26 Scharfe, *Education in Ancient India*, p. 244.

27 *Vasiṣtha Dharma Sūtra* 1.2.10, Patrick Olivelle, *Dharmasūtras* (Oxford: Oxford University Press, 1999).

This all sounds highly mechanistic, but although the discipline of memorisation requires immense commitment it does not necessarily turn the student into an automaton. The development of unwavering concentration should rather be seen as a discipline of unwavering trust. The student relinquishes his will and identifies with the will of the tradition, but this need not mean that he is dehumanised; for human-ness should not be defined by free-will alone. The student's extreme commitment can be understood to be beneficial to him in very human terms. For the student of the Vedas perfect obedience inherently contains its own reward, because it leads to perfect confidence or *śraddhā*. *Śraddhā* is derived from *śrat* (a root noun which means 'heart') and the verb *dhā* (to place). It therefore means to place one's heart on something.[28] Vaman Apte defines the term as 'trust, faith, belief, confidence, sedateness, composure of mind, intimacy, familiarity, respect and reverence.'[29] In the materials relating to ritual performance, according to Minoru Hara, *śraddhā* is 'considered as the innate nature of a human being, his nature to trust something objective.'[30] The Vedas are seen as an objective authority, and in the womb of the teacher the student's innate capacity to trust is allowed to develop to its fullest potential, completely uninhibited. The student inherits limitless confidence from his teacher. Perfect trust can be seen as a profoundly human virtue, and strict obedience should not be always judged to be oppressive, as inculturation or conditioning. The educational discipline of the Brahmanical student should be seen, as in the etymology, as something on which the heart rests, as a foundation for emotional stability and constancy of heart.

The recitation of the Vedas is not merely therapeutic on an emotional level, however, for the human dimension of the benefits of learning the Vedic hymns is overshadowed by a greater cosmic dimension. As Paul Hacker observes, '*mantras* when spoken are capable of bringing about a reality not only at the psychological level but even in the material order of things.'[31] The Vedic *mantra*

[28] Paul Hacker, 'śraddhā,' *Wiener Zeitschrift fur die Kunde Sud-und Ostasiens*, Band III (1963), p. 151–189.

[29] V. Apte, *A Practical Sanskrit Dictionary* (Delhi: Motilal Banarsidass, 1959). M. Hara defines it as a 'permanent dormant or innate instinct' in 'Note on Two Sanskrit Religious Terms: bhakti and śraddhā,' *Indo-Iranian Journal*, 7 (1964), pp. 124–145; p. 143.

[30] Hara, 'Note on Two Sanskrit Terms: bhakti and śraddhā', p. 143.

[31] Harold Coward, *Mantra* (Albany: State University of New York Press, 2004), p. 14.

are not seen as humanly authored hymns, but as pre-eternal sounds that are coextensive with the forces or laws governing the universe. All cosmic events are controlled by and mirror the Vedas. The truth that is passed down from teacher to pupil is greater than human wisdom; it was not invented or discovered by humans. Thus it was believed that the truth of the Vedas is an articulation that articulated itself, that the verses are elemental, and, like the laws of physics, that they reflect the self-expression of the cosmos.

Harold Coward observes that *mantras* express truth 'not just because they capture the truth of some cosmological occurrence but because they themselves have participated and continue to participate in the same cosmological events;'[32] not a sentence about an event, but are the event itself. This is most evident in the equivalence of the sound OM and the moment of creation.

Because a *mantra* has no human author it is perfect and completely incorrupt; unlike any human expression there is nothing that can be misunderstood, questioned or doubted in the Vedic hymns. In Brahmanical education a clear division is maintained between divine wisdom, the *mantra*, and human wisdom, which develops through the practice of judgement and decision-making. In the twelve years that the student lives with his teacher he focuses completely on inheriting divine wisdom, and he does not develop any critical faculty. Scharfe observes that it was often the case that 'the average reciter had little or no understanding of what he had learnt.'[33] This is not to denigrate this system of education, because the curative power of memorisation practice is not increased by questioning or analysing the linguistic meaning of what is learned.

Memorisation and the Socratic Elenchus

What would Socrates have said to a Vedic student absorbed in mantric recitation? Would he have reacted as he did to Ion, a professional performer of Homeric verse, when he criticised him for becoming hypnotised by his own performance? In his seminal study *Preface to Plato*, Eric Havelock interpreted many of Socrates' arguments in the *Republic* as a critique of educational practices based on memorisation. Havelock claims that Socrates' method of refutation (the *elenchus*) was designed to free his students from the 'state of emotional involvement and of emotional identification,'

[32] Coward, *Mantra*, p. 14.
[33] Scharfe, *Education in Ancient India*, p. 238.

described by Socrates as a kind of trance, that was a result of addiction to the recitation of Homeric verse. Havelock states that Socrates asks for a critical turn

> against centuries of habituation in rhythmic memorised experience. He asks of men that instead they should examine this experience and rearrange it, that they should think about what they say instead of just saying it. And that they should separate themselves from it instead of identifying with it; they themselves should become the 'subject' who stands apart from the 'object' and reconsiders it and analyses it and evaluates it, instead of just 'imitating' it.[34]

The 'subject' who stands apart from the 'object' is like the doctor that stands apart from the disease. Socrates argues that it is psychologically more beneficial to listen to a speech and analyse the inconsistencies within it, to diagnose and cure its internal problems, rather than to commit an inherited text to memory.

Following his medical model, as we have seen, Socrates developed a new metaphor for the teacher-pupil relationship, that of midwifery. When Theaetetus, his finest student, says that he can not stop worrying about the inadequacy of his ideas, Socrates replies 'Yes, those are the pains of labour, dear Theaetetus, it is because you are not barren but pregnant.' In the midwife metaphor Socrates teaches his pupils to give birth to their own truth by exercising their freedom to question, examine and diagnose or judge for themselves. Socrates charges each of his pupils to 'bring your own belief forth into the light.'[35] In this process, the student is not only giving birth to hypotheses and arguments, he is also giving birth to himself. The midwife watches over the student as he defines and styles his own identity. Full maturity is seen as the out-growing of all dependency. To inherit truth, to trust your teacher, to accept as the highest knowledge memorised text is judged by Socrates to impede progress towards full development. The true birth of the student occurs when all aspects of his soul have been thoroughly tested and chosen precisely because they are judged the best. As Hegel said of Socrates, 'such are not made but have formed themselves into what they are; they have become what they have wished to be, and are true to this.'[36]

[34] Eric Havelock, *Preface to Plato* (Oxford: Clarendon Press, 1963), p. 47.

[35] *Theaetetus* 157d. Cooper, *Plato*, p. 175.

[36] G. W. Hegel, *Lectures on the History of Philosophy* (Lincoln: University of Nebraska Press, 1995), Section 1.393.

The Socratic maxim that 'the unexamined life is not worth living' is one of the most familiar fragments of the philosophical tradition. Socrates would argue that the *Upanayana* ritual depicts rebirth into a life that is not worth living. Enclosure in the womb of the teacher would be for Socrates a form of imprisonment or entombment. He would argue that because the entire responsibility for the formation of the student's identity is held by the tradition, the student is never allowed to live his own life, that he never attains to full development or maturity because he is never allowed to take responsibility for himself.

In the midwife metaphor the student's progress rests on his own strength. He has to rely on his own inner resources in order to generate ideas that might, when tested, lead to what Socrates calls a '*discovery* worth the name of wisdom'. Socrates states that one's philosophical nature is 'self-made (*to autophues*) and owes its upbringing to no-one.'[37] In order to ensure that his pupils do not expect him to give birth for them, Socrates himself claims to be barren; he states:

> I myself am barren of wisdom. The common reproach against me is that I am always asking questions of other people but never express my own views about anything, because there is no wisdom in me; and that is true enough. ... I am not in any sense a wise man; I cannot claim as the child of my soul any discovery worth the name of wisdom.[38]

Throughout the Platonic Dialogues, there is no scene in which Plato dramatises the 'birth of wisdom'; instead he continually returns to the Oracle's pronouncement that Socrates is the wisest among men. However, Socrates always claims to be barren. In response to the Oracle, Socrates states that his wisdom amounts to this: 'I do not think I know what I do not know'. Socrates claims that his wisdom is merely 'human wisdom.'[39] He claims that the greatest possible human wisdom is to honestly admit that you know nothing. As a doctor or midwife, Socrates' main therapeutic technique is to remind people of their human limitation and at the same time to teach them how to be fully human. He aims to diagnose and cure the faults of the soul that result in people believing they have greater than human wisdom – these faults often include over-credulity, a weakness for flattery or lust for power. When Socrates finds

[37] *Republic* 520a. Cooper, Plato, p. 1137.
[38] *Theaetetus* 150c-d. Cooper, *Plato*, p. 167.
[39] *Apology* 20e. Cooper, *Plato*, p. 21.

these illnesses in the soul he attempts to correct them by means of arguments, reminding those who have delusions of grandeur of their human dimensions, using argument and questioning to humble and even humiliate them.

The Socratic dialogue ususally begins by a simple question: What is friendship? What is virtue? What is temperance? The student will answer this question as if it were obvious, then Socrates will ask more questions, getting the student to develop his definition, and during this process an essential contradiction inherent in the original answer will be exposed. The dialogue normally ends with both teacher and pupil agreeing they have returned to the beginning. The student's labour has been in vain. All his efforts have culminated in *aporia*. In ancient Greek, *poros* means path so *aporos* means lacking a path, a passage, a way. When a discussion ends in *aporia* it means that it has lost its bearings. The clear direction it seemed to be progressing in has revealed itself to be a dead end or impasse. In the dialogue named after him, Meno describes *aporia* as a state of pain and disorientation, and he compares Socrates to a stingray that numbs and paralyses its prey. Instead of passing down divine wisdom to his pupils, Socrates questions them relentlessly until they abandon all their preconceptions. One of Socrates' main responsibilities as a midwife is to diagnose false pregnancy. The midwife has a duty to abort students' ideas that are malformed. As an abortionist, the teacher's main responsibility is critical. Socrates teaches his students to examine their own ideas and be merciless in abandoning them if they are unfit.

Socrates claims to free his students from the form of life he most pities, the unexamined life. Here, however, it is vital to ask: Who, out of all Socrates' students, actually manages to give birth to a 'life worth living'? Which student is truly fertile, what conception is examined, tested by Socrates, and survives? The light-hearted way in which Socrates identifies himself with the happy image of the midwife disguises the real implications of the metaphor. Throughout the Socratic dialogues no student's pregnancy is brought to full birth' and all ideas are refuted and revealed to be what Socrates refers to as phantoms or false offspring. The only healthy birth that Socrates oversees is the birth of barrenness: the midwife's work is complete when the student realises that it is humanly impossible to give birth to truth. This is the way that Socrates teaches his students to be free; he frees them from any illusion of power or knowledge. There is no truth that has any power over the student, and the student has no special access to the truth that gives him power over others. The students are like Socrates, completely free from any authority that is greater than their own ignorance. But what does this really amount to in human terms? What is it like to live completely in the negative, holding on only to the central Socratic principle: 'I do not think I know what I do not know'? The barrenness of the student reflects his identification with *aporia*, understood as a pure state of not-knowing. In the midwife analogy Socrates promises his students that they are giving birth to their true selves, but the experience of *aporia* is one of loss of self.

Sarah Kofman observes that originally *poros* referred not to a land path but to a sea path. She states that a *poros* was a sea route, a passage opened up across a chaotic expanse. When there is no *poros* then the student is at sea. Kofman compares this aporetic sea to Hesiod's Tartarus, calling it 'a realm of wild, swirling squalls where there are no fixed directions, where one can find no landmarks, no bearings to travel by'.[40] Socrates claims to free his students to discover the truth for themselves, but he really teaches them to inherit a truth that is beyond questioning. This truth is the idea that the greatest possible experience of freedom is found in *aporia*, in a state where all ideas, beliefs, arguments and principles are equally negated, equally in free-fall. In the aporetic dialogues, Socrates' students experience the collapse of all their ideas into anxiety and grief, and fear the complete dissolution of their identity. Socrates himself experiences *aporia* as unlimited freedom and abandons himself to it. He allows every aporetic crisis to reduce him *afresh* to emptiness — this is the Socratic ritual of rebirth, which reoccurs continually.

In the *Phaedo* (112–114), Tartarus is depicted as a great ocean at the centre of the earth. Socrates states that 'into this chasm all rivers flow together' along with terrible winds. After death, condemned souls are thrown into this chasm and wracked about by great storms. By suspending his students' judgement in a constant state of *aporia*, Socrates trains them to endure Tartarus; he does not found their identity on perfect confidence in divine wisdom, but instead teaches them to cultivate perfect humility, to acknowledge the forces of chaos in the world and to develop courage in the face of the unknown.

In contrast, the educational paradigm of the womb of the teacher, which we have seen set out in the *Upanayana* ritual, works to seal the student away from the world. The student's perfect confidence is not merely based on an exchange of information, or words, or arguments,

[40] Sarah Kofman, 'Beyond Aporia,' in Andrew Benjamin, ed., *Post-Structuralist Classics* (New York: Routledge, 1988), p. 7.

but on the shaping of a sealed educational environment that forms a perfect whole around the student. We have seen that in the *Upanayana* ritual garments are given to the student that envelop him like womb-layers. In the womb of the teacher the student is taught to believe he is encompassed by completeness. He is never taught that there is anything missing, or that he should look for what is not right, nor to search for a mistake or an inconsistency. He has been given perfect confidence in his proximity to truth. It is a great virtue of this educational system that the student does not find himself left alone to search for a truth that might not even exist. Instead, he is brought up to believe that he is already in proximity to truth. Truth is so close it does not require explanation or analysis. The student does not struggle to give birth to ideas that approximate truth, instead he just has to listen, absorb and trust.

Martha Nussbaum states that:

> Philosophy heals human diseases, diseases produced by false beliefs. Its arguments are to the soul as the doctor's remedies are to the body. They can heal and they are to be evaluated in terms of their power to heal.[41]

In the Brahmanical *Upanayana*, argument is not seen as curative. Instead argument is seen as the disease, or at least a symptom of the disease.[42] The soul is healed not through argument, but by being held securely and surrounded completely by a sealed system of truth that is always already perfect; this is how the soul is healed in the womb of the teacher. The cure for human insufficiency and illness is to construct an nourishing environment of truth for every individual, a womb of truth consistent in all its parts. Every detail of the *Upanayana* and the student regimen combine to ensure that the student's memorisation of the Vedas frees him from any sense of deficiency. The recitation of *mantra* encapsulates the way that the student relates to his being, once he has been transformed by education. The *mantra* is the sound of perfect confidence in one's self and one's world. In his constant practice of questioning and refutation, the Socratic pupil learns humility and develops fortitude and courage in the face of the unknown. In his constant practice of Vedic recitation, the Brahmanical pupil rests in complete trust that

41 Martha Nussbaum, *The Therapy of Desire* (Princeton: Princeton University Press, 1994), p. 14.

42 See also Logi Gunnarsson, this volume, on the idea of 'philosophical maladies.'

he has inherited perfect knowledge and can never be separated from the truth.

In this chapter, I have argued that practices of education that rest on complete trust should be affirmed because they allow the student to see themselves not as an *aporia*, a problem that can never be solved, but as encompassed by truth. To borrow from another spiritual tradition, the essential message of the *Upanayana* ritual could be said to be: 'Be perfect, therefore as your heavenly father is perfect.'[43]

[43] Matthew 5:48.

A Return to the Self: Indians and Greeks on Life as Art and Philosophical Therapy

JONARDON GANERI

Spiritual Exercises and the Aesthetic Analogy

Of the many interrelated themes in Pierre Hadot's *Philosophy as a Way of Life: Spiritual Exercises from Socrates to Foucault*,[1] two strike me as having a particular centrality. First, there is the theme of attention to the present instant. Hadot describes this as the 'key to spiritual exercises' (p.84), and he finds the idea encapsulated in a quotation from Goethe's *Second Faust*: 'Only the present is our happiness' (p.217). The second theme is that of viewing the world from above: 'philosophy signified the attempt to raise up mankind from individuality and particularity to universality and objectivity' (p.242). Insofar as both attention to the present and raising oneself to an objective view imply the mastery of individual anxiety, passion and desire, they belong to a single conception, that conception being one of a 'return to the self':

> Thus, all spiritual exercises are, fundamentally, a return to the self, in which the self is liberated from the state of alienation into which it has been plunged by worries, passions, and desires. The 'self' liberated in this way is no longer merely our egoistic, passionate individuality: it is our moral person, open to universality and objectivity, and participating in universal nature or thought (p.103).

Richard Sorabji[2] has questioned the extent to which it is true to say *generally* of the ancient philosophers that they found value only in the present, conceding the idea principally to Marcus Aurelius, an

[1] Pierre Hadot, *Philosophy as a Way of Life: Spiritual Exercises from Socrates to Foucault* (Oxford: Blackwell, 1995), translated by Michael Chase from the original *Exercices spirituels et philosophie antique* (Paris: Etudes Augustiniennes, 1987).

[2] Richard Sorabji, *Emotion and Peace of Mind: From Stoic Agitation to Christian Temptation* (Oxford: Clarendon Press, 2002), pp. 238–9.

doi:10.1017/S1358246109990282

author to whom Hadot has given special attention.[3] Sorabji too, however, has spoken of what he terms the 'inwardness' of the ancient spiritual exercises, and he has pointed out that the idea of turning inward is more ancient than Augustine, who indeed says that he learned to look inward from the Platonists. For Hadot, the guiding metaphor seems to have been the one introduced by Plotinus, who likened the inward turn to the activity of a sculptor, chipping away at a block of marble in order to manifest the statue within. Thus *Ennead* 1.6.9:

> How then can you see the sort of beauty a good soul has? Go back into yourself and look; and if you do not yet see yourself beautiful, then, just as someone making a statue which has to be beautiful cuts away here and polishes there and makes one part smooth and clears another till he has given his statue a beautiful face, so you too must cut away excess and straighten the crooked and clear the dark and make it bright, and never stop 'working on your statue' till the divine glory of virtue shines out on you, till you see 'self-mastery enthroned upon its holy seat'.[4]

Hadot makes the point that for Plotinus a sculptor merely exposes something that pre-exists in the marble. This is the reason why he finds fault with the use to which Michel Foucault has put the ancient exercises, in Foucault's description of them as the 'cultivation of the self' through 'techniques'. Foucault, alleges Hadot, misunderstands the Plotinian metaphor as implying an exaggerated aestheticism, and even a Dandyism, according to which one fabricates a personality for oneself as if creating a work of art (pp. 102, 211). In an appraisal of the role of the aesthetic analogy in ancient ethics, Joseph Sen has pointed out that the Plotinian conception of the inward is based on a concept of subtraction: 'The ideal psychic state is not something to be newly made or created but is experienced with the removal of those accretions which have hidden and thus prevented a realization of the self which we already are.'[5]

[3] For example, Marcus Aurelius, *Meditations* 3.10: '[A]nd remember withall that it is only this present, a moment of time, that a man lives: all the rest either has been lived or may never be.' Translated by C. R. Haines, *Marcus Aurelius*, Loeb Classical Library (Cambridge, Mass. 1916).

[4] From the translation of A. H. Armstrong in the Loeb Classical Library edition (Cambridge, Mass. 1966). Stephen Clark, this volume, also discusses this passage.

[5] Joseph Sen, 'Good times and the timeless good,' *Journal of Neoplatonic Studies* 3 (1995), pp. 3–25; p. 24.

For some ancient Indians, the thought that death occurs not just once but many times over within the span of a single human life provides not comfort but additional anxiety. If one is to be cured of the fear that an endless chain of 're-deaths' is our fate, one remedy is to learn to see one's true self as something indestructible. That thought motivates the spiritual exercises described in the Upaniṣads. These typically involve precisely that 'return to the self' of which Hadot speaks, encouraging us to turn our attention inwards in order to re-acquaint ourselves with a universal, impartial self that indwells each of us. A couple of verses from the Katha Upaniṣad are enough to illustrate the point. Turning inward is the way to free oneself from sorrow and desire, to reach wisdom and even immortality:[6]

> Finer than the finest, larger than the largest,
> is the self that lies here hidden
> in the cave of a living being.
> Without desires and free from sorrow,
> a man perceives by the creator's grace
> the grandeur of the self. (Katha 2.20)

> The Self-existent One pierced the apertures outward,
> therefore, one looks out, and not into oneself.
> A certain wise man in search of immortality,
> turned his sight inward and saw the self within. (Katha 4.1)

Wilhelm Halbfass has observed that later philosophers in the Upaniṣadic tradition of Vedānta use the term *svāsthya*, 'coinciding with oneself; being in one's own true, natural state', to refer to a soteriological goal involving the removal of obstacles that distance us from an appreciation of our underlying self: ''Final release' (*mukti*) or 'isolation' (*kaivalya*) of the self is not to be produced or accomplished in a literal sense, but only in a figurative sense, just as the regaining of the natural state of health (*svāsthya*) through medical therapy is not the accomplishment or acquisition of something new, but only a return to a 'previous' state, a removal of disturbances and obstacles.'[7] The recovery of this natural state of the self is achieved by means of exercises whose function is to train one to regard apparent diversity as merely apparent, assenting to such appearances being regarded as a

[6] For other examples, see e.g. Chāndogya 6.1.1–7; 8.7.1–8.12.6.

[7] Wilhelm Halbfass, 'The therapeutic paradigm and the search for identity in Indian Philosophy,' in his *Traditions and Reflection: Explorations in Indian Thought* (Albany: State University of New York Press, 1991), p. 251. See also Martin Ganeri, this volume.

precondition for desire and other forms of emotional attachment. One way to accomplish this is to learn to 'withdraw' the senses. The most celebrated expression of the idea is found at *Bhagavadgītā* 2.58, though the same metaphor is found in Buddhist and other Indian texts too:

> And when he draws in on every side his senses from their proper objects,
> As a tortoise its limbs, – firm-stablished is the wisdom of such a man.

This idea of a 'return to the self' by way of a withdrawal of the senses has an echo in other of the spiritual exercises catalogued by Marcus Aurelius, who speaks of retreating to a 'daimon' within, as the Indians might to an 'ātman'.[8]

Philosophy and Therapy

Two philosophers belonging to the fourth or fifth century CE refer to a model of the discipline of philosophy that has four divisions: an account of what is sought to be removed or eliminated (*heya*, lit. 'what ought to be abandoned'); an account of its aetiology (*heya-hetu*, lit. 'that which produces *heya*'); an account of the state or condition achieved subsequent to this elimination (*hāna*; lit. 'abandonment'); and finally an account of the method to be employed to bring this condition about (*hāna-upāya*; lit. 'the means leading to *hāna*'). Their model of philosophical practice generalises and abstracts from two earlier four-fold accounts of practical disciplines. One is the soteriology made famous by the Buddha as the 'four noble truths', consisting in accounts of suffering (*duḥkha*), the causes of suffering (*samudaya*), liberation from suffering (*nirodha*), and the path from suffering to liberation (*mārga*) in the shape of eight sorts of 'right understanding'. The other is a model of medicine found in the treatises of the physicians, according to which there is an account of disease (*roga*), the causes of disease (*roga-hetu*), health or 'freedom from disease' (*ārogya*), and the treatment of disease

[8] *Meditations* 6.6: 'But if there appears nothing better than the very deity (*daimon*) enthroned in thee, which as brought into subjection to itself all individual desires, which scrutinizes the thoughts, and, in the words of Socrates, has withdrawn itself from all the enticements of the senses …'; compare 3.12, 3.16, and also 4.3: 'From now therefore bethink thee of the retreat into this little plot that is thyself.'

(*bhaiṣajya*).[9] One of the two philosophers who advance the model is the author of the *Yogasūtra*, Patañjali. Thus:

> What is to be abandoned is future suffering. What produces this is the self's contact with the perceived... the cause [in turn] of that is lack of knowledge. The state achieved by abandoning this is the isolation of the self; it consists in the non-presence of the self's contact [with the perceived] and follows when there is no lack of knowledge. The method to be employed is the persistent discrimination [between *buddhi* and *puruṣa*].[10]

So the 'spiritual exercise' here is a practice of discrimination which leads to a 'return to the self' in the form of the self's isolation from the perceptual world. Patañjali goes on to add that this practice of discrimination is supported by such things as postures (*āsana*), breathing control (*prāṇāyāma*), holding the mind steady (*dhāraṇā*), meditation (*dhyāna, samādhi*), ethical restraint (*yama*) and religious observance (*niyama*).[11]

The other philosopher to promote the model is Vātsyāyana, author of a commentary on the *Nyāyasūtra*, the foundational text of the most outwardly 'theoretical' of the Indian philosophical schools, Nyāya. In his commentary on the first sūtra, he says:

> The highest good is reached by means of knowledge of such knowables as the self, as will be explained in the next sūtra. One reaches the highest good, indeed, by rightly understanding the four *arthapadas*, namely what ought to be abandoned, that which produces it, its complete abandonment, [which is] the final goal, and the method for bringing that about.[12]

Vātsyāyana will go on to stress that the ideas of the highest good and the knowledge that leads to it are subject-specific; thus, while the highest good in medicine is health, the highest good in the 'science of the self' (*ātmavidyā*) is 'liberation' (*apavarga*). The next sūtra is

[9] For references: Albert Wezler, 'On the quadruple division of the Yogaśāstra, the *caturvyūhatva* of the Cikitsāśāstra and the 'four noble truths' of the Buddha,' *Indologica Taurinensia* 12 (1984), pp. 289–337.

[10] *Yogasūtra* 2.1.16–17, 24–26.

[11] *Yogasūtra* 2.1.29. Just as the modern idea of what it is to be stoical is comparatively impoverished, so similarly is the contemporary understanding of what is involved in the practice of yoga. See further Jayandra Soni, this volume.

[12] *Nyāyabhāṣya* 2, 14–16. Page and line numbers refer to *Gautamīyanyāyadarśana with Bhāṣya of Vātsyāyana*, critical ed. Anantalal Thakur (Delhi: Indian Council of Philosophical Research, 1997).

then read as identifying what ought to be abandoned as suffering (*duḥkha*), its cause as erroneous beliefs (*mithyājñāna*), the condition of the abandonment of suffering as liberation (*apavarga*), and the method as acquiring knowledge, including knowledge of the self (*ātmajñāna*). He explains that erroneous beliefs produce in us lusts (*rāga*) and revulsions (*dveṣa*), which lead first to greed (*lobha*) and thence to acts of harm (*hiṃsā*), stealing, and sexual indiscretion.[13] It is ironic, in view of the similarity of this scheme with the four noble truths of the Buddha, that the mistake about the self identified here is the error of thinking that it does not exist. The knowledge that is the antidote to such errors is knowledge of the 'real nature' (*tattva*) of the entity in question. Vātsyāyana concludes by noting that the condition of being without pain and suffering is also a condition of being without pleasure, because pleasure and pain are always intermixed, just as someone who wishes to administer a bitter poison, mixes it into honey.[14]

Another commentator, Uddyotakara, however, thinks that one should include as causes of suffering both erroneous beliefs and 'cravings' (*tṛṣṇā*), as well as merit and demerit. He considers that the condition of abandonment is having knowledge of the real nature of things, and the method for acquiring it to be the philosophical treatises (*śāstra*), and distinguishes that condition of abandonment from the final goal, liberation.[15] More generally, if it is knowledge of the 'real nature' of things which is sought, then the methods – the 'exercises' – will be ones of studying, debating, and examining with the help of evidence. These have approximate counterparts in the spiritual exercises documented by Hadot (pp. 84, 89, 153). Uddyotakara's remarks are clearly influenced by Buddhism, where all unwholesome emotions, it is claimed, have a possessive ingredient, which philosophical knowledge about the impossibility of possessing can eliminate.[16] Hatred, for example, is the belief that the person hated is preventing me from getting something I crave; if I come to know that the true nature of things is that everything is in flux and so there can be neither possessed nor possessor, then it is impossible (or at least irrational) to continue to feel that way.

13 *Nyāyabhāṣya* 7, 1–11.

14 *Nyāyabhāṣya* 8, 4.

15 *Nyāyavārttika* 3, 18–4, 1. Page and line numbers refer to *Nyāyabhāṣyavārttika of Uddyotakara*, critical ed. Anantalal Thakur (Delhi: Indian Council of Philosophical Research, 1997).

16 See the chapters by David Burton and Christopher Gowans, this volume.

If we return to our earlier discussion, the therapeutic model outlined in both the Yoga and Nyāya schools seems to be one of 'subtraction'. In every case, there is an elimination of suffering (in all its forms), leading to states of spiritual wholeness conceived of either as the self in isolation or the self as free from lusts and aversions, painful or pleasurable alike. A slightly later Nyāya philosopher has expressed the matter very clearly: 'In eliminating its particular qualities, the self rests in its own natural state – being permanent, it is not itself eliminated.'[17] In these systems, acquiring knowledge of a certain privileged sort is the key spiritual exercise, and so, as is perhaps most explicitly stated by Naiyāyikas, the study and practice of philosophy – reading philosophical texts, debating, arguing, and so on – is the fundamental activity in what Hadot has appropriately described as a 'return to the self'.

Plutarch and the Buddhists: Returning Oneself to The Present Moment

Instead of a model based on the activity of a sculptor, Plutarch speaks of weaving or painting a life with the help of active memory, allowing the memory of unpleasant things to form the muted backdrop against which more pleasant memories can shine out and be made prominent. I will quote Plutarch's important and densely argued passage in full:

> But just as the man pictured in Hades plaiting a rope allows a grazing donkey to consume what he is plaiting, so forgetfulness, unaware of most things and ungrateful, snatches and overruns things, obliterating every action and right act, every pleasant discussion, meeting, or enjoyment, and does not allow our life to be unified, through the past being woven together with the future... But those who do not preserve or retrieve the past in memory, but allow it to flow away from under them, make themselves needy every day in actual fact, and empty and dependent on tomorrow, as if last year and yesterday and the day before were nothing to them and had not actually happened to them... What we should do is make the bright and shining events prominent in the mind, like the colours in a picture, and hide and suppress

[17] Śrīdhara (c. 990 CE), in the *Nyāyakaṇḍalī: Praśastapādabhāṣyam of Praśastapāda with the commentary Nyāyakaṇḍalī by Śrīdhara Bhaṭṭa*, edited by Durgādhara Jhā (Varanasi: Sampurnanand Sanskrit University, 1997), p. 17.

> the gloomy ones, since we cannot rub them out or get rid of them altogether.[18]

I find in the contrast between Plotinus and Plutarch the reflection of a more general contrast between two interpretations of the spiritual exercises. In the first interpretation, the value of the spiritual exercises is restorative, returning the person to a state of psychological health from which they have departed. According to the second interpretation, the spiritual exercises are instead generative, producing in the person a condition (for example, an 'identity' or a 'character') that had not been there before.

It is not entirely clear whether Plutarch's view about weaving is that there is no self until one is woven, or if his view is that the weaving fashions, for a person who is already there, an 'identity' or 'character' or 'personality' that is their own.[19] Elsewhere, he speaks as if in favour of the view that there are no continuous selves:

> The man of yesterday has died and turned into the man of today, and the man of today is dying in turning into the man of tomorrow. No one stays still, or is a single person, but we become many, with matter whirling and sliding round a single image and a shared mould. ... Each of us is compounded of hundreds of different factors which arise in the course of our experience, a heterogeneous collection combined in a haphazard way.[20]

Sorabji has argued that this passage is incompatible with the earlier one about weaving, and possibly represents a poorly integrated acquaintance with Buddhist ideas about the self: 'Plutarch could have argued consistently, if he had chosen, that the short-term selves should be woven into a long-term biography. But in fact, when he recommends biographical weaving, he treats the short-term selves of the Growing Argument as no more than a simile. And in practice, it would not have been possible to combine the therapy of weaving, to produce tranquillity, with the therapy of dwelling on discontinuity to allay fear

[18] Plutarch, *On Tranquillity* 473 B – 474 B; translated by Richard Sorabji, *Emotion and Peace of Mind*, pp. 232–3.

[19] For a subtle and extensive discussion of Plutarch's view about the self, see Richard Sorabji, *Self: Ancient and Modern Insights about Individuality, Life and Death* (Oxford: Clarendon Press, 2006), chapter 9.

[20] Plutarch, *On the E at Delphi* 392 B, translated by Richard Sorabji, *Emotion and Peace of Mind*, p. 248; and 393 B, translated by Frank Babbitt, *Plutarch's Moralia*, volume V, Loeb Classical Library (Cambridge, Mass. 1936).

of death.'[21] And again, 'If [Plutarch and Seneca] really mean the same [as the Buddhists], it will be incompatible with the rest of what they say, which suggests that it could be an alien growth.. [I]t is incompatible with ... Plutarch's belief that we have genuine memories that we can use to weave our lives into a unity... Plutarch might be expected to say no more than that one acquires a new identity in an everyday sense.'[22] For Plutarch, the spiritual exercises help us not fret about the past or worry about the future, but they do so by encouraging us to see the good and the bad as belonging within a harmoniously unified whole life, with the bad providing a dim backdrop to the more pleasant. Plutarch sees no therapeutic value in thinking of our past miseries as simply flowing away and ceasing to belong to us.

It is open, of course, even for someone who thinks that the self is just a river of fleeting experience to find value in weaving together everything that is in their mind at a given moment, including the (merely apparent) memories they have; and indeed the possibility which Sorabji envisages but does not attribute to Plutarch might be what some Buddhists have in mind when they speak of constructing a sense of self by way of an activity involving the 'appropriation' (*upādāna*) of one's memory and experience.[23] More often, though, the resonance is with those spiritual exercises which involve an attention to the present moment, and indeed a reduction of oneself to a single point in time. Buddhists argue, unlike Plutarch, that there is therapeutic value in the idea that there are no continuous selves. The line of thought is roughly as follows: thinking that there are no continuous selves is an 'antidote' to the belief that the self is continuous or permanent, but this second belief is what makes it possible for us to 'crave' for things we do not yet have, or mourn that which we have lost. Since unsatisfied cravings are the source of 'suffering' in all its forms, we cure ourselves of suffering with the remedy that is the idea that there are no continuous selves (and that there are no continuous objects of craving either). Reminiscent, in a way, of Marcus Aurelius' advice to live each day as if it is one's last,[24] the idea is

[21] Sorabji, *Emotion and Peace of Mind*, p. 248.

[22] Sorabji, *Self: Ancient and Modern Insights about Individuality, Life and Death*, pp. 39–40.

[23] I have discussed this Buddhist view in my *The Concealed Art of the Soul: Theories of Self and Practices of Truth in Indian Ethics and Epistemology* (Oxford: Clarendon Press, 2007), chapters 6, 7.

[24] *Meditations* 2.5. Cf. also 8.5: 'Fret not thyself, for all things are as the Nature of the Universe would have them, and within a little thou shalt be non-existent.'

that it is hard to worry about the future if one does not expect to be there. For example, *Milinda-pañhā* 4.2.3:

> It was in regard to those beings who have defilements and in whom there is an excessively wrong view of self and in regard to those who are uplifted and downcast by pleasures and pains that it was said by the Lord [Buddha]: 'All tremble at punishment, all fear death.'[25]

Neither, perhaps, will one be greatly agitated by the memory of past calamities, although one will be able to feel compassion for that other one upon whom they fell. Another line of thought agrees that we do construct lives and characters and personae for ourselves, and sees the function of the spiritual exercises as one of dismantling these constructs, but in order to return us to a state in harmony with nature, rather than to the self. Many Buddhists, especially those within the Abhidharma school, have proposed the use of exercises of breakdown and dissolution, as did the Buddha himself. In the *Simile of the Lute*, for example, the Buddha explains that if one looks within and investigates, one will find only the psychological elements and not the self, just as one will search in vain among the components of a lute for the sound that the lute makes:

> 'This lute, sire, consists of numerous components, of a great many components, and it gives off a sound when it is played upon with its numerous components; that is, in dependence on the parchment sounding board, the belly, the arm, the head, the strings, the plectrum, and the appropriate effort of the musician…'. So too, bhikkhus, a bhikkhu investigates form… feeling… perception… volitional formations… consciousness. As he investigates form… feeling… perception… volitional formations… consciousness, whatever notions of 'I' or 'mine' or 'I am' had occurred to him before no longer occur to him. [26]

This is the way, the Buddha explains, for someone in whom lust, desire, hatred or delusion has arisen to acquire a mind that is steady, settled, unified and concentrated. The concept of self upon which those possessive emotions depend does not survive an analytical break-up of the mind into its components, any more than the

[25] Translated by I. B. Horner *Milinda's Questions* (Oxford: The Pali Text Society, reprinted1996), Volume 1, p. 204.

[26] Saṃyutta Nikāya iv 197–8; translated by Bhikkhu Bodhi in *The Connected Discourses of the Buddha* (Boston: Wisdom Publications, 2000), p. 1254.

sound made by the lute survives if the lute is broken into its parts. In the *Simile of the Lute*, the aesthetic analogy is used to compare the self with a piece of music in the air, and the point of the analogy is to emphasise that it has an ephemeral nature.

The idea that one should aim to reduce one's sense of self to a point in time is evident in Āryadeva's verse, 'What is called someone's life is nothing other than a moment of consciousness. People certainly do not know this; consequently self-knowledge is rare' (*Catuḥśataka* 1.10). The seventh century Buddhist Candrakīrti explains that

> People, with such misleading ideas as 'this is that' and 'the self is that,' attribute unity to a continuum of constructed things, a continuum that is not something different from the individual things that constitute it. For this reason, they act without understanding that it is momentary. Consequently, it is difficult to find among people anyone who understands the nature of the self. Someone who knows the nature of the self does not engage in harmful actions, because there is no longer a reason for error. Since people, for the most part, are prone to harmful actions, self-knowledge is rare in the world. Therefore, intelligent people, with great enthusiasm, should constantly exert themselves to analyze the nature of the self.[27]

Coming to know that there is no enduring self is thus clearly seen as a therapeutic philosophical achievement. No emotion that requires one to admit the existence of enduring self, such as regret or possessive desire, is able to survive the surgical removal of that commitment. Though possibly free of regret and anxiety, such a life may be, as Plutarch suggests, a 'needy' one, for one will need constantly to be affirmed in the present; one will have neither a past nor a future to sustain one. The therapy of 'dwelling on discontinuity' is intended to do more, certainly, than merely allay a fear of death, even if that fear is the basis of many others; it also produces tranquillity by removing unwelcome emotions. If anything, the problem is that it does too much – for will it not also eliminate wholesome emotions like hope?[28]

[27] Translated by Karen C. Lang in *Four Illusions: Candrakīrti's Advice to Travellers on the Bodhisattva Path* (New York: Oxford University Press, 2003), §41. There are many other Buddhist manuals of spiritual exercises, including notably Buddhaghoṣa's 'Path of Purification' (*Visuddhimagga*) and Śāntideva's 'Guide to the Path to Buddhist Awakening' (*Bodhicaryāvatāra*).

[28] The issue is very well discussed by David Burton, *Buddhism, Knowledge and Liberation: A Philosophical Study* (Aldershot: Ashgate, 2004), chapter 2 and in his chapter in this volume.

A Life Complete at Every Moment

There are, however, dissident voices. One of these rejects the aesthetic model altogether, whether it sees life as *sculpting* a self or *weaving* a persona and *narrating* a biography. For any artistic endeavour might be ended before it has reached completion, and any work of art might be left unfinished. A human life, however, it has sometimes been suggested, is complete at every moment; and if that is right, then the aesthetic analogy in any of its modes is singularly inappropriate.

Marcus Aurelius points to a disanalogy with aesthetic activities like drama and dancing:

> Nor is his life cut short, when the day of destiny overtakes him, as we might say of a tragedian's part, who leaves the stage before finishing his speech and playing out the piece. (3.8)
>
> In dancing and acting and such-like arts, if any break occurs, the whole action is rendered imperfect; but the rational soul in every part and wheresoever taken shews the work set before it fulfilled and all-sufficient for itself, so that it can say: *I have to the full what is my own.*' (11.1)

It is with the same idea, an idea antithetical to the aesthetic paradigm, that the *Meditations* are brought to an end (12.35–6). Among the Indians, the thought seems to me most clearly and beautifully expressed by Rabindranath Tagore:

> A young friend of mine comes to me this morning to inform me that it is his birthday and that he has just reached his nineteenth year. The distance between my age and his is great, and yet when I look at him it is not the incompleteness of his life which strikes me, but something which is complete in his youth. And in this differs the thing which grows, from the thing which is being made. A building in its unfinished stage is only too evidently unfinished. But *in life's growth every stage has its perfection*, the flower as well as the fruit.[29]
>
> There are men whose idea of life is static, who long for its continuation after death only because of their wish for permanence and not perfection; they love to imagine that the things to which they are accustomed will persist for ever. They completely identify themselves in their minds with their fixed surroundings

[29] Rabindranath Tagore, *Thought Relics* (New York: The Macmillan Company, 1912), p. 98; my italics.

> and with whatever they have gathered, and to have to leave these is death for them. They forget that *the true meaning of living is outliving, it is ever growing out of itself*. The fruit clings to its stem, its skin clings to the pulp and the pulp to the seed so long as the fruit is immature, so long as it is not ready for its course of further life. Its outer covering and its inner core are not yet differentiated and it only proves its life by its strength of tenacity. But when the seed is ripe its hold upon its surrounding is loosened, its pulp attains fragrance, sweetness and detachment, and is dedicated to all who need it. Birds peck at it and it is not hurt, the storm plucks it and flings it to the dust and it is not destroyed. It proves its immortality by its renunciation.[30]

As a mode of being-in-the-world, learning to think of one's life as complete at each moment seems to me to have many advantages. It does not require that one attach no value to the past or the future in order to allay dismay and anxiety, nor to think of oneself or the world as only momentary. Also, it does not expect of us the high-mindedness necessary to see oneself wholly objectively in terms of one's place in the cosmos. While I am not convinced that Tagore's analogy with *organic* growth is entirely successful, we may say that one's life is not so much a work of art as a work indefinitely extendable, adding to itself as a city might a new building or suburb, without any implication that what exists before the addition is unfinished.

Taming the self

A fascinating discussion of the ends of human life is to be found tucked away in four short sections of the *Śāntiparvan*, a voluminous book of philosophical reflection embedded within the body of the *Mahābhārata*. The text represents a clear attempt to absorb and integrate general ethical insights into the moral framework of the Hindu epic. It can be read, therefore, as an attempt to articulate a set of widespread ethical concerns. What is the 'highest good' (*niḥśreyasa*)? The *Śāntiparvan* gives a direct and unequivocal answer: it is the taming (*dama*) of the self (12.154.7).[31] Taming the self is a subduing, a rendering calm or tranquil, a pacification. What needs to be tamed is the

[30] Tagore, *Thought Relics*, p. 40; my italics.

[31] Vishnu S. Sukthankar, S.K. Belvalkar et al., *Mahābhārata*, critical edition (Poona: Bhandarkar Oriental Research Institute, 1933–66).

self's inclination to reach out to things that are 'external' to oneself (where 'external' means both physically exterior and outside of one's influence); so taming is a pulling back, a drawing in, a restraint (cf. *Bhagavad-gītā* 10.4); it is a form of self-control. One who achieves this is without fear, anger or envy, and has a profound steadiness of mind (*gāmbhīrya dhairya*; 12.156.12), that is an unpeturbability in the face of either pain or pleasure (12.156.9). This is because 'reaching out' is greed, a wish to obtain (*lobha*), and from this arises both anger and desire. With this in check, one lives the life glorified as one of wise conduct (*śiṣṭācāra*), namely the life of one who is fearless in the face of death, equal in the face of pleasure or pain, self-controlled, and impartial (12.152.20–26), delighting in no acquisition and pained by no loss. Such a person lives as one for whom acting well is just like a movement of one's body; in particular, there is no ulterior cause for such activity, such as wealth or fame (12.152.27). With the taming of self are also associated – perhaps optimistically – forgiveness, patience, abstention from injuring others, truth, sincerity, wisdom, mildness, modesty, liberality, contentment, pleasantness of speech, benevolence and freedom from malice (12.154).

It takes knowledge (*jñāna*) to achieve such a life, for greed and ignorance go hand in hand (12.153); and it takes 'spiritual austerity' (*tapas*) (12.155). What, though, is the role of knowledge in 'taming' the self? Greed is a failure to understand that none of things one seeks to obtain is going to last (12.157); it should also be understood that greed is, of its nature, insatiable (12.152). Anger is greed together with a sensitivity to other people's faults, and so is removed by tolerance (*kṣamā*), which comes from forbearance (*kṣānti*). The result of anger is desire (*kāma*), which arises from willfully wanting something (*saṃkalpa*).

A beautiful metaphor is used to illustrate this conception of the self-controlled life. One who lives wisely is said to tread softly on the earth: 'As the track of birds along the sky or of fowl over the surface of water cannot be discerned, even so the track of such a person does not attract notice.' Such a life has but one drawback, and this is that a person who lives thus is regarded by others as weak and simple. But for this, those others can be forgiven, and a life so lived is one from which one does not need to retreat: 'What need has a man of self-control for a forest? Similarly, of what use is a forest to him that has no self-control? That is a forest where the man of self-control dwells, and that is even a sacred asylum.' This, clearly, is not a transcendental, privative, ideal, but a way of living in the world, in a human community, one in which one can adopt either the practices of the cities or those of the forest. This life, the life of a *dānta*, a 'tamed' one, it is said, is one of tranquillity (*praśama*; 12.154.18).

Philosophy and the Ends of Life

That epistemic practices have a role in living a life well is asserted explicitly in the *Śāntiparvan* analysis: knowing that desires are insatiable and the things desired unstable is a solution to anger and greed. Yet it is not very explicit just how it is that knowledge, or philosophy more generally, can serve in this way as a 'therapy.' Perhaps that is not surprising, for the *Śāntiparvan* is not a work of academic philosophy; it is a work of epic literature. So let us turn next to the professional philosophers, specifically the practitioners of Nyāya. They say that the study of philosophy is indispensible in reaching the highest good: 'What leads to the highest good is knowledge (*tattvajnāña*),' specifically knowledge of the methods of inquiry and their objects, including the forms of debate (NS 1.1.1).[32] The connection is this: 'In the sequence of suffering, rebirth, activity, moral failing, and cognitive error, removing each by removing its successor leads to liberation (*apavarga*)' (NS 1.1.2). That is to say, moral failings are produced and sustained by cognitive errors, so if the error is removed, the moral failing will disappear too. Likewise, moral failings indirectly result in and sustain suffering, and a state free of suffering is the result of their removal.

One fundamental way in which we go wrong is to mistake a thing for its opposite. We 'mistake suffering for pleasure, the unreal for the real, that which is not a remedy for a remedy, the afraid for the fearless' and so on (*Nyāyabhāṣya* under 1.1.2). We mistakenly think of 'liberation' as a state of complete insentience, and so as quite undesirable. These cognitive errors instil in us wants and aversions, and that leads us to moral failings like falsehood, malice, deception and greed. Such failings in our moral psychology make us *act* immorally too; we engage in harmful acts towards others: theft, lies, rudeness and fault-finding. These contrast sharply with the virtues of thought, word and deed for which we strive.

Why, though, is it claimed that cognitive errors lead us to desire per se, rather than to desire *the wrong things*? Mistaking a sea shell for a piece of silver, I might want to go after it; and if I did, I would be desiring something which is not really there. But if it *really* had been a piece of silver, there seems to be nothing wrong with my wish to obtain it. The answer, presumably, is that we are not speaking here of ordinary empirical knowledge, but of that philosophical wisdom one derives from the *śāstras*, the texts. If I do not know

[32] Anantalal Thakur ed. *Gautamīyanyāyadarśana with Bhāṣya of Vātsyāyana* (Delhi: Indian Council of Philosophical Research, 1997).

what good evidence is, I cannot know if any of my beliefs matches up to it. But if I do not know this, then acting on anything I believe, true or false, would carry with it a degree of moral risk. The elimination of moral risk requires that I have 'theoretical' expertise in the arts of knowing. One might live a life that happened to be free from mistakes entirely by chance, but that would not be a good life. For a life to be a good one, the absence of suffering must rest on something more secure than chance.

How does one discriminate between a thing and a masquerade of it? How does one distinguish between a true pleasure and a pain that passes itself off as a pleasure? This, exactly, is what philosophy excels in, distinguishing between pretence and truth. For instance, the difference between a good argument and an argument that only pretends to be a good one, i.e. a piece of sophistry. Philosophy shows us how to see through the pretences of reason. Without a secure ability to do that, our attempts to live well in thought, deed and speech are subject to moral risk. Uddyotakara raises a further issue: incompatible beliefs cannot simultaneously be entertained, but what ensures that truth trumps error? According to him, it is only that true beliefs have a foundation that the false ones lack.

It is, of course, true that a great deal is said about such transcendental spiritual goals as *mokṣa, mukti* and *nirvāṇa*, and that these goals are represented as an ultimate, idealized aspiration for all. Mortal human beings, though, do not aspire actually to become sages; rather, they take the image of the sage as a *device* to help them pursue those goals that are properly their own. Thinking about *mokṣa* and *nirvāṇa*, as well as about the *buddhas* and the *ṛṣis*, helps us to actualize the human ends that are ours. Entertaining the idea that one is striving for a transcendent ideal might itself be a 'spiritual exercise,' a practice that forms a part of the good for a human being. If that is right, then it would be a mistake to read the descriptions of the transcendental states and the means to reach them as if they were literal expressions of a path from the world of men to the world of the gods. For the Indians, no doubt, these ideal states are given a characterization in largely privative terms, as states free from pain, free from suffering, free from anger and desire, and often indeed, free from pleasure too. The idea that what one should aim for is an existence that is so colourless has been one reason that European philosophers have struggled to engage with the Indian philosophical imagination. From my point of view, the very fact that the ideal states are described in such unappealing terms shows us that these are not really intended as descriptions of the good for human beings. The question to ask is a different one: namely, how might entertaining the idea that one is striving to achieve such a state help one get *somewhere*; and indeed, where might one be attempting to get for this to be an appropriate method for getting there? Might it be, for example, that reflecting on the nature of an existence entirely void of either pleasure or pain will help us to re-examine the relationship between these two? One might be led, for example, not to eschew pleasures altogether, but to be somewhat wary of them: to aim to live in such a way that pleasure is not itself the motivation of one's actions. Believing that the ideal state is a pleasureless state might lead me, not to give up all pleasure, for that is not a realistic human end, but to allow myself to be nourished by the pleasures I have and also to resist voluntarily seeking out new ones. That is, entertaining such an ideal might lead me to a life characterised as one of restraint and self-control.[33]

Philosophy, then, enables us to see through the pretences of reason, and so makes it possible for us to direct our efforts securely on their target, the living of a life free of suffering. This is not a life of insentient catatonia, for having as our outside aim a life free of suffering does not imply that the life which ensues is devoid of pleasure. It implies only that the pleasures are, as it were, collateral, that their presence does not distract us from our ultimate aims. A life of the restrained mind is a life in which pleasure provides neither the goal nor the motivating reason; but such need not be a life without pleasure.

I will conclude with a quotation from Henry Thoreau, very apt in the context of this chapter:

> The ancient philosophers, Chinese, Hindu, Persian, and Greek, were a class than which none has been poorer in outward riches, none so rich in inward… There are nowadays professors of philosophy, but not philosophers. Yet it is admirable to profess because it was once admirable to live. To be a philosopher is not merely to have subtle thoughts, nor even to found a school, but so to love wisdom as to live according to its dictates, a life of simplicity, independence, magnanimity, and trust. It is to solve some of the problems of life, not only theoretically, but practically…[34]

[33] See Keith Ansell Pearson, this volume, for related concerns in the thought of Nietzsche.
[34] Henry David Thoreau, *Walden, or, Life in the Woods* [1845] (New York: Pocket Books, 2004), pp. 15–16.

For Mortal Souls: Philosophy and Therapeia in Nietzsche's *Dawn*

KEITH ANSELL PEARSON

> *How one should turn to stone.* – Slowly slowly become hard like a precious stone – and finally lie there still and silent, to the joy of all eternity (*Dawn* 541)[1]

This chapter seeks to make a contribution to the growing interest in Nietzsche's relation to traditions of therapy in philosophy that has emerged in recent years.[2] It is in the texts of his middle period (1878–82) that Nietzsche's writing comes closest to being an exercise in philosophical therapeutics, and in this chapter I focus on *Dawn* from 1881 as a way of exploring this. *Dawn* is a text that has been admired in recent years for its ethical naturalism[3] and for its

[1] The following translations of Nietzsche are cited in my chapter: *The Anti-Christ* (AC), trans. Judith Norman (Cambridge: Cambridge University Press, 2005); *Beyond Good and Evil* (BGE), trans. Marion Faber (Oxford: Oxford University Press, 1998); *Dawn: Thoughts on the Prejudices of Morality*, (D) trans. Brittain Smith (Stanford: Stanford University Press, forthcoming) and *Daybreak: Thoughts on the Prejudices of Morality*, trans. R. J. Hollingdale (Cambridge: Cambridge University Press, 1986); *On the Genealogy of Morality*, trans. Carol Diethe (Cambridge: Cambridge University Press, 2006); *The Gay Science*, trans. Walter Kaufmann (New York, Random House, 1974); *Human, All too Human* (in two volumes), trans. R. J. Hollingdale (Cambridge: Cambridge University Press, 1984) [includes *Assorted Opinions and Maxims* (AOM) and *The Wanderer and His Shadow* (WS)]; *Nietzsche contra Wagner*, trans. Judith Norman (Cambridge: Cambridge University Press, 2005) *The Will to Power*, trans. Walter Kaufmann & R. J. Hollingdale (New York, Random House, 1968). For the German I have used, *Sämtiche Werke: Kritische Studienausgabe* in 15 Bänden (München, Berlin & New York, dtv/de Gruyter, 1988).

[2] See the two fine studies by Horst Hutter, *Shaping the Future: Nietzsche's New Regime of the Soul and Its Ascetic Practices* (Lanham:, Lexington Books, 2006) and Michael Ure, *Nietzsche's Therapy: Self-Cultivation in the Middle Works* (Lanham: Lexington Books, 2008). See also the essays collected in Jacob Golomb et al. *Nietzsche and Depth Psychology* (Albany: State University of New York Press, 1999).

[3] See Maudmarie Clark and Brian Leiter, 'Introduction' to F. Nietzsche, *Daybreak: Thoughts on the Prejudices of Morality*, trans.

doi:10.1017/S1358246109990294

anticipation of phenomenology.[4] My interest in the text in this chapter is in the way it revitalises for a modern age ancient philosophical concerns, notably a teaching for mortal souls who wish to be liberated from the fear and anguish of existence, as well as from God, the 'metaphysical need',[5] and romantic music,[6] and are able to affirm their mortal conditions of existence. As a general point of inspiration I have adopted Pierre Hadot's insight into the therapeutic ambitions of ancient philosophy which was, he claims, 'intended to cure mankind's anguish' (for example, anguish over our mortality).[7] This is evident in the teaching of Epicurus which sought to demonstrate the mortality of the soul and whose aim was, 'to free humans from "the fears of the mind".'[8] Similarly, Nietzsche's teaching in *Dawn* is for mortal souls. In the face of the loss of the dream of the soul's immortality, philosophy for Nietzsche, I shall show, has new

---

R. J. Hollingdale (Cambridge: Cambridge University Press, 1997), pp. vii–xxxiv. See also Ruth Abbey, *Nietzsche's Middle Period* (Oxford: Oxford University Press, 2000), pp. 7–10.

4 See Rüdiger Safranski, *Nietzsche. A Philosophical Biography*, trans. Shelley Frisch (New York: Norton, 2002), pp. 207–19.

5 In a note from the autumn of 1880 Nietzsche maintains that the metaphysical need is not the source of religion, as might be supposed, but rather the after effect of its decline: the 'need' is a result and not an origin. Nietzsche, *KSA* 9, 6 [290]. See also *GS* 151 where Nietzsche makes it clear that he is arguing contra Schopenhauer on this point.

6 The texts of the middle period find Nietzsche seeking to emancipate himself from Wagner and his youthful captivation by his music. In *HH* 153 he states that the free spirit's intellectual probity is put to the test in moments when it listens to something like Beethoven's *Ninth Symphony* which makes him feel that he is hovering above the earth in a dome of stars and with the dream of immortality in his heart: 'If he becomes aware of being in this condition he feels a profound stab in the heart and sighs for the man who will lead him back to his lost love, whether she be called religion or metaphysics'.

7 Pierre Hadot, *Philosophy as a Way of Life* (Oxford: Basil Blackwell, 1995), pp. 265–6. In a letter to Heinrich von Stein of December 1882 Nietzsche says he 'would like to take away from human existence some of its heartbreaking and cruel character'.

8 Catherine Wilson, *Epicureanism at the Origins of Modernity* (Oxford: New York, Oxford University Press, 2008), p. 7. See Epicurus in Brad Inwood and L. P. Gerson, *The Epicurus Reader* (Indianapolis: Hackett, 1994), p. 29: 'For there is nothing fearful in life for one who has grasped that there is nothing fearful in the absence of life...the wise man neither rejects life nor fears death'.

consolations to offer in the form of new sublimities.[9] Indeed, for Nietzsche it is by reflecting, with the aid of psychological observation, on what is 'human, all too human', that 'we can lighten the burden of life' (*HH* 35). Nietzsche's thinking in *Dawn* contains a number of proposals and recommendations of tremendous value to philosophical *therapeia*, including (a) a call for a new honesty about the human ego and human relations, including relations of self and other and love, so as to free us from certain delusions;[10] (b) the search for an authentic mode of existence which appreciates the value of solitude and independence; (c) the importance of having a rich and mature taste in order to eschew the fanatical. After an introduction to Nietzsche's text the chapter is divided into two main parts. In the first main part I explore various aspects of his conception of philosophical therapy, including purification of the higher feelings and liberation from the destructive effects of 'morality' and Christianity. In the second main part I explore his conception of 'the passion of knowledge', which is the passion that guides modern free spirits as they seek to overcome the need of religion and constraints of 'morality', and to access the new sublimities of philosophy.

Dawn's Therapy of Slowness

Dawn: Thoughts on the Prejudices of Morality was researched between January 1880 and March 1881 and published in the early summer of 1881. It is one of Nietzsche's 'yes-saying' books, a work of enlightenment which, Nietzsche tells his readers, seeks to pour out 'its light, its love, and its delicacy over nothing but bad things', giving back to these things the 'lofty right and *prerogative* of existence' (*EH* III 'Daybreak', 1). The Indian motto from the Rig Veda, 'there are so many dawns that have not yet broken' lies inscribed on the door to the book (ibid.). Nietzsche's amanuensis Peter Gast had written the

[9] We should note that Nietzsche confesses to not fearing death himself in a note of 1878: 'A prominent quality: a more refined heroism (which, by the way, I recognize in Epicurus). In my book there is not a word against the fear of death. I have little of that' (KSA 8, 28 [15]). There are a number of places in his published writings where Nietzsche writes in praise of the rational and voluntary death, and in a note from 1888 he writes of the need to 'convert the stupid psychological fact' of death 'into a moral necessity. So to live that one can also *will at the right time to die*!' (*KSA* 12, 10 [165]; *WP* 916).

[10] In *Dawn* 'Redlichkeit' (integrity or probity) is said to be mankind's youngest virtue (*D* 456).

motto on the title page whilst making a fair copy of the manuscript and this, in fact, inspired Nietzsche to adopt the new title and replace its original title of 'The Ploughshare'. In 1888 Nietzsche speaks of the book as amounting to a search for the new morning that ushers in a whole series of new days and he insists that not a single negative word is to be found in it, and no attack or malice either. In this book we encounter a thinker who lies in the sun, 'like a sea creature sunning itself among rocks' (ibid.) – and the book was largely conceived in the rocks near Genoa in solitude and where, so Nietzsche discloses, he 'had secrets to share with the sea'. *Dawn* is a book that journeys into the future, and which for Nietzsche constitutes, in fact, its true destination: 'Even now', he writes in a letter of March 1881 to his old friend Erwin Rohde, 'there are moments when I walk about on the heights above Genoa having glimpses and feelings such as Columbus once, perhaps from the very same place, sent out across the sea and into the future'. Nietzsche's appeal to Columbus is figurative; he is, in fact, critical of the real Columbus (D 37). The book concludes on an enigmatic note with Nietzsche asking his readers and fellow travellers whether it will be said of them one day that they too, 'steering toward the west, hoped to reach an India' but that it was their fate to shipwreck upon infinity (D 575).

At this point in his writings 'India' denotes for Nietzsche the path to self-enlightenment. Nietzsche holds that Europe remains behind Indian culture in terms of the progress it needs to make with respect to religious matters since it has not yet attained the 'free-minded naiveté' of the Brahmins. The priests of India demonstrated 'pleasure in thinking' in which observances – prayers, ceremonies, sacrifices, and hymns – are celebrated as the givers of all good things.[11] One step further, he adds, and one also throws aside the gods – 'which is what Europe will also have to do one day' (*D* 96). Europe remains distant, he muses, from the level of culture attained in the appearance of the Buddha, the teacher of self-redemption. Nietzsche anticipates an age when all the observances and customs of the old moralities and religions have come to an end. Instead of speculating on what will then emerge into existence, he calls for a new community of non-believers to make their sign and communicate with one another: 'There exist today among the different nations of Europe perhaps ten to twenty million people who no longer 'believe in God' – is it too much to ask that they *give a sign* to one another?' He imagines these people constituting a new

[11] See Kate Wharton, this volume.

power in Europe, between nations, classes, rulers and subjects, and between the un-peaceable and the most peaceable.

Dawn strikes me, at least in part, as a distinctly Epicurean moment in Nietzsche's development. In *The Wanderer and his Shadow* (1879) Nietzsche confesses to being inspired by the example of Epicurus whom he calls the inventor of an 'heroic-idyllic mode of philosophizing' (WS 295). We can follow Epicurus's example and learn to quieten ourselves by appreciating that it is not necessary to solve the ultimate and outermost theoretical questions; e.g. if the gods exist they do not concern themselves with us (*WS* 7).[12] In *Dawn* Epicurus is portrayed as the enemy of the idea of punishments in Hell *after* death, which was developed by numerous secret cults

[12] Melissa Lane has suggested that from *The Gay Science* (1882) on, that is, after *Dawn*, Nietzsche's preoccupation with Epicurus and Epicureans evaporates and that his subsequent remarks on them are almost relentlessly negative. M. Lane, 'Honesty as the Best Policy: Nietzsche on *Redlichkeit* and the Contrast between Stoic and Epicurean Strategies of the Self', in Mark Bevir, Jill Hargis, and Sara Rushing (eds), Histories of *Postmodernism* (London: Routledge, 2007), pp. 25–53. She also argues that the late Nietzsche favours Stoicism over Epicureanism. On her reading the difference is that whereas for Nietzsche Epicureanism is fatally flawed as a cognitive stance, the Stoics steel themselves cognitively and emotionally so as to confront reality and in the process they expand their knowledge to the whole of nature. Where the one restricts knowledge the other acknowledges reality in terms of a non-consolatory, non-delusional cognitive attitude towards it. Nietzsche's later appraisal of Epicurus is complex since he is identifying in him both a will to knowledge (in the form of knowledge of our actual mortal conditions of existence) and the denial of such a will (in the form of 'decadent' attempt to escape from the pain and tragic lot of human existence). In *GM* (1887) Nietzsche refers to the super cool but 'suffering Epicurus' as one who may have been hypnotized by the 'feeling of nothingness' and the 'repose of deepest sleep', that is, the *absence* of suffering (*GM* III. 17). In *NCW* (1888) Nietzsche notes that Epicurus may well have worn a *mask* and so may have been superficial out of profundity: 'Profound suffering makes you noble; it separates. – One of the most refined forms of disguise is Epicureanism, and a certain showy courage of taste that accepts suffering without a second thought and resists everything sad and profound. There are 'cheerful people' who use cheerfulness because it lets them be misunderstood: - they *want* to be misunderstood'. (*NCW* 'The Psychologist Has a Word,' 3) For further insight into Nietzsche's reading of Epicurus see also Howard Caygill 'The Consolation of Philosophy or 'Neither Dionysus nor the Crucified', *Journal of Nietzsche Studies* 7 (1994), pp. 131–51.

in the Roman Empire and was taken up by Christianity.[13] For Nietzsche the triumph of Epicurus's teaching resounds most beautifully in the mouth of the sombre Roman Lucretius but comes too early. Christianity takes the belief in 'subterranean terrors' under its special protection and this foray into heathendom enables it to carry the day over the popularity of the Mithras and Isis cults, winning to its side the rank of the timorous as the most zealous adherents of the new faith (Nietzsche notes that because of the extent of the Jews' attachment to life such an idea fell on barren ground). However, the teaching of Epicurus triumphs anew in the guise of modern science which has rejected 'any other representation of death and any life beyond it' (*D* 72; see also 150). Nietzsche is keen to encourage human beings to cultivate an attitude towards existence in which they accept their mortality and attain a new serenity about their dwelling on the earth, to conquer unjustified fears, and to reinstitute the role played by chance and chance events in the world and in human existence (*D* 13, 33, 36).[14]

Not only does Nietzsche subscribe at this time to much of the teaching of Epicurus on cosmology and philosophy, he was also inspired by Epicurus's conception of friendship and the ideal of withdrawing from society and cultivating one's own garden.[15] In a letter to Peter

[13] In *D* 202 Nietzsche encourages us to do with away with the concepts of 'sin' and 'punishment': 'May these banished monsters henceforth live somewhere other than among human beings, if they want to go on living at all and do not perish of disgust with themselves!' In *D* 208 entitled 'Question of Conscience' he states what he wishes to see changed: 'We want to cease making causes into sinners and consequences into executioners'. In *D* 53 he notes that it is the most conscientious who suffer so dreadfully from the fears of Hell: 'Thus life has been made gloomy precisely for those who had need of cheerfulness and pleasant pictures...'

[14] On Epicurus on fear and chance see P. Hadot, *Philosophy as a Way of Life*, p. 87, p. 223, and p. 252.

[15] Catherine Wilson neatly lays out the central tenets of the Epicurean system in her recent study. They include: the denial of supernatural agency engaged in the design and maintenance of the world; the view that self-moving, subvisible particles acting blindly bring about all growth, change, and decline; and the insistence that the goal of ethical self-discipline, which involves asceticism, is the minimization of mental and physical suffering', *Epicureanism at the Origins of Modernity*, p. 37. It is on this last point that Nietzsche will come to later criticize Epicureanism and describe Epicurus as a 'typical decadent'. See *AC* 30. In the same text Epicurus is once again prized on account of his battle against 'the subterranean cults, the whole of latent Christianity', his fight against the 'corruption of the soul' through notions of guilt, punishment, and immortality' (*AC* 58).

Gast of 1883 Nietzsche writes that Epicurus, 'is the best negative argument in favour of my challenge to all rare spirits to isolate themselves from the mass of their fellows'.[16] If philosophical therapeutics is centred on a concern with the healing of our own lives,[17] then in Nietzsche's texts of his middle period, including *Dawn*, can be seen to be an heir to this ancient tradition. The difference is that he is developing a therapy for the sicknesses of the soul under peculiarly modern conditions of existence of social control and indoctrination.[18] Like Epicurus, Nietzsche's philosophical therapy is in search of pupils and disciples: 'What I envy in Epicurus are the disciples in his garden; in *such circumstances* one could certainly forget noble Greece and more certainly still ignoble Germany!'[19]

In *Dawn* Nietzsche is tracing a history of human fear and self-torment. However, his evaluations of our inheritance—of the origins and sources of human identity in fear; of the cruel practices employed by the ancient discipline of customary morality; and of Christianity—are not simply negative but subtle and nuanced (which does not prevent him from making certain key decisions about the future direction of humanity).[20] Nietzsche notes that cultural institutions and mores instil in the passions, and contrary to their nature, a belief in their duration and responsibility for this duration, and gives the example of the institution of marriage which has this effect on the passion of love. Whilst such transformations introduce much hypocrisy and lying into the world they also bring with them 'a *suprahuman*, human-exalting concept' (*D* 27). On the one hand, and on a wider scale, an 'obscure fear and awe' has directed humanity in its consideration of 'higher and weightier affairs', and in the process a fearful humanity has prejudged and paralysed thinking, choosing instead to enslave itself to self-abasement, self-torture,

16 See Oscar Levy (ed.), *Friedrich Nietzsche. Selected Letters*, trans. A. N. Ludovici (London: Soho Book Company, 1921), pp. 157–8.

17 Hadot, *Philosophy as a Way of Life*, 1995, p. 87.

18 In a note from 1881 Nietzsche states that he considers the various moral schools of antiquity to be 'experimental laboratories' containing a number of recipes for worldly wisdom or the art of living and holds that these experiments now belong to us as our legitimate property: 'we shall not hesitate to adopt a Stoic recipe just because we have profited in the past from Epicurean recipes' (*KSA* 9, 15 [59]; cited in Hadot, *Philosophy as a Way of Life*, p. 277).

19 Letter to Gast in Levy, *Selected Letters*, p. 164.

20 In *D* 18 Nietzsche writes: 'Nothing has been purchased more dearly than that little bit of human reason and feeling of freedom that now constitutes our pride'.

and much torment of body and soul (*D* 107; see also 142). On the other hand, however, it is possible to locate in the history of human rituals, including rituals of sacrifice, a 'prodigious training ground of the intellect' (*D* 40). As Nietzsche notes, it is not only religions that have been hatched and nurtured on this soil but also the 'prehistoric world of science' as well as the poet, the thinker, the physician, and the lawgiver: 'The fear of the incomprehensible, which, in ambiguous fashion, demanded ceremonies from us, metamorphosed gradually into a fascination with the hardly-comprehensible, and where one knew not how to explicate, one learned to create' (ibid.). He goes so far as to claim that it is fear and not love that has furthered the universal knowledge of humanity – where love is deceptive and blind (it harbours a secret impulse to elevate the other as high as possible), fear has a capacity for genuine discernment, for example, discerning the powers and desires of a person or an object (*D* 309).

For Nietzsche we are both heirs to, and continuers of, a history of sacrifice and of the sublime; the difference is that now for us the promise of happiness—which centres on a strengthening and elevation of 'the general feeling of human *power*'—seeks to remain true to our mortal dwelling on the earth. Our task is now to take our time in our search; we are no longer looking for a single answer to our questions or some ultimate solution to the riddles of existence. Nietzsche advises us to go slowly and wisely:

> *Small doses.* – If you want to effect the most profound transformation possible, then administer the means in the smallest doses, but unremittingly and over long periods of time! What great things can be accomplished at one fell swoop? Thus we want to guard against exchanging head over heels and with acts of violence the moral condition we are used to for a new evaluation of things – no, we want to keep on living in that condition for a long, long time – until we, very late, presumably, become fully aware that the *new evaluation* has become the predominant force and that the small doses of it, *to which we will have to grow accustomed from now on*, have laid down in us a new nature (*D* 534).

Purification of the Higher Feelings

For Nietzsche a chief task is to purify ourselves of the origins and sources of our desire for the sublime, since the higher feelings associated with it are bound up with humanity's investment in an imaginary world: an 'exalted humanity' is full of self-loathing and this needs to be conquered. However, he does not propose that we simply transcend the sublime, but that we go in search of new experiences of it. As we shall see, these will centre on knowledge and self-experimentation. Through knowledge a purified humanity can conquer the fear and anxiety that has captivated previous humanity and taught it to kneel down before the incomprehensible. In accordance with the tradition stretching from Longinus to Kant and Schiller, Nietzsche employs the sublime in connection with notions of elevation, exaltation, loftiness, ennoblement and the attainment of newly-discovered heights of experience. At the same time it is bound up for him with practices of purification and sublimation that involve the conquest and overcoming of traditional and conventional conceptions of reality and of what is possible in experience. In *Dawn* Nietzsche's concern is with a transitional humanity that is moving from a heritage of religions and moralities to something new, in fact, to uncharted conditions of existence. He is keen to militate against the sublime of dread and terror and to configure the sublime in a more modest and even humbling manner.[21] For Nietzsche the new sublimities of philosophy are bound up with a new comportment towards existence as it now concerns us as searchers of knowledge—and a new fearlessness is required as we embark on this search free of 'the prejudices of morality'.[22] We are in the process of becoming creatures that exist largely to know and who seek to conquer the elevation offered by 'morality'.

In *Dawn* Nietzsche operates with two main critical conceptions of morality: (a) the ancient morality of custom which characterizes eras that precede world history and are decisive for determining the character of humanity (*D* 9, 16, 18); (b) the modern emphasis on self-sacrifice in which it is supposed that we have defined the essence of the moral (*D* 132). In addition, he is keen to attack the view that everything that exists has a connection with morality and thus an ethical significance can be projected onto the world (*D* 3, 100). Hitherto individuals have lived in fear and as conforming herd animals; they have concealed themselves in the communal generality

[21] The link between the sublime and terror is, of course, the one made by Edmund Burke, *A Philosophical Enquiry into the Origin of our Ideas of the Sublime and Beautiful* (Oxford: Oxford University Press, 1998), part 1, section VII and part II, section II. Compare Immanuel Kant *Critique of Judgment*, trans. Werner S. Pluhar (Indianapolis: Hackett, 1987), section 28.

[22] Book five of *GS*, which Nietzsche added to the text's second edition in 1887, is entitled 'We Fearless Ones'.

of the concepts 'human being' and 'society'. Even our distinctive sense for truth is a sense for security and is a need we share with other animals: 'one doesn't want to let oneself be deceived, be led astray by one's actions' (*D* 26). In short, human existence has been constrained by its evolutionary conditions of adaptation: 'everything to which we give the name *Socratic virtues is bestial*' (ibid.). Today the prejudice holds sway in Europe that the sympathetic affects and compassion define the moral, such as actions deemed to be congenial, disinterested, of general utility, and so on. Although Nietzsche mentions Schopenhauer and Mill as famous teachers of this conception of morality, he holds that they merely echo doctrines that have been sprouting up in both fine and crude forms since the French Revolution (*D* 132). Central to modernity, as Nietzsche perceives it, is the idea that the ego must deny itself and adapt itself to the whole and as a result the 'individual' is debilitated and cancelled: 'one never tires of enumerating and excoriating everything evil and malicious, prodigal, costly, and extravagant in the prior form of individual existence...compassion for the individual and passion for society here go hand in hand' (ibid.). Nietzsche contests the morality of self-sacrifice and looks ahead to a different morality, one that is in keeping with the spirit of the book as a whole. In contrast to a narrow, petty bourgeois morality a higher and freer manner of thinking will now look beyond the immediate consequences our actions have for others and seek to further more distant aims. Under some circumstances this will be at the expense of the suffering of others, for example, by furthering genuine knowledge: does not 'free thinking' initially plunge people into doubt and distress? In seeking victory over ourselves we need '*to get beyond our compassion*' (*D* 146). The grief, despair, blunderings and fearful footstep of individuals will form part of 'a new ploughshare' that will 'cleave the ground, rendering it fruitful for all...' (ibid.)

In one of the text's opening aphorisms Nietzsche argues that 'We must again rid the world of much *false* grandeur' simply because 'it offends against the justice which all things may lay claim to from us' (*D* 4). In fact, the task goes much deeper than this since we are in the process of unlearning an inherited symbolism. The task of purifying ourselves of this inheritance involves inquiring into the origins and sources of the sublime. This is something Nietzsche had already begun to undertake in the previous text, *Human, all too Human*, where, for example, he had located the origins of the sublime in the religious cult (*HH* 130). Several aphorisms of *Dawn* continue this inquiry. In *D* 33 Nietzsche notes that for primitive humanity some evil chance event is interpreted in terms of a demonic power and caprice; there is no investigation into the natural causes of the phenomenon since the demonic cause is taken for granted. In this mental schema we have a demonic cause and a supernatural consequence, such as the punishments and mercies administered by the divinity, in which the sense for reality and taking pleasure in it is spoiled: reality only has value to the extent that '*it is capable of being a symbol*'. It is, therefore, under the spell of the ancient morality of custom that man disdains the causes, the effects, and reality of events and 'spins all his higher feelings of reverence, sublime exaltation, pride, gratitude, and love *from an imaginary world*: the so-called higher world' (*D* 33). The results of the process are, Nietzsche thinks, perceptible today: 'wherever a man's feelings are *exalted*, the imaginary world is involved in some way'. It is for this reason that the scientific human being has to be suspicious of all higher feelings, so tremendously nourished are they by delusion and nonsense: 'Not that they necessarily are or forever have to be: but of all the gradual purifications awaiting humanity, the purification of the higher feelings will no doubt be one of the most gradual' (*D* 3). In *D* 32 Nietzsche clearly indicates that the feeling of being '*sublimely exalted* above reality' grew out of the experience of suffering for the sake of morality: humanity developed the consciousness that suffering brought it closer to a deeper world of truth (*D* 32). We now have a pride in morality that stands in the way of a new understanding of morality, and only a new pride stemming from the tasks of knowledge can break with this inheritance.

In aphorism 45 entitled 'A Tragic Ending for Knowledge' Nietzsche notes that it is human sacrifice that has traditionally served as the means of producing exaltation; this sacrifice has both elevated and exalted the human being. What if mankind were to now sacrifice itself: to whom would it make the sacrifice? Nietzsche suggests that it would be 'the knowledge of truth' since only here could the goal be said to be commensurate with the sacrifice, 'because for this goal no sacrifice is too great'.[23] But this goal remains too distant and lofty; much closer to home is the task of working out the extent to which humanity can take steps towards the advancement of knowledge and ascertaining what kind of knowledge-drive could impel it to the point of extinction 'with the light of

[23] See also on this *GM* II. 7, in which Nietzsche notes that life has always known how to play tricks so as to justify itself, including its 'evil', and today, for us moderns and free spirits, this takes the form of 'life as a riddle, life as a problem of knowledge'.

an anticipatory wisdom in its eyes'. But perhaps here we discover the madness of such a drive if divorced from human ends of cultivation:

> Perhaps one day, once an alliance for the purpose of knowledge has been established with inhabitants of other planets and one has communicated one's knowledge from star to star for a few millennia: perhaps then enthusiasm for knowledge will swell to such a high tide! (*D* 45)

Nietzsche reflects on how a person's experience of the world and existence assumes the form of a 'revelation' and suggests that this is the problem that underlies the origin of all religions. He imagines the disclosure of the world through human consciousness amounting to a blissful experience. However, the ancient religious human being is so overwhelmed by the experience that they are unable to credit themselves as the source of insight and of such bliss; rather, they feel compelled to credit God (or some superior godlike human being) as the source of the world's revelation. In this process the experience is removed from the domain of doubt and critique and is rendered something holy. Humanity has come to experience itself as being indebted to what can be described as a law of the father: 'whenever we elevate our creation over ourselves and seemingly disregard our own worth, we then experience the exultation of paternal love and pride, which compensates and more than compensates for everything' (*D* 62). The problem goes deep because from its history of elevation and exaltation humanity has developed within itself much self-abasement, self-hatred, and self-loathing. He notes, for example, that those who live for exalted and enraptured moments are usually wretched and disconsolate. They view these moments of intoxication as their true self, whilst the thought of their environment, their age, their entire world fills them with vengeful emotions. He continues:

> Humanity has these rapturous drunkards to thank for a great deal of evil: for they are insatiable sowers of the weeds of dissatisfaction with self and neighbour, of disdain for this world and this time, especially of world-weariness. Perhaps a whole Hell of *criminals* could not muster an impact as sinister and uncanny, as oppressive and ruinous of earth and air into the farthest future as that tiny, noble community of intractable, half-mad fantasists, people of genius who cannot control themselves and who take all possible pleasure in themselves only at the point where they have completely lost themselves...(*D* 50)

The morality that humanity has cultivated and dedicated itself to is one of 'enthusiastic devotion' and 'self-sacrifice' in which it looks down from sublime heights on the more sober morality of self-control (which is regarded as egotistical). Nietzsche suggests the reason why morality has been developed in this way is owing to the enjoyment of the state of intoxication which has stemmed from the thought that the person is at one with the powerful being to whom it consecrates itself; in this way 'the feeling of power' is enjoyed and is confirmed by a sacrifice of the self. For Nietzsche such an overcoming of the 'self' is impossible: 'In truth you only *seem* to sacrifice yourselves; instead, in your thoughts you transform yourselves into gods and take pleasure in yourselves as such' (*D* 215; see also *D* 269).

Nietzsche is dealing with a problem that preoccupies him in his middle and late periods: the problem of fanaticism (*D* 57–8, 68, 298, 511; see also *AOM* 15; *GS* 347; *BGE* 10).[24] As he notes, such 'enthusiasts' will seek to implant the faith in intoxication 'as being that which is actually living in life: a dreadful faith!' (ibid.). Such is the extent of Nietzsche's anxiety that he wonders whether humanity as a whole will one day perish by its 'spiritual fire-waters' and those who keep alive the desire for them. The 'strange madness of moral judgements' is bound up with states of exaltation and 'the most exalted language' (*D* 189). Nietzsche is advising us to be on our guard, to be vigilant as philosophers against 'the half-mad, the fantastic, the fanatical', including so-called human beings of genius who claim to have 'visions' and to have seen things others do not see. We are to be cautious, not credulous, when confronted with the claims of visions, that is to say, 'of a profound mental disturbance...' (*D* 66) The problem with the consolations that have been offered to humanity by religions to date is that they have imparted to life the fundamental character of suffering: 'the human being's greatest diseases grew out of the battle against its diseases, and the apparent remedies have, in the long run, produced something much worse

[24] At this time Nietzsche is reading Voltaire's *Mahomet* (see *HH* 221) and recommending to people, including his sister Elisabeth, that they read it (see letter to her dated 13 February 1881, *Friedrich Nietzsche Briefe* III. 1 (Berlin: Walter de Gruyter, 1981), p. 62). However, we need to read carefully here since there is the danger of turning Nietzsche's championing of the Enlightenment against forces of reaction into an all-too timely position against Islam. To avoid this requires a careful analysis of Nietzsche's comments on different religions. In *GS* 347, for example, it is not Islam but Christianity and Buddhism that he describes as teaching fanaticism. In *D* 68 Saint Paul is described as a fanatic whilst in *D* 546 Epictetus is presented as an example of a non-fanatical person.

that what they were supposed to eliminate' (*D* 52). Humanity has mistaken 'the momentarily effective, anesthetizing and intoxicating means, the so-called consolations, for the actual remedies' (ibid.). It is under the most 'scandalous quackery' that humanity has come to treat its diseases of the soul.

Nietzsche appeals to Epictetus for an example of a non-fanatical mode of living and as a counterweight to modern idealists who are greedy for expansion. Epictetus's ideal human being, lacking all fear of God and believing strictly in reason, 'is no penitential preacher' (*D* 546). Although this ancient thinker was a slave, the exemplar he invokes is without class and is possible in every class. Nietzsche notes, moreover, that while Christianity was made for a different species of antique slave (one weak in will and mind), Epictetus neither lives in hope nor accepts the best he knows as a gift but 'possesses it, he holds it bravely in his own hand, he defends it against the whole world if the world wants to rob him of it' (ibid.). Epictetus is also admired by Nietzsche on account of his dedication to his own ego and for resisting the glorification of thinking and living for others (*D* 131). He serves as a useful contrast to Christian thinkers such as Pascal, who considered the ego to be something hateful:

> If, as Pascal and Christianity claim, our ego is always *hateful*, how might we possibly ever allow or assume that someone else could love it – be it God or a human being! It would go against all decency to let oneself be loved knowing full well that one only *deserves* hate – not to mention other feelings of repulsion. - 'But this is precisely the kingdom of mercy'. – So is your love-thy-neighbour mercy? Your compassion mercy? Well, if these things are possible for you, go still one step further: love yourselves out of mercy – then you won't need your God any more at all, and the whole drama of original sin and redemption will play itself out to the end in you yourselves (*D* 79).

In an aphorism on 'pseudo-egotism' Nietzsche notes how most people do nothing for their ego, but rather live in accordance with the 'phantom ego' that has been formed in the opinions of those around them. The result is that we live in a fog of impersonal or half-personal opinions and arbitrary evaluations: 'one person always in the head of another and then again this head in other heads: a curious world of phantasms that nonetheless knows how to don such a sensible appearance!' (*D* 105) We live within the effect of general opinions about the 'human being', which is a 'bloodless abstraction' and 'fiction' (ibid.). Even the modern glorification of work and talk of its blessings can be interpreted as a fear of everything individual. The subjection to hard industriousness from early until late serves as 'the best policeman' since it keeps everyone in bounds and hinders the development of reason, desire, and the craving for independence. It uses vast amounts of nervous energy which could be given over to reflection, brooding, dreaming, loving and hating and working through our experiences: '...a society in which there is continuous hard work will have more security: and security is currently worshipped as the supreme divinity' (*D* 173). Nietzsche claims that it is the moral fashion of a commercial society to value actions aimed at common security and to cultivate above all the sympathetic affections. At work here is a collective drive toward timidity which desires that life be rid of all the dangers it might have once held: 'Are we not, with this prodigious intent to grate off all the rough and sharp edges of life, well on the way to turning humanity into *sand*!' (*D* 174) In place of the ruling ethic of sympathy and self-sacrifice, which can assume the form of a 'tyrannical encroachment', Nietzsche invites individuals to engage in self-fashioning, cultivating a self that the other can behold with pleasure, a 'lovely, peaceful, self-enclosed garden...with high walls to protect against the dangers and dust of the roadway, but with a hospitable gate as well' (ibid). Before an individual can practise benevolence towards others he has to be beneficently disposed towards himself, otherwise he is running from and hating himself, and seeking to rescue himself from himself in others (*D* 516).

Clearly, Nietzsche is not advocating the abolition of all possible types or forms of morality. Where morality centres on 'continual self-command and self-overcoming... in great things and in the smallest', Nietzsche is a champion of it (*WS* 45). His concern is that 'morality' in the forms it has assumed in the greater part of human history, right up to Kant's moral law, has opened up an abundance of sources of displeasure and with every refinement of morals the human being has only become more discontented with itself, its neighbour, and its lot (*D* 106).[25] The individual in search of happiness, and who wishes to become its own lawgiver, cannot be treated with prescriptions to the path to happiness simply because individual happiness springs from one's own unknown laws and external prescriptions only serve to obstruct and hinder it: 'The so-called 'moral' precepts are, in truth, directed against individuals and are in no way aimed at

[25] Nietzsche considers Kant an important figure because he stands outside the movement within modernity that places the stress on the sympathetic affects (*D* 132). The problem is that his conception of the rational moral law conceals a remnant of ascetic cruelty (*D* 338; see also *D* 187 & 207).

promoting their happiness' (*D* 108). Up to now, Nietzsche notes, the moral law has been supposed to stand above our personal likes and dislikes; we did not want to impose this law upon ourselves but preferred to take it from somewhere or have it commanded to us.

Christianity brought into the world 'a completely new and unlimited *imperilment*', creating new securities, enjoyments, recreations, and evaluations. Although we moderns may be in the process of emancipating ourselves from such an imperilment we keep dragging into our existence the old habits associated with these securities and evaluations, even into our noblest arts and philosophies (*D* 57). Nietzsche holds that in wanting to return to the affects 'in their utmost grandeur and strength' – for example, as *love* of God, *fear* of God, fanatical *faith* in God, and so on – Christianity represents a popular protest against philosophy and he appeals to the ancient sages against it since they advocated the triumph of reason over the affects (*D* 58). Christianity has sought to transform the great passions and powers, such as Eros and Aphrodite, which are capable of idealisation, into 'infernal kobolds and phantoms of deceit', arousing in the conscience of the believer tremendous torments at the slightest sexual excitation (*D* 76). The result is to fill human beings with a feeling of dread at the sight of their natural animal conditions of existence, turning necessary and regularly recurring sensations into a source of inner misery to the point where inner misery becomes a necessary and regularly recurring phenomenon in human beings. This may even be a misery that we keep secret and is more deeply rooted than we care to admit (Nietzsche mentions in this regard Shakespeare's confession of Christian gloominess in the *Sonnets*). Christianity has contempt for the world and makes a new virtue of ignorance, namely 'innocence', the most frequent result of which is the feeling of guilt and despair: 'a virtue which leads to Heaven via the detour through Hell' (*D* 321; see also *D* 89).

Nietzsche notes, quite seriously, that Christianity has wanted to free human beings from the burden of the demands of sober morality by showing a shorter way to perfection, perhaps imitating philosophers who wanted a 'royal road to truth' that would avoid wearisome and tedious dialectics or the gathering of rigorously tested facts. In both cases a profound error is at work even though such an error has provided comfort to those caught exhausted and despairing in the wilderness of existence (*D* 59). Christianity has emerged from a 'rustic rudeness' by incorporating the spirit of countless people whose need is to take joy in submission, 'all those subtle and crude enthusiasts of self-mortification and other-idolization'. As a result Christianity has evolved into a 'very *spirited* religion' that has made

European humanity something sharp-witted and not only theologically cunning. The creation of a mode of life which tames the beast in man, which is the noble end of Christianity, has succeeded in keeping awake 'the feeling of a superhuman mission' in the soul and in the body. Here one takes pride in obeying, and this, Nietzsche notes, is the distinguishing mark of all aristocrats. It is with their 'surpassing beauty and refinement' that the princes of the church prove to the people the church's 'truth' and which is itself the result of a harmony between figure, spirit, and task. Nietzsche then asks whether this attempt at an aristocratic harmony must also go to the grave with the end of religions: 'can nothing higher be attained, or even imagined?' (*D* 60) When in the next aphorism Nietzsche invites sensitive people who are still Christians from the heart to attempt the experiment of living without Christianity he is in search of an authentic mode of life: 'they owe it to *their faith* in this way for once to sojourn 'in the wilderness' – if only to win for themselves the right to a voice on the question whether Christianity is necessary. For the present they cling to their native soil and thence revile the world beyond it...' (*D* 61) After such a wandering beyond his little corner of existence, a Christian may return home, not out of homesickness, but out of sound and honest judgement.

Nietzsche sees here a model for future human beings who will live in this way with respect to all evaluations of the past: 'one must voluntarily *live through* them once again, and likewise their opposite – in order, in the final analysis, to have the *right* to let them fall through the sieve' (*D* 62).

The Passion of Knowledge and the Sublimities of Philosophy

According to Nietzsche philosophy's love of knowledge is now assuming the form of a passion which shrinks at no sacrifice. He notes that our drive to knowledge has become so strong for us that we now cannot tolerate the idea of happiness without knowledge: 'Restless discovering and divining has such an attraction for us, and has grown as indispensable to us as is to the lover his unrequited love...' (*D* 429) We now honestly believe, Nietzsche writes, that 'under the pressure and suffering of this passion the whole of humanity must believe itself to be more sublime and more consoled than previously, when it had not yet overcome its envy of the cruder pleasure and contentment that result from barbarism' (ibid.). We even entertain the thought that humanity might perish of its newfound passion for knowledge, though clearly Nietzsche is not an advocate of this. As he notes, such a thought can hold no sway over us. Our evolution is now bound up with this passion, however, and the task is to allow ourselves to be ennobled and elevated by it: '...if humanity is not destroyed by a *passion* it will be destroyed by a *weakness*: which does one prefer? This is the main question. Do we desire for humanity an end in fire and light or in sand?' (ibid.).

Nietzsche notes that it is errors that have hitherto served as forces of consolation for humanity. If today we are seekers of truth and idealists of knowledge may we *not*, then, expect the same from truth? But can truths be capable of producing the effect of consolation? Is it not in the nature of truth precisely not to console? If human beings exist as truthful beings but employ philosophy as a cure for themselves, does this not suggest that they are not, in fact, seeking truth at all? But if the character of truth as a whole is one that makes us ill should we not abolish it in the same way the Greeks abolished gods once they were unable to offer consolation? Nietzsche spells out the reason for our ambivalent stance towards errors. On the one hand it is on their basis that humanity has been elevated and has excelled itself again and again, for example, through errors as to its descent, uniqueness, and destiny. On the other hand, it has to be noted that it is through the same errors that unspeakable amounts of suffering, persecution, suspicion, and misery have come into the world (*D* 425). Our moralities and religions do not wed us to the earth as a site of dwelling and thinking; rather, we consider ourselves 'too good and too significant for the earth', as if we were paying it only a passing visit. The 'proud sufferer' has thus become in the course of human development the highest type of human being that is revered. We cannot assume that truth will offer remedies and in the future, then, truth '*as a whole* and something wholly coherent' will have to exist only for those souls that are full of joy and peace, at once powerful and harmless.[26] Nevertheless, in spite of its cold, dry and inhuman character knowledge can offer genuine instruction and aid the coming into being of a mature humanity, showing that we are not what we take ourselves to be as subjects and agents (see *D* 115–117). We will grow in power by now making sacrifices of ourselves to knowledge.

In an aphorism entitled 'Mortal souls' Nietzsche suggests that it is a question of relearning what it is to be human, including human time as mortal time. Several aphorisms in the book consider humanity's

[26] Nietzsche mentions Aristotle as an example of a philosopher full of joyfulness and peace (*D* 424).

misguided dream of an immortal existence. 211 is an especially witty aphorism in which Nietzsche considers the impertinent nature of the dream. He notes that the actual existence of a single immortal human being would be enough to drive everyone else on earth into a rampage of death and suicide out of being sick and tired of it. The better strategy is for us to take more seriously the creature that lives typically for seventy years and give it back the actual time it has hitherto lacked for itself. Nietzsche is inviting us to replace the sublime dream of immortality with a new sobriety towards existence, as this aphorism from book five makes clear:

> With regard to knowledge the most useful accomplishment is perhaps: that the belief in the immortality of the soul has been abandoned. Now humanity is allowed to wait; now it no longer needs to rush headlong into things and choke down half-examined ideas as formerly it was forced to do. For in those days the salvation of poor 'eternal souls' depended on the extent of their knowledge acquired during a short lifetime; they had to *make a decision* overnight – 'knowledge' took on a dreadful importance. (*D* 501)

Nietzsche argues we are now in a new situation with regard to knowledge and as a result we can conquer anew our courage for mistakes, for experimentation, and for accepting things provisionally. Without the sanction of the old moralities and religions, individuals and entire generations 'can now fix their eyes on tasks of a vastness that would to earlier ages have seemed madness' (ibid.). Humanity has earned the right to self-experimentation: 'The greatest sacrifices to knowledge have not yet been made – indeed, previously it would have meant blasphemy and the surrender of one's eternal salvation even to *have a presentiment* of the thoughts that precede our actions' (ibid.).

Aphorism 507 entitled 'Against the Tyranny of the True' signals a warning however concerning our devotion to knowledge through experimentation. Here Nietzsche stages an anxiety that takes on a more dramatic form in his later writings and their questioning of the will to truth. In this aphorism he asks why it should be considered desirable that truth alone should rule and be omnipotent. We can esteem it as a 'great power' but we should not allow it to rule over us in some tyrannical fashion. Much healthier is to allow truth to have opponents and for us to find relief from it from time to time, and be at liberty to reside knowingly in 'untruth'. Failure to place truth within a rich economy of life will make truth, and ourselves in the process, 'boring, powerless, and tasteless' (*D* 507). In the next work, *The Gay Science* Nietzsche focuses on the task of the 'incorporation' (*Einverleibung*) of truth and knowledge and holds this to be our new experiment (*GS* 110). Ultimately, the task of the passion of knowledge is to give existence an 'aesthetic meaning', that is, to increase our taste for it (*KSA* 9, 11 [162]).

Nietzsche observes that, as the world becomes more comprehensible to us, the more solemnity of all kinds decreases. Hitherto, he notes, it was fear that informed humanity's attitude of reverence as it found itself overcome in the face of the unknown and the mysterious, forcing it to sink down before the incomprehensible. He then asks whether the world will lose some its appeal once a new humanity comes into being that has grown less fearful in the face of the character of the world: might it not also result in our own fearsomeness becoming slighter? His answer is negative and it is such because of the courage that he sees as amongst our new virtues; this is a species of courage so courageous that it feels itself to be '*above* people and things', it is a kind of 'excessive magnanimity' and, Nietzsche notes, has hitherto been lacking in humanity. He declares the age of 'harmless counterfeiting' to be over and looks ahead to the 'astronomers of the ideal' who will take over the role of the poets whose task was to be seers who could recount to us 'something of the *possible*!' If, as might be supposed, there are reasons for nihilism there are also equally good reasons for its exact opposite:

> If only they wanted to let us experience in advance something of the *future virtues*! Or of virtues that will never exist on earth, although they could exist somewhere in the world – of purple-glowing galaxies and the whole Milky Ways of the beautiful! Where are you, you astronomers of the ideal? (*D* 551)

Nietzsche does not, then, align his thinking with the cause of spreading fear or terror but instead commits himself to expanding our appreciation of the beautiful:

> The pessimist, who gives all things the blackest and gloomiest colours, makes use of only flames and bolts of lightning, celestial effulgence, and everything that has glaring brilliance and confuses the eye; brightness is only there for him to increase the horror and to make us sense that things are more terrifying than they really are (*D* 561).

In aphorism 469 entitled 'The Realm of Beauty is Bigger', Nietzsche suggests that new appreciations of beauty are becoming possible now that we no longer accept the limitation of restricting beauty to the morally good: 'Just as surely as evil people have a hundred types of happiness about which the virtuous have no clue, they also have a hundred types of beauty: and many have not yet been discovered' (*D* 468). In aphorism 550 on 'Knowledge and Beauty' Nietzsche suggests a reorientation in our thinking about beauty and reality. He notes that hitherto people have reserved their veneration and feeling of happiness for works of imagination and dissemblance whilst the opposite phenomena leave them cold. Pleasure or delight is taken only by plunging into the depths of semblance and by taking leave of reality. This developed taste for semblance and appearance over reality has encouraged the aesthetic attitude that takes reality to be something ugly. Contra this development Nietzsche suggests that knowledge of the ugliest reality can be something beautiful for us and the discovery of reality generates for us so many subtle pleasures. Do we not need to ask whether the 'beautiful in itself' makes any sense? Nietzsche appeals to a number of philosophers who have *enjoyed* knowledge and sought the highest happiness in the activity of a well-trained, inquisitive, and inventive understanding, including Plato and Aristotle, Descartes and Spinoza:

> The happiness of those who seek knowledge increases the amount of beauty in the world and makes everything that is here sunnier; knowledge does not merely place its beauty around things but, in the long run, into things – may future humanity bear witness to this proposition!...What danger for their honesty of becoming, through this enjoyment, a panegyrist of things! (*D* 550)

Nietzsche addresses what philosophy now does in relation to the emerging science of knowledge. He draws a comparison with rococo horticulture which arose from the feeling that nature is ugly, savage, and boring and thus the aim was to beautify it. This is now what philosophy does with science, beautifying what strikes us as ugly, dry, cheerless, and laborious. Philosophy is a species of art and poetry and thus a form of 'entertainment': it wants to entertain 'but, in accordance with its inherited pride, it wants to do this in a more sublime and elevated manner and before a select audience' (*D* 427). Nietzsche already has here, then, the conception of the project of the 'gay science' with its mixture of poetry, song, the philosophical aphorism, and dedication to science. In this aphorism from *Dawn* Nietzsche speaks of philosophy enabling us to wander in science as in 'wild nature' and without effort or boredom. Such an ambition for philosophy is one that makes religion, hitherto the highest species of the art of entertainment, superfluous. Eventually a cry of dissent against philosophy may emerge, one voiced by pure scientism and naturalism: '"back to science," to the nature and naturalness of science!' At this point, Nietzsche notes, an age of humanity's history may then commence that discovers the mightiest beauty in precisely the wild and ugly sides of science, 'just as it was only from the time of Rousseau that one discovered a sense for the beauty of high mountains and the desert' (*D* 427). In short, Nietzsche can see no good reason why humanity cannot grow in strength and insight with science: even when science deflates it humanity can experience an elevation above itself.

Nietzsche appeals to the 'spiritually needy' and considers how the new tasks and new modes of knowledge suppose solitude as their condition. He imagines a time for higher festivals when one freely gives away one's spiritual house and possessions to ones in need. In this condition of solitude the satiated soul lightens the burden of its own soul, eschewing both praise for what it does and avoiding gratitude which is invasive and fails to respect solitude and silence. This is to speak of a new kind of teacher who, armed with a handful of knowledge and a bag full of experiences, becomes 'a doctor of the spirit to the indigent and to aid people here and there whose head *is disturbed by opinions*...' (*D* 449). The aim is not to prove that one is right before such a person, but rather 'to speak with him in such a way that...he himself says what is right and, proud of the fact, walks away!' Such a teacher exists like a beacon of light offering illumination. Nietzsche imagines this teacher existing in the manner of a new kind of Stoic and inspired by a new sublime:

> To have no advantage, neither better food, nor purer air, nor a more joyful spirit – but to share, to give back, to communicate, to grow poorer! To be able to be humble so as to be accessible to many and humiliating to none! To have experienced much injustice and have crawled through the worm-tunnels of every kind of error in order to be able to reach many hidden souls along their secret paths! Always in a type of love and a type of self-interest and self-enjoyment! To be in possession of a dominion and at the same time inconspicuous and renouncing! To lie constantly in the sun and the kindness of grace and yet to know that the paths rising to the sublime are right at hand! – That would be a life! That would be a reason to live, to live a long time. (ibid)

Nietzsche in fact raises the question whether the philosopher of the morning is really renouncing things or gaining a new cheerfulness or serenity:

> To relinquish the world without knowing it, like a *nun* – that leads to an infertile, perhaps melancholic solitude. This has nothing in common with the solitude of the thinker's *vita contemplativa*: when he elects it, he in no way wishes to renounce; on the contrary, it would amount to renunciation, melancholy, downfall of his self for him to have to endure the *vita practica*: he relinquishes the latter because he knows it, because he knows himself. Thus he leaps into *his* water, thus he attains *his* serenity. (*D* 440)

For the thinker who now has the new dedication to knowledge existence is lived magnanimously. In aphorism 459 entitled 'The thinker's magnanimity' Nietzsche writes:

> Rousseau and Schopenhauer – both were proud enough to inscribe upon their existence the motto: *vitam impendere vero* ('to dedicate one's life to truth'). And again – how they both must have suffered in their pride that they could not succeed in making *verum impendere vitae*! ('to dedicate truth to life') – *verum*, as each of them understood it – in that their lives tagged along beside their knowledge like a temperamental bass that refuses to stay in tune with the melody! But knowledge would be in a sorry state if it was meted out to every thinker only as it suited his person! And thinkers would be in a sorry state if their vanity were so great that they could only endure this! The great thinker's most beautiful virtue radiates precisely from: the magnanimity with which he, as a person of knowledge, undauntedly, often shamed, often with sublime mockery and smiling – offers himself and his life in sacrifice (*D* 459).

Neither Rousseau nor Schopenhauer, Nietzsche is arguing, had the cognitive maturity needed to allow for knowledge and life to enter into a new marriage in which knowledge elevates and pulls life up with it: their emotional personalities interfered too much to permit this process to take place.

Nietzsche suggests that we should no longer feel the need to rush knowledge along to some end point. There is no longer the need, he holds, to approach questions and experiments as if the solutions to them had to correspond to a typical human time span. The course of science is no longer being crossed by the accidental fact that people live to be approximately seventy years old. We are now free to take our time and go slowly: 'To solve everything at one fell swoop, with one single word – that was the secret wish: this was the task one imagined in the image of the Gordian knot or of Columbus' egg; one did not doubt that in the realm of knowledge as well it was possible to reach one's goal after the manner of an Alexander or a Columbus and to solve all questions with *one answer*' (*D* 547). The idea evolved that there was a riddle to solve for the philosopher and that the task was to compress the problem of the world into the simplest riddle-form: 'The boundless ambition and jubilation of being the 'unriddler of the world' were the stuff of thinker's dreams' (ibid). Under such a schema of the task of thinking philosophy assumed the guise of being a supreme struggle for the tyrannical rule of spirit reserved for a single individual (Nietzsche thinks that it is Schopenhauer who has most recently fancied themselves as such an individual).

The lesson to be drawn from this inheritance is that the quest for knowledge has been retarded by the moral narrow-mindedness of its disciples. In the future, Nietzsche declares, it needs to be pursued with a higher and more magnanimous feeling: '"What do I matter!" stands over the door of the future thinker' (ibid).

For Nietzsche the consolations of religion are rapidly disappearing from our consciousness (*AOM* 169; *D* 68). The new sublimities of philosophy he is fashioning can be understood, I think, as affording new consolations (for example, the personal sacrifices we make to knowledge may contribute to the greater health of a future humanity). What has gone for us free spirited moderns are precisely those things Boethius sought as consolation from philosophy: belief in ultimate goodness, in an avenger and a final improver, belief in Providence, resting in endless trust, and so on (*GS* 285).[27] Whilst the passion of knowledge does not exist in order to console us or to satisfy the heart's desire – indeed, it challenge us to the very core of our being since truth and knowledge reveal that we are not what we take ourselves to be as agents or subjects – philosophy can entertain us (hold our attention) in new ways and by reflecting on the 'human, all too human' through psychological observation it will help 'lighten the burden of life' (*HH* 35).

Conclusion

What, ultimately, is it that drives Nietzsche's project in the texts of his middle period and as we encounter it in *Dawn*? I believe it is

[27] What Boethius wants from philosophy is assurance that the wicked will not go unpunished and knowledge that the world is a rational order and guided by Providence. See Boethius, *The Consolation of Philosophy*, trans. V. E. Watts (Middlesex: Penguin, 1969).

the search for an authentic mode of existence: 'We, however, want to become the ones that we are: ones who are new, unique, incomparable, self-creating, self-legislating' (*GS* 335). In *Dawn* Nietzsche notes that we typically adopt out of fear the evaluations which guide our actions, and only pretend that they are our own; we then grow so accustomed to the pretence that this ends up being our nature. To have one's own evaluation of things is something exceedingly rare (*D* 104). It is necessary to contest the idea that there is a single moral-making morality; every code of ethics that affirms itself in an exclusive manner 'destroys too much valuable energy and costs humanity much too dearly' (*D* 164). In the future, Nietzsche hopes, the inventive and fructifying person shall no longer be sacrificed and numerous new attempts at living life and creating community shall be undertaken. When this takes place we will find that an enormous load of guilty conscience has been purged from the world. Humanity has suffered for too long from teachers of morality who wanted too much all at once and sought to lay down precepts for everyone (*D* 194). In the future the care of truth will need to centre on the most personal questions and create time for them: 'what is it that I actually do? What is it precisely that I wish to accomplish thereby?' (*D* 196). Small individual questions and experiments are no longer to be viewed with contempt and impatience (*D* 547). We will grow and become the ones that we are, however, only by experiencing dissatisfaction with ourselves and assuming the risk of experimenting in life, even to the point of living unwisely,[28] freely taking the journey through our wastelands, quagmires, and icy glaciers. The ones who don't take the risk of life 'will never make the journey around the world (that you yourselves are!), but will remain trapped within yourselves like a knot on the log you were born to, a mere happenstance' (*D* 343).

In *Dawn* Nietzsche makes numerous practical recommendations for how we might go about cultivating and practising such an authentic existence. When we are tired and fed up with ourselves and require fresh stimulation the best practice is to sleep a lot, 'literally and figuratively! That way one will also awaken again upon a new morning!' (*D* 376) An essential test to learn is the endurance of solitude (*D* 443). Solitude has the advantage of providing us with the distant perspective we need to think well of things: 'on my own I seem to see my friends more clearly and more appealingly than

[28] See *BGE* 205: '...the true philosopher...lives 'unphilosophically' and 'unwisely' and above all *imprudently* and feels the burdensome duty of a hundred tests and temptations in life – he is continually risking *himself*...'

when together with them; and at the time when I loved music most and was most sensitive to it, I loved at a distance from it' (*D* 485). We need solitude 'so as not to drink out of everyone's cisterns' for amongst the many we simply do not think as an 'I'. Not only is such solitude of benefit to ourselves it also improves our relation to others; when we turn angry towards people and fear them we need the desert to become good again (*D* 491).

Nietzsche seeks to counsel us in the wisdom of 'slow cures' (*D* 462). He notes that chronic diseases of the soul, like those of the body, rarely emerge through one-time large offences against the rationality of body and soul, but rather through countless undetected little acts of negligence. If this is the case then the cure has to be equally subtle and entail countless little offsetting exercises and the unwitting cultivation of different habits: 'Many a person has a cold, malicious word to say for his environment ten times a day and doesn't think anything of it, especially since, after a few years, he has created for himself a *law* of habit that from now on *compels* him ten times every day to sour his environment. But he can also accustom himself to doing it a kindness ten times!' (ibid).

Finally, if we are to grow as a species and attain a new human maturity we need a new honesty about matters of love. Nietzsche wonders whether people speak with such idolatry about love – the 'food of the gods' - simply because they have had so little of it. But would not a utopia of universal love be something ludicrous? – 'each person flocked around, pestered, longed for not by one love...but by thousands, indeed by each and everyone' (*D* 147). Instead, Nietzsche wants us to favour a future of solitude, quietude, and even being unpopular. In addition, he proposes that individuals should be discouraged from reaching a decision affecting their life while in the state of being in love; marriage needs to be taken much more seriously and not allowed to grow on the basis of the whim of lovers (*D* 151; see also *D* 532). The imperatives of philosophies of universal love and compassion will serve only to destroy us. If we are tempted by them we should put them to the test and stop all our fantasizing (*D* 137).

It goes without saying perhaps that Nietzsche's emphasis on the individual's self-development entails a corresponding devaluation of economics and politics. He considers these to represent a squandering of spirit: 'Our age, no matter how much it talks and talks about economy, is a squanderer: it squanders what is most precious, spirit' (*D* 179). Today, he holds, we are in a state of 'colossal and ridiculous lunacy' with everybody feeling obliged to know what is going on day in and day out and longing at every instant to be actively involved to the point of abandoning the work of their own therapy. The philosophical therapy he is proposing in *Dawn* is thus reserved for those solitaries who have seceded from society and who wish to be the harbingers of a new earth and new peoples to come:

> To build anew the laws of life and of behaviour – for this task our sciences of physiology, medicine, sociology, and solitude are not yet sure of themselves: and only from them can we can take the foundation-stones for new ideals (if not the new ideals themselves). Thus we are living either a *preliminary* or *posterior* existence, depending on taste and talent, and it is best in this interregnum to be to every possible extent our own *reges* and to found little *experimental states*. We are experiments: let us also want to be such! (*D* 453)

The Philosopher as Pathogenic Agent, Patient, and Therapist: The Case of William James

LOGI GUNNARSSON

> However, in Teufelsdröckh, there is always the strangest Dualism: light dancing, with guitar-music, will be going on in the forecourt, while by fits from within comes the faint whimpering of woe and wail.
>
> Carlyle, *Sartor Resartus*

One way to understand philosophy as a form of therapy is this: it involves a philosopher who is trying to cure himself. He has been drawn into a certain philosophical frame of mind—the 'disease'—and has thus infected himself with this illness. Now he is sick and trying to employ philosophy to cure himself. So philosophy is both: the ailment and the cure. And the philosopher is all three: pathogenic agent, patient, and therapist.

The young William James was such a philosopher. I want to show that, according to James himself, the trouble he got himself into was not just a philosophical puzzle. Rather, he made himself truly melancholic by his philosophical frame of mind. I shall also argue that—contrary to common misconceptions of James—the cure he prescribed to himself did not consist in an arbitrary act of will. Rather, the cure was a radical reconception of how to justify a solution to a philosophical question as the one true answer.[1]

Employing philosophy as therapy implies a certain duality of the mind. The philosopher is genuinely drawn to a certain way of thinking and a part of him wants to continue in this frame of mind. But another part of him doesn't. From this perspective, he sees himself as sick and wants to cure himself. So it would seem that the goal of philosophy as therapy must be the unity of the person: unless the philosopher manages to rid himself of the tendency to think in a certain way, he is not cured. In the final section of this chapter, I will briefly

[1] I am only concerned with the early James: his writings until *The Will to Believe*. In fact, the reconception in question is compatible with a rejection of the pragmatic theory of truth.

doi:10.1017/S1358246109990300

address the issue of whether this is right—whether the goal of philosophy as therapy should be the unity of the person.

The Illness: Philosophical Melancholy

On April 30, 1870, William James wrote in his diary:

> I think that yesterday was a crisis in my life. I finished the first part of [Charles] Renouvier's second 'Essais' and see no reason why his definition of Free Will—'the sustaining of a thought *because I choose to* when I might have other thoughts'—need be the definition of an illusion. At any rate, I will assume for the present—until next year—that it is no illusion. My first act of free will shall be to believe in free will. For the remainder of the year, I will abstain from the mere speculation and the contemplative *Grüblei* in which my nature takes most delight, and voluntarily cultivate the feeling of moral freedom, by reading books favorable to it, as well as by acting. After the first of January, my callow skin being somewhat fledged, I may perhaps return to metaphysical study and skepticism without danger to my powers of action. For the present then remember: care little for speculation; much for the *form* of my action; recollect that only when habits of order are formed can we advance to really interesting fields of action—and consequently accumulate grain on grain of willful choice like a very miser; never forgetting how one link dropped undoes an indefinite number. *Principiis obsta*—Today has furnished the exceptionally passionate initiative which [Alexander] Bain posits as needful for the acquisition of habits. I will see to the sequel. Not in maxims, not in *Anschauungen*, but in accumulated acts of thought lies salvation. *Passer outre.* Hitherto, when I have felt like taking a free initiative, like daring to act originally, without carefully waiting for contemplation of the external world to determine all for me, suicide seemed the most manly form to put my daring into; now, I will go a step further with my will, not only act with it, but believe as well; believe in my individual reality and creative power. My belief, to be sure, *can't* be optimistic—but I will posit life (the real, the good) in the self-governing *resistance* of the ego to the world.[2]

This is not the statement of a person playing around with philosophical problems. It is also not the report of somebody who suffered a singular 'crisis' yesterday that he has now resolved today. James writes this note

[2] Henry James (son of WJ), ed., *The Letters of William James*, vol. 1 (Boston: Atlantic Monthly Press, 1926), pp. 147–148.

in an attempt to work his way out of a severe crisis. Yesterday, in struggling with his crisis, he had an insight that he now resolves to hold on to as a way of 'salvation.' (I shall call this entry 'the crisis note.')

What sort of a crisis is it? If James had been alive today, he is likely to have been diagnosed with 'Bipolar Mood Disorder.'[3] For brief periods in 1870–1871, he may or may not have checked himself into a mental asylum.[4] Be that as it may, James certainly was in a severe psychological crisis of some sort in the late 1860s and early 1870s. In 1870 James had not yet found his place or direction in life. Born in 1842, he first studied painting in New Port in 1860–61 before devoting himself to chemistry and comparative anatomy at Harvard (1861–1863). In 1863 he took up the study of medicine. Having realized that the practice of medicine was not his calling, he took a break from medical studies to serve as assistant to the acclaimed geologist Louis Agassiz on a scientific field trip on the Amazon (1865–1866).[5] In Brazil he discovered that he hated 'collecting'[6] and, back in Cambridge in 1866, he resumed the study of medicine—only to interrupt his program once again to go to Germany to study experimental physiology and seek relief for his poor physical health (1867–1868). In 1868 he moved back to his parents' house in Cambridge and finally completed his medical degree (1869), but he was never to practice medicine. So at the time of the 'crisis note' in April 1870, he was twenty-eight years old, living again with his parents, suffering from poor physical condition (e.g. insomnia, a difficulty reading for more than a few hours, a bad back), and had no partner in sight (he married in 1878 at the age of thirty-six). He had been in continual conflict with his father about his intellectual development and still had no profession, even though he, the eldest child, had once been the star among the James children.[7] Now time had passed and his brother Wilky had fought heroically in the civil war—his own physical weakness had

3 Howard Feinstein, *Becoming William James*, with a new introduction (Ithaca: Cornell University Press, 1999), p. 13.

4 See Linda Simon, *Genuine Reality: A Life of William James* (New York: Harcourt Brace, 1998), pp. 121–122n.

5 See Ralph Barton Perry, *The Thought and Character of William James*, vol. 1 (Boston: Little, Brown, 1935), pp. 216–217.

6 Ignas K. Skrupskelis and Elizabeth M. Berkeley, eds., *The Correspondence of William James*, vol. 4 (Charlottesville: University Press of Virginia, 1995), p. 128.

7 See Henry James (brother of WJ), *A Small Boy and Others* (London: Gibson Square Books, 2001), pp. 108, 136–137; Simon, *Genuine Reality: A Life of William James*, pp. 39–40.

disqualified him as a soldier (and made it impossible to do laboratory work). And another of his brothers, Henry, was settling into the career of a writer. His sister, Alice, was also living at their parents' house after recently suffering a nervous breakdown, and in her mental condition she exhibited some of the same symptoms as he.[8] It is easy to see that, at the time of the crisis note, James had good reason to worry about his prospects and his physical and mental health.

Another event highly detrimental to his mental condition was the death of his cousin, Minny Temple, at the age of just twenty-five in the month prior to James's crisis note. After returning from Germany, James had been emotionally and intellectually intensely concerned with the terminally ill Minny. Her person, her death, and her correspondence with him about religious matters in the last months and days of her life had a deep impact on James and his mental condition. Her death was a terrible loss for him.[9]

Erik H. Erikson describes James's development from his art education to his appointment as an instructor at Harvard in 1872 as a 'particularly prolonged identity crisis.'[10] Leaving aside the question of whether this is the best way to describe James's life during these years, there can be no doubt that he was in a serious psychological crisis during the late 1860s and the early 1870s, in particular around the time of the crisis note. However, I am not interested in this crisis as a psychiatric crisis, as a period in a depression disorder or any other psychiatric disorder, or as a purely biographical crisis. Rather, it is of interest to me here as a philosophical crisis with a psychological dimension.

In the essay 'Is Life Worth Living?' which was originally delivered as a lecture in 1895, James briefly mentions 'melancholy' as symptom of a mental condition neither caused by philosophy nor curable by it: 'We are not magicians to make the optimistic temperament universal; and alongside of the deliverances of temperamental optimism concerning life, those of temperamental pessimism always exist .... In what is called 'circular insanity,' phases of melancholy succeed

[8] See Simon, *Genuine Reality: A Life of William James*, p. 114.

[9] See Henry James (brother of WJ), *Notes of a Son and Brother* (London: MacMillan, 1914), pp. 422–423, 478–479; Simon, *Genuine Reality: A Life of William James*, pp 116–123; Richard D. Richardson, *William James: In the Maelstrom of American Modernism* (Boston: Houghton Mifflin, 2007), pp. 96–100, 111–113

[10] Erik H. Erikson, *Identity: Youth and Crisis* (New York: W. W. Norton, 1968), p. 151.

phases of mania, with no outward cause that we can discover.'[11] This he distinguishes from 'philosophical melancholy':[12]

> My task, let me say now, is practically narrow, and my words are to deal only with that metaphysical *tedium vitae* which is peculiar to reflecting men. Most of you are devoted, for good or ill, to the reflective life. Many of you are students of philosophy, and have already felt in your own persons the skepticism and unreality that too much grubbing in the abstract roots of things will breed. This is, indeed, one of the regular fruits of the over-studious career. Too much questioning and too little active responsibility lead ... to the edge of the slope, at the bottom of which lie pessimism and the nightmare or suicidal view of life. But to the diseases which reflection breeds, still further reflection can oppose effective remedies; and it is of the melancholy and *Weltschmerz* bred of reflection that I now proceed to speak.[13]

This distinction between two kinds of melancholy, which James made in 1895, can be seen as a comment on his own life, particularly in the 1860s and the early 1870s. As I have said above, he himself may have been subject to a 'circular insanity' and, as I shall show, philosophical melancholy surfaces not only in the crisis note during these years. It is philosophical melancholy—melancholy bred of reflection—that interests me in this chapter. [14]

What is the nature of the philosophical melancholy bred of reflection? One may distinguish three components that James invokes to characterize it: judgment, emotion or sentiment, and action. The judgment is that life is not worth living, and the action that the philosophically melancholic person is disposed to perform is suicide.[15] Finally, the emotion or sentiment may be characterized as

[11] William James, *The Will to Believe and Other Essays in Popular Philosophy* (Cambridge, Mass.: Harvard University Press, 1979), p. 36; see also p. 39.

[12] James, *The Will to Believe*, p. 44. He also speaks of 'speculative melancholy' (p. 42).

[13] James, *The Will to Believe*, pp. 39–40.

[14] This understanding of philosophical melancholy evinced in James's 'Is Life Worth Living?' must be distinguished from the narrower use of the term also employed in this article. According to this narrower interpretation, philosophical melancholy is specifically related to a 'contradiction' between a certain idea of nature and a 'craving of the hearth' (*The Will to Believe*, pp. 40–41; see also pp. 42–44). I am only interested in the broader understanding of philosophical melancholy.

[15] See James, *The Will to Believe*, pp. 34–45.

'melancholy and *Weltschmerz*,' a feeling of 'unreality,' sadness,[16] the 'sentiment' of '*tedium vitae*,'[17] and as a feeling of uncanniness, or '*unheimlichkeit*.'[18]

In the crisis note, James formulates a certain resolution. I now want to argue that James hopes with this resolution to cure himself of philosophical melancholy. To do so, I must show that the description of philosophical melancholy and the remedy given in 'Is Life Worth Living?' apply to the ailment and the cure discussed both in the crisis note and at other moments in James's life around that time. I shall consider all three elements: judgment, action, and emotion.

James says in the passage from 'Is Life Worth Living?' that 'too much questioning' leads to 'the edge of the slope, at the bottom of which lie[s] ... the ... suicidal view of life.' Philosophical melancholy can render one prone to suicide. In a letter written to Thomas Ward in January 1868, James confides that 'all last winter' he 'was on the continual verge of suicide.'[19] He suggests that he was prevented from committing suicide by the thought that he might make his '*nick* ... in the raw stuff the race has got to shape' and in this way 'assert' his 'reality.' [20] This comment corresponds to remarks in both the crisis note and in 'Is Life Worth Living?'

In the crisis note, he writes that, instead of suicide, he will believe in his 'individual reality and creative power.' This is not only an expression of the hope that he will be creative. According to James, it would be impossible to make a difference to the course of history if determinism were true: free will and determinism are incompatible.[21] Thus, in saying in the crisis note that he will believe in free will—in the 'self-governing *resistance* of the ego to the world'—he is saying that he will believe in a necessary presupposition of the truth of a thought that prevented him from committing suicide: the thought that he might make his '*nick* ... in the raw stuff the race has got to shape.'

16 James, *The Will to Believe*, p. 34.

17 James, *The Will to Believe*, p. 130. This description seems justified on account of the context of this quote and the mention of 'metaphysical *tedium vitae*' in the passage under discussion.

18 James, *The Will to Believe*, p. 41.

19 Skrupskelis and Berkeley, eds., *The Correspondence of William James*, vol. 4, p. 248.

20 Skrupskelis and Berkeley, eds., *The Correspondence of William James*, vol. 4, p. 250.

21 See James, *The Will to Believe*, p. 117; Ignas K. Skrupskelis and Elizabeth M. Berkeley, eds., *The Correspondence of William James*, vol. 6 (Charlottesville: University Press of Virginia, 1998), pp. 98–100, 163.

This thought expressed in the letter to Ward is similar to a thought he offers to the 'reflective would-be suicide'[22] in 'Is Life Worth Living?' as a way of making him see that life can be worth living. In both cases, James appeals to the fact that we owe so much to other people, dead and living, as a way of motivating us to act for the sake of others.[23] In the letter, he describes actions for the sake of others as adding 'to the property of the race,' modifying other people's lives, and thus as enabling one to enter into '*real* relations with them.'[24] This will allow a person to make his '*nick* ... in the raw stuff the race has got to shape.' Moreover, in both cases James is offering a solution to the same difficulty. In the letter to Ward, James ponders how either of them can manage to feel that through work they take 'hold of the reality of things.' James says that this is 'hard theoretically.'[25] He is thus saying that this difficulty of his life has a theoretical root. And this root is the same as the one in 'Is Life Worth Living?': how are we to motivate ourselves to act in a world which we do not believe expresses God's purposes?[26]

The letter to Ward is a good example of how James's own melancholic state of mind has—at least according to James himself—two different causes. In speaking about finding work that makes Ward and him feel as if they take 'hold of the reality of things,' James also addresses his and Ward's difficulty in finding 'work wh. shall by its mere *exercise* interest' them. He proposes a practical solution to this problem before turning to the theoretical difficulty just mentioned. Philosophical melancholy arises from reflection, but the state of mind—melancholy—may be the same as the melancholy caused by the difficulty of opting for a vocation in life. In struggling with his own melancholy, James typically fights on both fronts, often without making a clear distinction between them.

After proposing in 'Is Life Worth Living?' that the 'reflective would-be suicide' act for the sake of others, James explains that this proposal is meant for 'men who have cast away all metaphysics in order to get rid of hypochondria.'[27] As used by James, the term

[22] James, *The Will to Believe*, p. 47.

[23] See Skrupskelis and Berkeley, eds., *The Correspondence of William James*, vol. 4, pp. 248–250; James, *The Will to Believe*, pp. 47–48.

[24] Skrupskelis and Berkeley, eds., *The Correspondence of William James*, vol. 4, p. 249.

[25] Skrupskelis and Berkeley, eds., *The Correspondence of William James*, vol. 4, p. 248.

[26] See Skrupskelis and Berkeley, eds., *The Correspondence of William James*, vol. 4, p. 248; James, *The Will to Believe*, pp. 40–45.

[27] James, *The Will to Believe*, p. 48.

'philosophical hypochondria' seems to mean the same thing as 'philosophical melancholy.' Furthermore, he frequently applies it to himself, as when he writes to his brother Henry in 1872 about his appointment as an instructor giving him 'diversion from these introspective studies which had bred a sort of philosophical hypochondria in me of late.'[28] This echoes the resolution he makes in the crisis note to 'abstain from the mere speculation and the contemplative *Grüblei*.'

But why does 'mere speculation' breed philosophical melancholy? The problem is that 'mere speculation' cannot settle central philosophical questions such as the issue of free will. Philosophical questions are not puzzles to be solved as part of a game. Rather, they force themselves on a person as he leads his life. They pertain to a person's understanding of himself and his place in the world, and the significance of the life he lives will turn on the person's answers to these questions. If no answers to these questions are forthcoming, then the person will be at a loss as to how to lead his life or whether to go on living at all. This is at least how James treats many philosophical questions. Given this role of philosophical questions in a person's life, the problem with 'mere speculation'—if it does not deliver answers to philosophical questions—is that it naturally gives rise to melancholy: 'Hitherto, when I have felt like taking a free initiative, like daring to act originally, without carefully waiting for contemplation of the external world to determine all for me, suicide seemed the most manly form to put my daring into.' The problem with pure 'contemplation' is that it will not answer the philosophical questions 'for' the person asking them. 'Hitherto,' when contemplation failed to deliver answers, 'suicide' seemed to James the most appropriate response to this situation.

In the crisis note, he resolves to hold on to an insight that makes an entirely different kind of response possible. The insight is that his mistake consisted in 'waiting for contemplation of the external world' to decide philosophical questions. In 'Is Life Worth Living?' James says that 'to diseases which reflection breeds, still further reflection can oppose effective remedies.' However, the reflective remedy that the crisis note offers is to stop thinking that reflection *alone* should settle the relevant issue: 'Without carefully waiting for contemplation of the external world to determine all for

[28] Ignas K. Skrupskelis and Elizabeth M. Berkeley, eds., *The Correspondence of William James*, vol. 1 (Charlottesville: University Press of Virginia, 1992), p. 167. See also Henry James (son of WJ), ed., *The Letters of William James*, vol. 1, pp. 169–171.

me … I will go a step further with my will, not only act with it, but believe as well.'[29]

What he resolves to believe in is free will: 'My first act of free will shall be to believe in free will.' As already hinted at in the crisis passage, the belief in free will is crucial for 'moral freedom' and belief in the 'good.' As I will elaborate later, according to James, free will is incompatible with determinism and a deterministic world is a world devoid of meaning, a world in which life is not worth living. The problem with 'mere speculation' is not simply that it cannot resolve the question of free will. Rather, there are many philosophical questions it cannot settle. These are often questions, if settled one way rather than another, that lead to the view that life is not worth living. One such question, which James connects closely with the issue of determinism, is whether actions are objectively good or have an objective significance, or whether their goodness or significance is simply relative to subjective feeling. It is the possibility of the latter answer that breeds philosophical melancholy, expressing itself, for example, in a feeling of uncanniness.

This question is one of the topics in the philosophical lectures that James delivered in the late 1870s, the 1880s, and the 1890s, and that are collected in *The Will to Believe*, published in 1897. It is also a central issue in the notes he made to himself in the late 1860s and early 1870s. In a note addressed to Oliver Wendell Holmes, James records some thoughts he had been 'groping for the other evening' in a discussion with Holmes, perhaps during the winter of 1866–67: he states that a theory which implies that it is impossible to 'authenticate' a person's 'most pleasurable feelings' by 'guaranteeing the objective significance' of these feelings is 'inconsistent with a high degree of happiness,' given that 'a man's happiness depends on his feelings.'[30] In a note written sometime between 1873 and 1875, James rejects Chauncey Wright's 'nihilism,' which denies that there is a 'relation of reality, which implies not only that we feel so

[29] I had been assuming that the passage from 'Is Life Worth Living?' should be read as saying that 'further reflection' can provide 'effective remedies' to the 'diseases which reflection breeds.' I am grateful to Jonardon Ganeri for pointing out to me that the sentence can also be read as saying that 'further reflection' is an obstacle to 'effective remedies.' In that case, the remedies that James is proposing would presumably not be 'reflective' at all.

[30] Henry James (son of WJ), ed., *The Letters of William James*, vol. 1, pp. 82–83.

& so, but that we *should* feel so.'[31] James says in a note (possibly from 1873) that 'to human nature there is something uncanny, *unheimlich*' about reality as interpreted by such an approach.[32] James expresses this in even more personal terms in the following passage about this 'Humean' view: 'I for one must confess that if by an effort of abstraction I am able for a moment to conceive of the world in Humean terms ... I feel as if the breath was leaving my body.'[33] Later, in a letter written to Shadworth Hodgson in 1886, James responds to Hodgson's criticism of 'The Dilemma of Determinism' by repeating his claim about uncanniness: the act of excluding 'moral categories altogether from a place in the world's definition ... leaves the world *unheimlich*, reptilian, and foreign to man.'[34] From this view, which makes James 'feel as if the breath was leaving' his body and experience the world as uncanny, there is 'no possible *theoretic* escape.' This, at least, is how James puts it in 'The Dilemma of Determinism' (1884) when describing a related view: 'The only escape is by the practical way.'[35] James's own crisis note is a record of an 'escape by the practical way': having realized that 'mere speculation' will not settle the issue for him, he resolves to believe in a view which does not render the world uncanny to him. One can only conclude that the crisis note is part of James's attempt to cure himself of a condition that has all the essential elements of philosophical melancholy: the judgment that life is not worth living, the tendency to commit suicide, and emotional reactions such as the feeling of uncanniness.

The Cure: The 'Whole Man'

In the 'Dilemma of Determinism,' James says that it is an 'issue of fact' whether determinism or indeterminism is true.[36] However, it is an issue that is insoluble 'from any strict theoretical point of view.'[37] James thus turns to unraveling the consequences of the belief that determinism is true. He offers a complicated argument

[31] William James, *Manuscript Essay and Notes* (Cambridge, Mass.: Harvard University Press, 1988), p. 154.

[32] Perry, *The Thought and Character of William James*, vol. 1, p. 499.

[33] Perry, *The Thought and Character of William James*, vol. 1, p. 500.

[34] Skrupskelis and Berkeley, eds., *The Correspondence of William James*, vol. 6, p. 163; see also James, *The Will to Believe*, p. 71.

[35] James, *The Will to Believe*, pp. 133–134.

[36] James, *The Will to Believe*, p. 117.

[37] James, *The Will to Believe*, p. 124.

which I must simplify here: that, from a 'strictly theoretical point of view,' subjectivism is the most 'rational' reaction to the assumption that determinism is true.[38] Subjectivism is the view—to simplify further—that actions and events are in themselves neither good nor bad.[39] The acceptance of subjectivism, in turn, leads to 'romanticism.' In other words, if one believes that determinism is true, then one is rationally led to become a romantic. James refers to Ernest Renan and Emile Zola to explain what the 'romantic state of mind' amounts to:

> Both [Renan and Zola] are athirst for the facts of life, and both think the facts of human sensibility to be of all facts the most worthy of attention. Both agree, moreover, that sensibility seems to be there for no higher purpose—certainly not … for the sake of bringing mere outward rights to pass and frustrating outward wrongs … under the pages of both [Renan and Zola] there sounds incessantly the hoarse bass of *vanitas vanitatum, omnia vanitas*, which the reader may hear, whenever he will, between the lines. No writer of this French romantic school has a word of rescue from the hour of satiety with the things of life—the hour in which we say 'I take no pleasure in them'—or from the hour of terror at the world's vast meaningless grinding, if perchance such hours should come. For terror and satiety are facts of sensibility like any others; and at their own hour they reign in their own right. The heart of the romantic utterances, whether poetical, critical, or historical, is this inward remedilessness, what [Thomas] Carlyle calls this far-off whimpering of wail and woe. And from this romantic state of mind there is absolutely no possible *theoretic* escape. Whether, like Renan, we look upon life in a more refined manner, as a romance of the spirit; or whether, like the friends of M. Zola we … prefer to be cynical, and call the world a 'roman experimental' on an infinite scale—in either case the world appears to us potentially as what the same Carlyle once called it, a vast, gloomy, solitary Golgotha and mill of death.[40]

As a version of subjectivism, romanticism assumes that no action is objectively worthy of being performed. Actions only have a worth relative to our sensibilities. Likewise, the sensibilities themselves have no objective worth. As such, one sensibility is no more worthy

38 James, *The Will to Believe*, p. 131.
39 See James, *The Will to Believe*, pp. 128–130.
40 James, *The Will to Believe*, pp. 133–134.

of being had than any other. Although the romantic rejoices in the observation of the multiplicity of facts and human sensibilities, objectively speaking, all that exists is 'the world's vast meaningless grinding.' Thus, romanticism accepts the judgment at the core of philosophical melancholy: that there is nothing about life that, objectively speaking, renders it worth living. This means that the romantic is entirely defenseless against feelings of philosophical melancholy if they overcome him: in experiencing life as meaningless, the romantic's feeling has—in his own view—placed him in touch with the way things really are: objectively speaking, nothing is worthy of being done.

James's two references in this passage to Thomas Carlyle's *Sartor Resartus* are particularly noteworthy. Carlyle's book presents itself as an edition of, and commentary on, a work on the philosophy of clothes by 'Professor Teufelsdröckh of Weissnichtwo.'[41] However, the book also recounts the biography of Teufelsdröckh. The reference to Golgotha is part of an autobiographical comment by Teufelsdröckh: 'To me the Universe was all void of Life, of Purpose, of Volition, even of Hostility: it was one huge, dead, immeasurable Steam-engine, rolling on, in its dead indifference, to grind me to limb from limb. O vast, gloomy, solitary Golgotha, and Mill of Death!'[42] Such thoughts and the events of his life drive Teufeldröckh to the verge of suicide.[43] Now, James knew his Carlyle inside and out.[44] The reference to the world as a 'solitary Golgotha' should therefore not be understood as a reference to a purely theoretical work. Rather, it is a reference to a particular person who describes his own experiences of the world in this way and is almost pushed to suicide on account of this way of seeing the world. In other words, James wants to demonstrate that romanticism drives people to the verge of suicide—a condition from which 'there is absolutely no possible *theoretic* escape.'

The other reference to Carlyle is no less important. In drawing attention to 'what Carlyle calls this far-off whimpering of wail and woe,' James quotes him out of context. The relevant passage is part of the editor's description of Teufeldröckh: 'However, in Teufelsdröckh, there is always the strangest Dualism: light

[41] Thomas Carlyle, *Sartor Resartus*, edited by K. McSweeney and P. Sabor (Oxford: Oxford University Press, 1987), p. 6.

[42] Carlyle, *Sartor Resartus*, p. 127.

[43] See Carlyle, *Sartor Resartus*, pp. 127–128.

[44] See, e.g., the quotes from *Sartor Resartus* in James, *The Will to Believe*, pp. 42–44.

dancing, with guitar-music, will be going on in the forecourt, while by fits from within comes the faint whimpering of woe and wail.'[45] Thus, although it is not how James uses the quote, the 'whimpering of woe and wail' is something that continues to occur within a person who is trying to escape this very condition. This description of Teufelsdröckh is presented just after Teufelsdröckh's own account of his first success in pulling himself away from the 'CENTRE OF INDIFFERENCE' by a 'first preliminary moral Act.'[46] This means that, here, Teufelsdröckh attempts to perform something very similar to James's act, as reported in the crisis note. The question is whether the editor's description of Teufelsdröckh is not just as true of James: despite his positive assertion of life by the performance of 'light dancing, with guitar-music ... in the forecourt,' there is 'whimpering of woe and wail' going on underneath. In other words, the question is whether James's attempts to cure himself of philosophical melancholy are and can be a success. I will return to this question in the final section.

So if there is no 'theoretic escape' from the melancholy of romanticism, what sort of escape is possible? According to James, 'the only escape is by the practical way.'[47] In making this proposal, James draws again on Carlyle. To escape, one must take 'conduct, and not sensibility,' as 'the ultimate fact for our recognition.'[48] We must assume that there are actions to be performed—actions that are good irrespective of our subjective feeling—and we must act accordingly. The passages in Carlyle's work to which James refers at this point are part of a discussion in which Carlyle quotes from Goethe's *Wilhelm Meisters Lehrjahre* as follows: 'Doubt of any sort cannot be removed except by Action.'[49] In *Wilhelm Meisters Lehrjahre*, it is not purely theoretical doubt that is at issue. On the contrary, the advice that doubt should be eliminated by action is presented as part of a method for curing the mad.[50] Although Carlyle does not explicitly identify the context of the quote from Goethe, it would have been clear to James. He wrote to his correspondents about reading *Wilhelm Meisters Lehrjahre* while he himself was

45 Carlyle, *Sartor Resartus*, p. 142.
46 Carlyle, *Sartor Resartus*, p. 142.
47 James, *The Will to Believe*, p. 134.
48 James, *The Will to Believe*, p. 134.
49 Carlyle, *Sartor Resartus*, p. 148.
50 See Johann Wolfgang Goethe, *Wilhelm Meisters Lehrjahre* (Munich: Insel, 1980), pp. 358–359.

fighting melancholy during his stay in Berlin in 1868.[51] Again, the trouble for which James proposes a cure is not some theoretical puzzle: it is the cure to a madness fed by too much reflection—a madness to which James felt he was subject.

Summing up, one can say that, in the 'Dilemma of Determinism,' James reports that he opts for indeterminism by an act of belief. By showing that the acceptance of determinism leads rationally to romanticism, a state that drives a person to the verge of suicide, James has given us grounds for deciding to believe in indeterminism. However, does James not make it much too easy for himself? He spells out the practical consequences of accepting determinism. Finding these emotionally unacceptable, he decides to believe in indeterminism. This, at least, is a common criticism leveled at James. The following passage is exemplary of such criticism. It is taken from Jean-Paul Sartre's novel *Nausea* and consists in a dialogue between the main character of the novel, Antoine Roquentin, and the so-called 'autodidact.' Roquentin has the first word:

> 'I was just thinking,' I tell him, 'that here we are, all of us, eating and drinking to preserve our precious existence, and that there's nothing, nothing, absolutely no reason for existing.'
>
> The Autodidact … repeats slowly:
>
> 'No reason for existing … I suppose, Monsieur, you mean that life has no object. Isn't that what people call pessimism?'
>
> He goes on thinking for a moment, then he says gently:
>
> 'A few years ago I read a book by an American author, called *Is Life Worth Living*? Isn't that the question you are asking yourself?'
>
> No, that obviously isn't the question I'm asking myself. But I don't want to explain anything.
>
> 'He concluded,' the Autodidact tells me in a consoling voice, 'in favour of deliberate optimism. Life has a meaning if you choose to give it one. First of all you must act, you must throw yourself into some enterprise. If you think about it later on, the die is cast, you are already involved. I don't know what you think about that, Monsieur?'
>
> 'Nothing,' I say.
>
> Or rather I think that that is precisely the sort of lie that the commercial traveler, the two young people, and the white-haired gentleman keep on telling themselves.[52]

[51] See Skrupskelis and Berkeley, eds., *The Correspondence of William James*, vol. 1, pp. 49–51; vol. 4, pp. 305–308.

[52] Jean-Paul Sartre, *Nausea*, translated by R. Baldick (London: Penguin, 2000), p. 162.

'Life has a meaning if you choose to give it one.' That is the thesis attributed to James in this passage.[53] According to Roquentin, this is a 'lie'—a lie that the people in the café where he is sitting 'keep on telling themselves.' Believing that life is meaningful may make people 'happy,' as Roquentin observes about the young people he mentions in this passage.[54] They invent their lies in order to 'conceal the enormous absurdity of their existence' and to keep themselves from noticing that they exist. Contrary to them, Roquentin knows that he and they exist and there is 'absolutely no reason for existing.'[55] This is not the place to analyze the precise content of Roquentin's thesis about existence, but it surely includes the claim that the world is devoid of meaning. The point to notice is that Roquentin thinks that this is something he knows. He has discovered that the world is devoid of meaning. It is simply true. The tragicomic fact about James and the people in the café is that they believe something that, though it may make them happy, is simply false.

Despite Roquentin's mockery of James, they in fact have much in common. *Nausea* is written in the form of Roquentin's diary. Roquentin's impetus for keeping the diary is to try to understand the nature and implications of the unsettling emotional reaction he has been having to things. He, like James, fears that these reactions may be a sign of insanity.[56] However, as with James, these emotional reactions are part and parcel of a philosophical engagement with the world. Both of them expect important philosophical truths to come to light through emotion. Roquentin comes to describe this emotional reaction as 'nausea,' which is also the title of Sartre's book. However, Sartre originally planned to call the work *Melancholia*.[57] Although it would be wrong to identify nausea with melancholy, Roquentin is surely a philosophical melancholic.

Roquentin thinks that his nausea has revealed to him (though this is not his terminology) the metaphysical nature of reality. Moreover, he thinks that one can gain access to this deepest of metaphysical truths *only* through, first, having had a certain emotional revelation and, second, having understood it: 'Existence is not something which allows itself to be thought of from a distance; it has to invade you suddenly, pounce upon you, weigh heavily on your heart like a

53 See Martin Suhr, *Jean-Paul Sartre zur Einführung* (Hamburg: Junius, 2001), p. 42.
54 Sartre, *Nausea*, p. 156.
55 Sartre, *Nausea*, pp. 161–162.
56 See Sartre, *Nausea*, pp. 9–15.
57 See Suhr, *Jean-Paul Sartre zur Einführung*, pp. 29–32.

huge motionless animal.'[58] It is through his nausea that this invasion of existence happens, and through understanding his nausea, he understands existence and his own life.[59]

This Roquentin shares with James: a proper metaphysical understanding of reality is only possible through an emotional relationship to reality. However, there are important differences. The emotion that reveals existence to Roquentin is a *passive* emotion: something that overcomes him. One may suppose that this is part of the reason Roquentin thinks it is so revealing: when he experiences this emotion, reality impresses itself upon him. He just needs to correctly apprehend what has imposed itself on him. Thus, as James might put it, Roquentin misunderstands the role of reflection: he thinks that he has simply reflected upon an emotion that was there independent of reflection. In fact—as James might continue—the opposite is the case. Nausea—or melancholy if you will—is bred by reflection. More specifically, it is bred by the assumption that only by reflecting on the world at a distance can we arrive at the truth about it. If reflection fails to deliver any determinate results, we may be overwhelmed with the same kind of emotion as triggered by Roquentin's experience of existence as a huge and superfluous presence suffocating him in its arbitrariness.[60] Such experiences are overwhelming precisely because we suppose them to amount to a neutral access to the way things are. This is precisely not what they are. Rather, as James might elaborate, melancholy is just one of many possible emotional relationships with the world.

So, one might think that James's cure for philosophical melancholy can be summarized as follows: philosophical melancholy is bred by the assumption that pure reflection can unravel the nature of reality. When a person realizes that pure reflection cannot deliver definite answers, that person develops a melancholic relationship with the world. The cure is to stop searching for definite answers. Instead, one should playfully take up the different perspectives that exist without assuming that any of them represents the correct way of looking at things. In other words, the cure for philosophical melancholy is to become an 'ironist' in Richard Rorty's sense.[61]

Yet this is not the cure James proposes. The ironist makes the very mistake that James wants to avoid. The ironist thinks that reflection

[58] Sartre, *Nausea*, p. 189.
[59] See Sartre, *Nausea*, pp. 182–185.
[60] See Sartre, *Nausea*, pp. 182–193.
[61] See Richard Rorty, *Contingency, Irony, and Solidarity* (Cambridge: Cambridge University Press, 1985).

alone delivers truth. Failing to arrive at the truth through reflection alone, the ironist does not give up the idea that reflection alone delivers truth, but instead gives up the idea of a single truth and proposes—like James's romantics—that we rejoice in the different perspectives that exist. The James I love—the young James—advocates a different course.

To understand James, it is extremely important to distinguish between two possible interpretations. The first way of interpreting him is in accord with the main line of argumentation in his essay 'The Will to Believe': 'Our passional nature not only lawfully may, but must, decide an option between propositions, whenever it is a genuine option that cannot by its nature be decided on intellectual grounds.'[62] Applying this maxim to the issue of determinism, we might say: the question of whether determinism is true cannot be decided on intellectual grounds alone. So we are permitted to decide to believe in determinism or indeterminism. We may have certain practical reasons for making this choice, but these reasons have nothing to do with the question of whether determinism is true or not. That remains an open question.

This is certainly a strand in James's thinking. However, there is also another one. First of all, one needs to note that, according to James, an emotional reaction is a way of expressing how the world is. By reacting in this way, one is saying that the world is such that it calls for a reaction of this kind. If an opposite reaction were appropriate, the world would be different. The emotional reaction may also be the only way of capturing the relevant feature of the world. In particular, a purely intellectual description of the world could not adequately capture it.[63]

Now, if two opposite emotional reactions amount to different descriptions of the world, and these emotional reactions are the only way of bringing out the differences between the two accounts of the world, how are we to decide which of these emotional reactions correctly captures the way the world is? James has a remarkable answer to this question:

> My action is the complement which, by proving congruous or not, reveals the latent nature of the mass to which it is applied. The world may ... be likened unto a lock, whose inward nature, moral or unmoral, will never reveal itself to our simply expectant gaze ... nature has put into our hands two keys, by

62 James, *The Will to Believe*, p. 20 (italics deleted).
63 See James, *The Will to Believe*, pp. 73, 84–87, 106–111.

which we may test the lock. If we try the moral key *and it fits*, it is a moral lock. If we try the unmoral key and *it* fits, it is an unmoral lock.[64]

The issue—is this a moral or an unmoral world?—is the same as the one touched upon in our previous discussion of 'The Dilemma of Determinism.' To assume that the world is unmoral is to take the subjectivist position presupposed by romanticism. In other words, it is the position one is rationally led to if one is a determinist. In contrast, the assumption that we live in a 'moral universe' amounts to the objectivist view that the 'moral order' rests on 'an absolute and ultimate *should*, or on a series of *shoulds* all the way down.'[65] According to James, this objectivist view presupposes indeterminism.[66]

This passage is a philosophical elaboration of the position taken in the crisis note and stands in a marked contrast to Roquentin's approach and Rorty's ironism. In the crisis note, James records his refusal to wait 'for contemplation of the external world to determine all for me.' He says in this passage that the 'world ... will never reveal itself to our simply expectant gaze.' Several features of James's alternative approach must be stressed: (1.) The world does not reveal itself to the simple passive observer. *Action* is called for. (2.) Certain features of the world cannot be discovered through purely theoretic deliberation. Rather, these features are only accessible through *emotion*. (3.) However, to get at the truth, it is not enough to analyze these emotions. The relevant *emotional attitudes* must be lived out *in action*. (4.) Objectivism and subjectivism call for different courses of action.[67] An inquiry into the truth of these theories requires that one follow these *different courses of action*. (5.) James is really proposing a *test*: by acting on theories, we can find out which one is true.[68] (6.) The world is *responsive to our action*. By acting in a certain way, we can find out *how the world is*. (7.) The test involves 'all *three departments of the mind*': the 'impressions of sense,' 'the theoretic and defining department,' and the 'active and emotional powers.'[69] (8.) The 'verification' of the relevant theory does not 'occur in the life of a single philosopher.' Rather, 'the *experience of the entire human race* must make the

[64] James, *The Will to Believe*, p. 88.
[65] James, *The Will to Believe*, p. 85.
[66] See James, *The Will to Believe*, p. 135.
[67] See James, *The Will to Believe*, pp. 85–87.
[68] See James, *The Will to Believe*, pp. 86–89.
[69] James, *The Will to Believe*, p. 100 (emphasis added).

verification.'[70] The important task of elaborating on these points is something that cannot be undertaken here.[71] Explicating these points would be to explain what James means by his claim that the 'entire nature of the man,'[72] the 'entire man,'[73] or the 'whole man within us'[74] is required to confirm certain philosophical theories.[75]

An important ambiguity in the metaphor of the world as a 'lock' should be emphasized. One way of understanding this metaphor stresses the fact that the lock and its key are two independent objects. For example, if the key is destroyed, the lock still exists and we may make another key to fit the lock. According to this interpretation, our emotional reaction—the key—seeks to fit a world which is independent of such emotional reactions.

The other understanding of the metaphor is that the concept of a key and the concept of a lock are interdependent: a hole can only be understood as a lock if we understand it as something into which a key fits that opens some object such as a door. Likewise, an object which can be stuck into a hole can only be understood as a key if it has the function of opening an object such as a door. In light of this, James's metaphor can now be interpreted as follows: the world in question is a world whose nature cannot be understood independently of the emotional reaction through which the world's nature is revealed.

According to both interpretations, acting on an emotional attitude plays an important role in revealing the nature of the world. However, only the second interpretation can provide a straightforward explanation of the success of testing theories in this way: if the world in question is something whose nature cannot be understood independently of emotional reactions, then it is not surprising that emotional reactions play a role in revealing the nature of the world. Taking this interpretation further, one can argue that, in the passage under discussion, James is not talking about the world as a whole. Rather, he is interested in certain philosophical questions such as the issue of the objectivity of values and the freedom of will. The world is either such that the will is free or it is such that the will is not free.

70 James, *The Will to Believe*, p. 87 (emphasis added).

71 This chapter is part of a larger project on the early William James and this and many other points will be elaborated in the longer work.

72 William James, *Essays, Comments, and Reviews* (Cambridge, Mass.: Harvard University Press, 1987), p. 325.

73 James, *The Will to Believe*, p. 61.

74 James, *The Will to Believe*, p. 77.

75 See William James, *Essays in Philosophy* (Cambridge, Mass.: Harvard University Press, 1978), p. 360.

However, the world in question here is a world whose nature is not independent of our emotional reactions to it. If it turns out that one emotional reaction is appropriate, then the world is such that the will is free. If another emotional reaction is appropriate, the will is not free. The purpose of James's test is to find out which reaction is appropriate.

Is The Cured Philosopher a Unified Person?

James writes that 'to the diseases which reflection breeds, still further reflection can oppose effective remedies.'[76] Reflection is the source of philosophical melancholy: a person assumes that reflection alone—theoretical reasoning alone—should be able to solve all philosophical questions and then discovers that it alone cannot settle some philosophical issues. James's proposed cure, which he prescribed to himself, was to give up this assumption. The cure consists in coming to realize that some philosophical questions can only be answered by relying on much more than theoretical reason. The 'entire man' must be involved. In particular, emotions play an important role in the justification of a particular solution. Philosophical melancholy is an emotional reaction to a refusal to allow emotions their proper say in solving certain problems. Thus, one might say that philosophical melancholy is caused by a certain imbalance of the soul. Theoretical reason has claimed too much territory for itself. The cure lies in restoring the harmony between the different aspects of a person—in making the man 'whole' again.

Or so it would seem. But does James really believe that philosophical melancholy can be entirely overcome? Does he think that we can and should become unified persons in this way? And would he be right? Should we strive to avoid philosophical melancholy and to become unified persons? Let me conclude this chapter by saying just a few words about these difficult issues.

James states that 'reflection' provides 'effective remedies' to the 'diseases which reflection breeds.' But is it theoretical reason alone that recognizes its own limits and allows emotions to have their say? More specifically, is it theoretical reason alone that realizes that the question of the objectivity of value cannot be settled by theoretical reason alone and should be settled by acting on the different theories and allowing emotions have their say in the matter? Or, in contrast, do we only come to this realization on the basis of all the

[76] James, *The Will to Believe*, p. 40.

departments of human reason? If the former is the case, theoretical reason has, as it were, cured itself. However, if the latter is the case, then the tendency to rely on theoretical reason alone has been corrected by something other than theoretical reason. If that is the case, will this tendency not continue to exercise its influence? In other words, will there not continue to be two opposite sentiments within the reflective person: the longing to have all problems settled by theoretical reason and the desire to achieve intellectual peace by giving emotions their say? Is it not proper that these two opposite sentiments should exist? Is philosophical melancholy not simply an expression of our appropriate sadness about the impotence of theoretical reason to solve central questions of life? Our melancholy would be proper because—as reflective people—we should never rest assured that theoretical reason cannot solve the problems we are facing. To rest assured would be to stop being truly reflective. So perhaps philosophical melancholy—or at least a certain kind of sadness—is simply the price we need to pay for reflection.

As far as I know, James himself never explicitly addressed this issue. However, in other related contexts he recognizes that we are subject to opposite philosophical sentiments without a clear way of solving the conflict. In his introduction to *The Literary Remains of the Late Henry James* (1884), a book containing works by his father, James describes the acceptance of a position such as the one he advocates in 'The Dilemma of Determinism' as an expression of 'healthy-mindedness.' James continues:

> But healthy-mindedness is not the whole of life; and the *morbid* view ... asks for a philosophy very different from that of absolute moralism ... What he [the morbid-minded person] craves is to be consoled in his very impotence, to feel that the Powers of the Universe recognize and secure him, all passive and failing as he is. Well, we are all *potentially* such sick men. The sanest and best of us are of one clay with lunatics and prison-inmates.[77]

The morbid position—his father's theological doctrine—is close to the optimistic position rejected in 'The Dilemma of Determinism.'[78] However, this morbid view is also just one possible

[77] William James, *Essays in Religion and Morality* (Cambridge, Mass.: Harvard University Press, 1982), p. 62.

[78] Given my focus on the early James, I have refrained from discussing *The Varieties of Religious Experience*. However, the work is of course relevant to our topic: In his discussion of healthy-mindedness, morbidity and melancholy, James illustrates the 'worst kind of melancholy'—that is, the one

expression of the longing to have pure reflection solve the problems of life all on its own. James recognizes that he himself has been subject to such a sentiment. The question remains whether he thinks he has entirely overcome it—or whether he should.[79]

'which takes the form of panic fear'—by describing a terrifying experience he himself had 'whilst in this state of philosophic pessimism and general depression of spirits about my prospect' (William James, *The Varieties of Religious Experience* [Cambridge: Harvard University Press, 1985], p. 134). In this work, James attributed the experience to a French correspondent, but he later admitted that he had described his own experience (James [son of WJ], ed., *The Letters of William James*, vol. 1, p. 145). It is a subject of debate when the episode occurred, but it is not unlikely that it took place around the time of the crisis note or perhaps a few years later (see Richardson, *William James: In the Maelstrom of American Modernism*, p. 543n4).

79 I am greatly indebted to Róbert Haraldsson for the discussions we have had about James over the years, in particular during the course we co-taught about James at the University of Iceland. I would also like to thank Adam Blauhut for his diligent editorial work and the audience at the University of Liverpool for their helpful remarks on a previous version of this chapter.

Curing Diseases of Belief and Desire: Buddhist Philosophical Therapy

DAVID BURTON

A Philosophical Therapy?

It seems uncontroversial that Buddhism is therapeutic in intent.[1] The word 'therapy' is often used, however, to denote methods of treating medically defined mental illnesses, while in the Buddhist context it refers to the treatment of deep-seated dissatisfaction and confusion that, it is claimed, afflict us all. The Buddha is likened to a doctor who offers a medicine to cure the spiritual ills of the suffering world. In the Pāli scriptures, one of the epithets of the Buddha is 'the Great Physician' and the therapeutic regimen or healing treatment is his teaching, the *Dhamma*.[2] This metaphor is continued in later literature, most famously in the *Saddharmapuṇḍarīka Sūtra*, where the Buddha is said to be like a benevolent doctor who attempts to administer appropriate medicine to his sons. In the Mahāyāna pantheon, one of the most popular of the celestial Buddhas is Bhaiṣajyaguru, the master of healing, who is believed to offer cures for both the spiritual and more mundane ailments of sentient beings.[3] The four truths, possibly the most pervasive of all Buddhist teachings, are expressed in the form of a medical diagnosis. The first truth, that there is suffering (*dukkha*), is the diagnosis of the disease. The second truth, that suffering arises from a cause (or causes), seeks to identify the root source of the disease. The third

[1] I use the umbrella term 'Buddhism' to refer to a wide variety of traditions and schools without intending to deny their very significant diversity of belief and practice.

[2] See *Theragāthā* 1111. Trans. Kenneth Roy Norman, *Poems of Early Buddhist Monks: Theragāthā* (Oxford: The Pali Text Society, 1997), p. 106; *Milindapañha* 334–336. Trans. Thomas William Rhys Davids, *The Questions of King Milinda, Part II*, (Oxford: Oxford University Press, 1894), pp. 216–220.

[3] See Raoul Birnbaum, *The Healing Buddha* (Boulder: Shambala, 1979).

doi:10.1017/S1358246109990312

truth, that suffering can be ended, is a prognosis that the disease is curable. The fourth truth describes the path to end suffering, and is the prescription of treatment.[4]

That this Buddhist therapy might appropriately be labelled as 'philosophy' is more controversial, requiring some explanation and defence. Of course, there is no consensus about the nature and purpose of philosophy. It might be objected that the Buddha's teaching is vehemently anti-philosophical, given his negative attitude to the metaphysical enquiries that have so often been the staple of the philosopher's trade. Buddhist sources commonly exhibit a dismissive response to questions about metaphysical matters—such as the origin and extent of the universe and the post-mortem state of the person who has achieved enlightenment (*bodhi*)—which, it is claimed, have no bearing on the issue of curing suffering. The Buddha famously compares someone who is preoccupied with these speculative concerns to a person who is struck by a poisoned arrow and, instead of letting the surgeon immediately operate to remove it, hinders him with irrelevant questions about the origin and type of arrow. The questions are beside the point, and pursuing them is a distraction from the pressing existential task at hand. The Buddha claims that he does not offer answers to such questions; his teachings are pre-eminently practical, focused on the reality of suffering and the need to identify and overcome its causes.[5] Moreover, it can be argued that the term 'philosophy' is of Western (European) provenance and has a particular cultural heritage; applying it to Buddhism could smack of the imperialist appropriation and subjugation of foreign world-views by presenting them in terms of a familiar but distorting concept from Western intellectual discourse.

These objections clearly have some validity and thus we should proceed with caution. Nevertheless, there is a good case for considering the Buddhist therapy to be a form of philosophy, even if it is one with its own peculiar characteristics. Not all philosophy is obsessed by metaphysical issues and some philosophies—for example, various forms of Empiricism and Existentialism—have eschewed such speculation. Furthermore, philosophy need not be, and often has not been, construed as an 'ivory tower' activity of intellectual cleverness divorced from everyday life; it sometimes offers solutions to

[4] See Rupert Gethin, *The Foundations of Buddhism* (Oxford: Oxford University Press, 1998), pp. 59–84.

[5] *Majjhima Nikāya* I, 426–437. Trans. Bhikkhu Ñāṇamoli and Bhikkhu Bodhi, *The Middle Length Discourses of the Buddha*, (Boston: Wisdom Books, 1995), pp. 533–541.

people's most troubling and personal dissatisfactions and crises. Moreover, the claim that Buddhist and other types of 'Eastern' thought are not philosophy can itself be symptomatic of a Western arrogance which sees only European and European-derived cultures as capable of the argumentative and logical skills that are frequently considered to be the hallmarks of genuine philosophy.[6] This contention seems unsustainable and parochial given that many Indian forms of thought, including Buddhism, often have been attentive to the rules of correct thinking and rigorous debate.

Richard King argues that the conception of philosophy as a highly abstruse, technical and specialist activity with little or no bearing on the individual's experience has become dominant only in comparatively recent times. King contends that this tendency for philosophy to be divorced from the concerns of everyday life has occurred especially since the European Enlightenment and the advent of professionalised philosophy as an academic, secular discipline which often allies itself with scientific analysis and has been, with some notable exceptions, keen to distance itself from any topic which might be considered religious or spiritual. By contrast, far from eschewing interest in matters of ultimate concern to individuals—what might be termed 'meaning of life' questions—pre-Enlightenment thinkers in many cases saw it as the purpose of philosophy to address these issues.

In the *Alagaddūpama Sutta*[7], the Buddha discusses some 'misguided men' who 'learn the *Dhamma*' in the sense of becoming familiar with the Buddha's various sermons, sayings, expositions and so forth. However, they 'do not examine the meaning of those teachings with wisdom' and fail to achieve 'a reflective acceptance' of them. As a result 'they do not experience the good (*attha*) for the sake of which they learned the *Dhamma*.' Instead, they make use of the *Dhamma* only 'for the sake of criticising others and for winning debates.' The Buddha declares that such an attitude to the *Dhamma* is not simply useless; it actively will 'conduce to their harm and suffering for a long time.' In his commentary, Buddhaghosa (5th century CE) claims that the purpose of this passage is to explain the seriousness of the error of 'wrongly motivated acquisition of intellectual knowledge of the *Dhamma*.'[8]

6 Western thinkers have frequently regarded only their own tradition to be authentic philosophy. For a discussion of this point, see Richard King, *Indian Philosophy: An Introduction to Hindu and Buddhist Thought* (Edinburgh: Edinburgh University Press, 1999), Chapters 2 and 10.

7 *Majjhima Nikāya* I, 132–142. Trans. Ñāṇamoli and Bodhi, op. cit., pp. 224–236.

8 Ñāṇamoli and Bodhi, op. cit., p. 1208.

The Buddha proceeds to give the famous simile of the snake, in which the misguided man is compared to someone who grasps a venomous serpent in the wrong way, allowing it to bite him. Such a deluded person uses the Buddha's teaching for the sake of self-assertion and to exhibit his superior intelligence and knowledge. He employs his knowledge about the *Dhamma*, which is meant to be a therapy for wise living, to unwittingly demonstrate his lack of wisdom. The misguided person treats the truth as an intellectual acquisition and does not let it permeate his entire being. By contrast, the Buddha extols 'those disciples who examine the meaning' of his teachings 'with wisdom', achieve 'reflective acceptance' of them and, consequently, 'experience the good for the sake of which they learned the *Dhamma*'. Rather than seeking simply to criticise others and win debates, such people put into practice the Buddha's prescriptions and, therefore, 'those teachings, being rightly grasped by them, conduce to their welfare and happiness for a long time.' They use the Buddhist teachings as vehicles for self-transformation and correctly regard them as offering practical solutions to their keenly felt experience of suffering.

Commenting on this *sutta*, Jonardon Ganeri writes that the misguided man has a 'professional interest' in the truth and considers it to be of merely instrumental value—that is, as a means to win debates, demonstrate his intellectual prowess and achieve fame. By contrast, the disciple who genuinely pursues wisdom has a very different attitude to the truth; he is receptive to its power to affect him and re-orientate his mind. He allows the truth to 'blow through him', 'to run riot in the soul', letting it 'saturate the whole of his mental life' so that it reshapes 'not only his beliefs but also his hopes, his ideals, the stories he tells about himself, the concerns he has for himself and others.'[9]

Diseases of Belief and Desire

Buddhism teaches that our affective states are closely connected to our views and that erroneous beliefs lie at the root of human unhappiness. A common Buddhist theme is that all things are

[9] Jonardon Ganeri, *The Concealed Art of the Soul: Theories of Self and Practices of Truth in Indian Ethics and Epistemology* (Oxford: Oxford University Press, 2007), pp. 44–45 and 52.

impermanent[10] and lack independent existence. The world is an unceasing flux of interconnected phenomena. However, we do not understand things as they really are (*yathābhūta*). Pāli texts provide extensive catalogues of the various ways in which people can hold wrong views (*micchādiṭṭhi*), for example, by accepting the existence of an eternal, unchanging soul or self.[11] These erroneous opinions have a deleterious effect on our values, so that we cherish things which, if we really understood their insubstantial nature, we would not endow with such significance. We find them desirable, sometimes highly desirable, and get caught in a web of attachments to them. Nāgārjuna (second to third centuries CE) declares that: 'As a child with his notion of truth, falls in love with a mirror image, worldly people, due to delusion, are trapped in a thicket of objects.'[12] Given that things are impermanent, this reliance on them inevitably leads to suffering. Particularly pernicious is attachment to sensual things, dependent as it is on objects which are especially unreliable: 'The Blessed One has stated how sensual pleasures provide little gratification, much suffering, and much despair, and how great is the danger in them'.[13] Attachment can also be to wealth, fame, friends, family, and so on. But it is not just attachment to external things that is problematic. One's own self is actually a concatenation of transient events; it is one's failure to recognise this fact and to adjust one's values accordingly which, the Buddhists contend, often causes suffering, as one fails to come to terms with sickness, ageing and death.

It is evident that the Buddhists think that desires are not brute forces and it would be incorrect to consider them to be non-cognitive. Rather, they are intelligent in the sense that they are based on and responsive to beliefs, although, in another sense, the Buddhists think that many of our desires are decidedly not intelligent, in that they are based on erroneous views. Desires have a close relationship to views about what is valuable. We consider possessions, wealth, fame, one's sense of self and so forth to have more value than they actually have, and thus we desire them inappropriately and get

10 To be precise, the Pāli and other early Buddhist sources usually claim that all conditioned (*saṅkhata*) things are impermanent. The contrast here is with *nibbāna*, which is said to be unconditioned (*asaṅkhata*) and permanent.

11 For example, see *Dīgha Nikāya* I, 1–46. Trans. Maurice Walshe, *Thus Have I Heard: The Long Discourses of the Buddha*, (London: Wisdom Publications, 1987), pp. 67–90.

12 *Yuktiṣaṣṭikā* 53. Trans. Joseph Loizzo, *Nāgārjuna's Reason Sixty (Yuktiṣaṣṭikā) with Candrakīrti's Commentary (Yuktiṣaṣṭikāvṛtti)* (New York: American Institute of Buddhist Studies, 2007). p. 203.

13 *Majjhima Nikāya* I, 130. Trans. Ñāṇamoli and Bodhi, op. cit., p. 225.

attached to them which, given the reality of impermanence and insubstantiality, the Buddhists deems harmful to our well-being.[14]

Buddhism argues that our suffering is a result of deep attachment to uncontrollable and unreliable things. Buddhist philosophical therapy is, in this respect, about cultivating an attitude of 'letting go'. The things that we think matter so much are not worth being anxious, unhappy, and angry about. This solution should be cognitive, in the sense that the ignorance needs to be removed in order for the emotional relaxation to occur. This should rectify our values, so that impermanent, insubstantial things are no longer relied upon for a comfort and security which, in fact, they cannot give. Emotions and desires are expressions of our interpretation of the world; if our interpretation is out of accord with the way the world really is, then unhappiness will result. The Buddhist therapy therefore aims to align our interpretations with reality, thereby diminishing and eventually stopping the discontentment that results from unrealisable expectations.

This account indicates that, for Buddhism, the relationship between emotions and beliefs is causal. Moreover, the Buddhists do not think that the causal relationship between views and one's affective states is one-way. While beliefs influence desires and emotions, it is also the case that desires and emotions have an impact on beliefs. There is a psychological tendency for us to believe what we wish to be the case and not to accept beliefs that are unattractive to us. Desire often leads to rationalisation. So, it may be that I want to believe that things are permanent and substantial, and thus I am inclined to form this belief. It is because I want my desire for these things to be a source of happiness that I overlook the painful consequences of my craving and attachment. I am reluctant to believe things to be impermanent and insubstantial because I would then

[14] If the Buddhists claim that the problem is that that we overvalue these things, this implies that they might still have some value. Their value would presumably depend in part on whether the Buddhist is a monastic or layperson. Thus, possessions, wealth, family, career and so forth would have value to a layperson and, ideally, would not have value to monastics. However, the Buddhist would object that this is because the layperson is still in the grip of attachment and thus still endows these things with more value than they actually have. But even the strictest monastic Buddhist would give at least instrumental value to some basic possessions such as robes and alms bowl, for they are the implements which enable the monk or nun to live and continue to practise Buddhism. Moreover, the monastic communities in many cases rely on the wealth generated by the laity, which means that such wealth is valued at least as a means to support the continuation of Buddhism.

have to modify my emotional attachments to them. Even if I do assent to the truth of impermanence and the folly of my attachments, I tend to ignore or marginalise this belief. I push it to the periphery of my awareness, because it is an inconvenient and uncomfortable truth that contradicts my wishes. Furthermore, desires blind us to the way things really are; they make us forgetful, distracted by the objects of our passions. Ignorance and desire are thus mutually assisting causes of suffering. They are intertwined and reinforce one another. This a point which is made most vividly in the Buddhist Wheel of Existence (*bhavacakra*) paintings, which, at the hub of the wheel, depict ignorance as a pig, hatred as a snake and greed as a cockerel, biting each others tails to symbolise that they are inseparably connected.[15] Consequently, the Buddhist therapy is intended not only to inform one of the way things really are, but to provide techniques to stop one's misguided desires and emotions from rebelling against the truth that one already knows.

Contrary to a popular misconception, this Buddhist therapy is not intended to remove desire per se, but rather the particular types of desire that cause suffering. Buddhism considers desire to be a complex phenomenon, with both positive and negative forms. This complexity is evident in a verse from the *Udāna* in which the authentic monk (*bhikkhu*) is described as simultaneously desireless (*nirāso*) and desiring the goal (*atthakāmo*) of enlightenment:

> Who lives by no craft, unburdened, desiring the goal,
> With restrained faculties, wholly released,
> Wandering homeless, unselfish, desireless,
> Conceit abandoned, solitary—he is a bhikkhu.[16]

Buddhist texts use many different terms for the varieties of desire. One of the most common is *chanda*, which is classified as 'ethically variable', meaning that it can have both ethically unwholesome (*akusala*) and wholesome (*kusala*) forms.[17] For example, *chanda* is considered to be unwholesome when directed at sensual objects

15 Gethin, op. cit., pp. 158–159.

16 *Udāna* 3.9. Trans. John D. Ireland, *The Udāna: Inspired Utterances of the Buddha and The Itivuttaka: The Buddha's Sayings* (Kandy: Buddhist Publication Society, 2007), p. 48. See also David Webster, *The Philosophy of Desire in the Buddhist Pāli Canon* (London: Routledge, 2005), p. 191.

17 *Abhidhammattha Sangaha* II, 9. Trans. Mahāthera Nārada and Bhikkhu Bodhi, *A Comprehensive Manual of Abhidhamma. The Abhidhammattha Sangaha of Acariya Anuruddha* (Kandy: Buddhist Publication Society, 1993), pp. 91–94.

(*kāmachanda*)[18] whereas it can be wholesome when focused on ethical behaviour and spiritual progress. Thus, *chanda* is identified as one of the four bases of power (*iddhipāda*) which the Buddha claims to be necessary in order to achieve enlightenment.[19] Śāntideva (8th century CE) encourages the cultivation of this type of desire: 'The powers of desire [*chanda*], perseverance, delight, and letting go, all lead to the fulfilment of the needs of living beings. Out of the fear of suffering, and while meditating on the praises, one should create desire.'[20] As Śāntideva indicates here, not only is desire for enlightenment necessary, but the desire to help other sentient beings is central to the Mahāyāna Bodhisattva ideal. This means that the supposed paradox of desire—that is, that the Buddhist is encouraged to desire to end all desire—is not real, because Buddhism does not promote the ending of all desire.[21]

Although various terms are employed to refer to desires that are unwholesome, one of the most widely used and best known is *taṇhā*—that is, craving or grasping. *Taṇhā* is a particular way of desiring which is productive of suffering and rooted in ignorance. As an impulse to possess the objects towards which it is directed, it is inherently selfish and appropriative, latching on to the object and sticking like glue. Thus, *taṇhā* is said to give rise to attachment (*upādāna*). Most obviously, *taṇhā* occurs in relation to mundane things such as sensual objects, wealth, fame, and so forth. However, the dangers of craving and attachment to non-sensual objects and experiences—such as sublime states of meditative absorption (*jhāna*)—are also warned against.[22] A traditional classification divides *taṇhā* into three types. First, there is the craving for sensual gratification (*kāmataṇhā*). Second, there is the craving for self-preservation

[18] *Visuddhimagga* IV, 85. Trans. Bhikkhu Ñāṇamoli, *The Path of Purification: Visuddhimagga by Bhadantācariya Buddhaghosa* (Kandy: Buddhist Publication Society, 1991, 5th edn.), p. 138.

[19] See *Saṃyutta Nikāya* V, 254–293. Trans. Bhikkhu Bodhi, *The Connected Discourses of the Buddha: A New Translation of the Saṃyutta Nikāya* (Boston: Wisdom Publications, 2000), pp. 1718–1749.

[20] *Bodhicaryāvatāra* VII, 31. Trans. Kate Crosby and Andrew Skilton, *The Bodhicaryāvatāra: A Guide to the Buddhist Path to Awakening* (Oxford: Oxford Paperbacks, 1998), p. 69.

[21] On the apparent paradox of desire, see A.L. Herman, 'A Solution to the Paradox of Desire in Buddhism', *Philosophy East and West*, Vol. 29, No. 1 (Jan., 1979), pp. 91–94; Wayne Alt, 'There Is No Paradox of Desire in Buddhism', *Philosophy East and West* 30.4 (1980), pp. 521–528.

[22] See *Majjhima Nikāya* II, 228–238. Trans. Ñāṇamoli and Bodhi, op. cit., pp. 839–846.

(*bhavataṇhā*). As Padmasiri De Silva explains, this form of craving is closely connected to 'the need for self-assertion, power, fame, wealth, recognition etc.'[23] Third, there is the craving for non-existence or destruction (*vibhavataṇhā*) which lies at the root of aggressive impulses such as anger and hatred.

David Webster has pointed to evidence in the Pāli sources that even *taṇhā* may have a positive role at the beginning of the Buddhist path, given that grasping after spiritual truths is presumably better than grasping after sensual objects, fame and so forth. Craving for enlightenment might be the initial motivation for adopting the Buddhist therapy. However, *taṇhā* must eventually be replaced by, or transformed into, an unselfish, unattached form of desire, perhaps best described as an aspiration.[24]

Another common misconception is that the Buddhist therapy aims to extinguish all emotions. On the contrary, Buddhism is careful to distinguish between those affective states that are ethically unwholesome—such as hatred, jealousy, and avarice—and those that are ethically wholesome and have a positive role in the pursuit of enlightenment and are, in some cases, constitutive of the enlightened state itself. Psychological states with an affective dimension that are said to be very important on the path to enlightenment include faith or confidence (*saddhā*)[25] and the feeling of agitation, thrill or anxiety (*saṃvega*) produced by the realisation that liberation is an urgent requirement, given the extreme miseries of this world.[26] Buddhists also find a positive role for moral shame (*hiri*) and fear of doing wrong (*ottappa*), as emotions of conscience that deter one from performing morally unwholesome acts.[27] There are also the four divine abodes (*brahmavihāras*): a group of mental states which seem to be emotions or at least have some emotional content. They are friendliness (*mettā*), sympathetic joy (*muditā*), compassion (*karuṇā*), and equanimity (*upekkhā*), all of which are highly valued and considered to be perfected in enlightenment.[28] It might be objected that *upekkhā* is not rightly named an emotion given that

[23] Padmasiri De Silva, *An Introduction to Buddhist Psychology* (London: Palgrave Macmillan, 2005, 4th edn), p. 36.

[24] Webster, op. cit., p. 139.

[25] *Abhidhammattha Sangaha* II, 5. Trans. Nārada and Bodhi, op. cit., pp. 83–84.

[26] De Silva, op. cit., p. 50.

[27] *Abhidhammattha Sangaha* II, 5. Trans. Nārada and Bodhi, op. cit., p. 86.

[28] See *Dīgha Nikāya* I, 235–252. Trans. Walshe, op. cit., pp. 187–195.

Buddhaghosa says it is a state of peaceful neutrality and impartiality, neither pleasant nor painful, and without either joy or grief.[29] If this is an emotion, it is of an unusual, pacific type. Alternatively, it might be characterised as the absence of emotion. At any rate, the other three divine abodes are recognisably akin to what we think of as emotions, or at least have an affective dimension. So, it seems accurate to claim that the enlightened person is not devoid of emotions, but has used the Buddhist therapy to eradicate all affective states that are rooted in delusion.

Emotional and Cognitive Dispositions

There are numerous Buddhist critiques of the mistaken beliefs in the permanence and substantiality of the self and other things. Nor do the Buddhists tire of pointing out the irrationality of reliance on that which is transient. In addition, they devote considerable energy to positive demonstrations of the coherence and rationality of their own beliefs that there is no self and all things are impermanent and insubstantial.[30] These are attempts to persuade using reason and to replace error with truth in order to remove both the ignorance and the attachment that cause suffering.

However, the mere rehearsal of arguments can be a fairly ineffective way of changing beliefs, desires and emotions that are, in many cases, deeply engrained. Simply announcing that all things are impermanent and insubstantial, and that one should not desire them, is unlikely to provide liberation, nor does listening to a logical argument usually have great existential impact. Such rational analysis commonly has relatively little effect on our attitudes and personality. Our convictions, desires and emotions are often unruly, and not so easily convinced by the voice of reason.

This recalcitrance is recognised in numerous Buddhist sources, according to which our minds are under the sway of deeply engrained emotional and cognitive habits which it can be extremely difficult to remove or transform through straightforward rational considerations. For example, in fourteenth and fifteenth century Tibet, there was a popular notion that there are two forms of ignorance, one which is non-linguistic and unlearned, and the other linguistic and acquired

29 *Visuddhimagga* IV, 155–197. Trans. Ñāṇamoli, op. cit., pp. 156–164.

30 For an analysis of the Buddhist arguments, see Mark Siderits, *Empty Persons: Personal Identity and Buddhist Philosophy* (Aldershot: Ashgate, 2003).

through learning. This is a distinction made by Tsong kha pa, Sakya mchog ldan and others.[31] A particularly articulate exposition of the difference between these two types of ignorance is found in mKhas grub rje's *Stong thun chen mo*:

> There are two kinds of mistaken conceptions: the philosophical (*kun brtags*) and the innate (*lhan skyes*). The philosophical [kind] refers to the philosopher's belief (*dam bcha' ba*) regarding the variety of ways in which things could inherently exist [that is, have permanent and substantial existence], arrived at through the invention (*sgro brtags*) of a host of reasons that [they claim] prove that things inherently exist. The innate kind is something that has been part and parcel of every sentient being without distinction since beginningless time.[32]

Philosophical misconceptions are the theories and doctrines developed by philosophers and religious thinkers positing the existence of permanent and substantial entities such as the soul, God, eternal atoms and so forth. However, most sentient beings are not philosophers, and many do not have any explicitly held beliefs of the aforementioned type. Yet they do possess an innate misconception even if it is not, in most cases, made explicit through language and conceptuality. And the philosopher's mistaken theories are simply explications and rationalisations of a deeply rooted innate ignorance which he or she shares with all other unenlightened sentient beings. Even animals, mKhas grub rje contends, have this innate misconception.

He claims that, while it is important to eradicate both philosophical and innate misconceptions, the chief object to be removed must be the innate misconception, because it is this which traps sentient beings in a state of suffering. In other words, the philosophers' misguided theories are a relatively superficial problem; at best, mKhas grub rje says, refuting them through various arguments can be a 'stepping stone' (*yan lag*) to the more important eradication of the innate misconception. The philosophical misconceptions are more symptom than cause of our predicament. To support this position, mKhas grub rje quotes an amusing passage from the

[31] José Cabezón, *Dose of Emptiness: An Annotated Translation of the sTong thun chen mo of mKhas grub dGe legs dpal bzang* (Albany: State University of New York Press, 1992), pp. 456–457.

[32] *Stong thun chen mo* 132. Trans. Cabezón, op. cit., pp. 128–129. Slightly modified. mKhas grub rje's entire analysis of innate and philosophical misconceptions occurs in the *Stong thun chen mo* 132–140. Trans. Cabezón, op. cit., pp. 128–135.

Madhyamakāvatāra by Candrakīrti (7th century CE) who writes that refutation of the view that there is a permanent self will not destroy one's attachment to the ego. To claim otherwise is comparable to the absurd belief that the realisation that there is no elephant in a room will destroy all fear of a snake that is lurking along the far wall![33] mKhas grub rje evidently interprets this passage to mean that the refutation of the rather obvious philosophical misconceptions (the elephant) will not eradicate the less obvious and deep rooted innate misconception (the snake).

The notion that there are entrenched cognitive and emotional habitual tendencies that contribute to suffering was not new to Buddhism in fourteenth and fifteenth century Tibet. On the contrary, the idea has ancient roots. In the Pāli scriptures, the term '*anusaya*' is used to refer to dispositions which, it is claimed, initially lie dormant in the mind. The dialogues of the Buddha identify various *anusayas* including dispositions to sensuous craving or lust (*kāmarāga*), aversion (*paṭigha*), conceit (*māna*), wrong view (*diṭṭhi*), attachment to rules and observances (*sīlabbataparāmāsa*), doubt (*vicikicchā*), craving for existence (*bhavarāga*), and ignorance (*avijjā*). They represent the potential for the corresponding active emotional and cognitive afflictions (*kilesa*) to arise. De Silva writes that these *anusayas* are 'basically dormant passions which become excited into action by suitable stimuli'.[34] They represent our inclination to respond to certain types of stimulation in habitual ways. For instance, lust and aversion are said to be the inveterate responses to pleasant and painful feelings respectively.[35]

The question arises as to the origin of these *anusayas*. It seems likely that they are in part the result of a long history of socialisation, responses to experiences that have been learned since early childhood. It is also highly plausible that tendencies to aggression, lust and so forth are due in part to our genetic inheritance, although this explanation was not open to Buddhists in pre-Mendelian times. The Pāli scriptures state the Buddha's view that the *anusayas* exist even in small children, as a result of *kamma* from previous lives. A very young child, the Buddha contends, has not yet developed concepts such as 'self', 'lust' and 'hatred', and has not yet started to respond

33 *Madhyamakāvatāra* VI, 140–141. Cited in *Stong thun chen mo* 134. Trans. Cabezón, op. cit., pp. 130.

34 De Silva, op. cit., p. 73.

35 *Majjhima Nikāya*, III, 285. Trans. Ñāṇamoli and Bodhi, op. cit., p. 1134; See also *Majjhima Nikāya* I, 303. Trans. Ñāṇamoli and Bodhi, op. cit., p. 401.

to the world in terms of these ideas and emotions. Nevertheless, they exist within the child as dispositions ready to be activated once the child's cognitive capacities have developed and the appropriate stimulus occurs.[36] Moreover, he claims that without removing these dispositions, liberation from suffering cannot be achieved.[37]

The notion of underlying psychological tendencies is further developed by the Sautrāntika Buddhists, as recorded in the *Abhidharmakośabhāṣya*. They distinguish between the afflictions (*kleśa*) as latent dispositions (*anuśaya*), which are a hibernating karmic residue from past existences, and the manifest *kleśas* which are the actual occurrences of the afflictions of greed, hatred, delusion and so forth. A latent disposition when stimulated by an appropriate object causes a manifest affliction to occur. The Sautrāntikas' most significant and suggestive innovation was the introduction of the seed (*bhīja*) as a metaphor representing the latent dispositions.[38] It appears that this metaphor developed into the Yogācāra notion of the storehouse consciousness (*ālayavijñāna*), a subterranean torrent of mental events which functions as a repository for the seeds which are the latent dispositions.[39]

From a therapeutic perspective, the most important point is that liberation from suffering is said to require that the seeds be eradicated. The *Abhidharmakośabhāṣya* says that the enlightened person's 'destroyed afflictions will not be able to sprout again' and that the afflictions have been destroyed completely, 'like seeds burned by fire.'[40] So, the task for Buddhist philosophical therapy is to eradicate not just the active manifestations of greed, hatred and delusion, but also the dispositions which give rise to them.

Therapeutic Techniques

Buddhism employs a range of methods intended to remove the harmful, stubborn dispositions. For instance, the efficacy of verbal

[36] *Majjhima Nikāya* I, 432–433. Trans. Ñāṇamoli and Bodhi, op. cit., pp. 537–538.

[37] *Majjhima Nikāya* III, 285. Trans. Ñāṇamoli and Bodhi, op. cit., pp. 1134–1135.

[38] *Abhidharmakośabhāṣya* V 1d-2a. Trans. William S. Waldron, *The Buddhist Unconscious. The Ālaya-vijñāna in the Context of Indian Buddhist Thought* (London: RoutledgeCurzon, 2003), p. 73.

[39] On the *ālaya-vijñāna*, see Waldron, op. cit., pp. 89–169.

[40] *Abhidharmakośabhāṣya* II 36d. Trans. Waldron, op. cit., p. 75.

communication is highlighted. Buddhist teachings were originally preserved in an oral form. Many of the Buddhist scriptures are purportedly records of dialogues that took place between the Buddha and various disciples. In these conversations, the Buddha is represented as responding to the particular questions and spiritual needs of his interlocutors. The importance of 'spiritual' or 'beautiful' friendship (*kalyāṇamitratā*) is emphasised, particularly between an experienced teacher and pupil. The teacher, in intimate communication with the student, can formulate guidance in dependence upon the student's particular requirements.

Buddhist writings also make copious use of literary forms such as parable, metaphor, and contextualised descriptions. Some of the most popular Buddhist scriptures in the Theravāda tradition are the *Jātakas*, colourful and often poignant stories about the Buddha's previous lives which teach lessons about Buddhist virtues such as wisdom, generosity and compassion. The parables of the *Saddharmapuṇḍarīka Sūtra* and the *Avataṃsaka Sūtra* as well as various stories of exemplary Buddhist saints play a similar role in Mahāyāna traditions. Buddhist teachings commonly incorporate familiar imagery from everyday life. Images of streams and rivers, local flora and fauna, agricultural husbandry and so forth are used to explain various Buddhist ideas. These metaphors would have been especially rich in meaning for the intended audience, living in a predominantly agrarian society and thus in close association with the natural environment. For example, the Buddhist view of consciousness is frequently illustrated by means of the metaphor of the stream or river and, as we have seen already, the image of the seed is employed to elucidate the notion of underlying dispositions.[41] Such literary styles are highly effective ways of making abstract teachings comprehensible and pertinent, thus making it more likely that they will have a transformative effect on the personality.

In addition, non-literary forms of therapy are very widely employed in Buddhism. Memorisation through recitation is commonly practised: teachings will be chanted in rituals often with the intention (among others) of lodging them firmly in the practitioners' minds. Frequently repeated views about impermanence and the harmfulness of craving and so forth are less likely to be forgotten, and more likely to be brought to mind when they are needed to combat the onslaught of the afflictions. In insight meditation

[41] Steven Collins, *Selfless Persons: Imagery and Thought in Theravāda Buddhism* (Cambridge: Cambridge University Press, 1982), pp. 165–176; 218–224; 247–261.

(*vipaśyana*) a common method employed is repeated reflection on important Buddhist teachings and the arguments in support of these teachings while in a concentrated state of consciousness. This is a technique which is meant to penetrate the deeper layers of delusion which cloud the mind. There are also many examples of confession used as a spiritual practice. The Theravāda Vinaya requires the monastic community to undertake confession in which individuals make public their transgressions of monastic precepts and rules.[42] In Mahāyāna Buddhism, confession of one's faults (*pāpadeśanā*) is one of the key elements of the liturgy referred to as 'the Supreme Worship' (*anuttarapūjā*).[43] Perhaps the best known example of this Mahāyāna confessional practice is found in Śāntideva's *Bodhicaryāvatāra*, who laments and reflects on the seriousness of the various evil deeds he has committed, and uses this confessional mood to commit himself more firmly to the Buddhist path.[44] Confession, then, is viewed as a means for honest recognition of the grip that the afflictions of greed, hatred and delusion have upon one's mind. This to be coupled with a resolve to observe ethical precepts intended to prevent future ethically unwholesome behaviour and thoughts.

One of the most important Buddhist therapeutic methods is introspection and self-analysis. In Pāli sources, terms such as mindfulness (*sati*) and thorough attention (*yoniso manasikāra*) are commonly used to refer to the ability to be aware of the desires, emotions, and beliefs that arise in the mind. The Buddha recommends the application of constant mindfulness to one's body, sensations and thoughts.[45] And he compares the capacity to introspect to the reflective power of a mirror. Just as a mirror will reveal the true appearance of the face with all its blemishes, so introspective awareness allows one to examine the mind and notice its imperfections, that is, the afflictions of greed, hatred and delusion. Presumably, by devoting sustained attention to the contents of the mind, those dispositions of which we may have been previously unaware will become apparent. He goes on to advise that, having reflected in this way, only those

[42] See *Mahāvagga* 27, 1–15. Trans. Isaline B. Horner, *The Book of Discipline, volume IV* (London: Luzac, 1971), p. 167; *Cullavagga* IV 30–34. Trans. Isaline B. Horner, *The Book of Discipline, volume V* (London: Luzac, 1963), pp. 138–140.

[43] See Crosby and Skilton, op. cit., pp. 9–13.

[44] *Bodhicaryāvatāra* II, 27–66. Trans. Crosby and Skilton, op. cit., pp. 16–19.

[45] *Dīgha Nikāya* II, 290–315. Trans. Walshe, op. cit., pp. 335–350.

actions of body, speech and mind that are harmful to neither oneself nor others should be performed.[46]

The *Abhidharmakośabhāṣya* says that it is the lack of this thorough attention (*ayoniso manaskāra*) that allows outbursts of the afflictions to occur.[47] Without mindfulness, the afflictions will go unnoticed, and there will be no possibility of taking effective action to remove them. With mindfulness, the opportunity arises to exert oneself to restrain and abandon ethically unwholesome states of mind, and to cultivate and maintain those that are wholesome. In this respect, the Buddhist therapy has both a purgative and a tonic aspect. The afflictions are vices to be purged from the mind like poison that needs to be completely expelled from the body; their opposites are virtues to be actively encouraged and strengthened, like muscles that need to be toned up.[48]

Mindfulness enables the Buddhist practitioner to identify the various feelings (*vedanā*) that are experienced and to stop them giving rise to affective responses of craving, aversion and so forth. According to the Buddhist analysis, pleasant and painful feelings are reactions to contact with objects. The Buddhists claim that once contact with the object has occurred, the feeling experienced is not within our control. However, pleasant feelings normally arouse in us the craving to possess the object whereas unpleasant feelings give rise to aversion and hatred. It is precisely here that the mind can intervene by stopping the habitual responses of craving or aversion. These responses are strong dispositions, so it is difficult to change them. But the Buddhists contend that is possible to remove them over time through attentiveness and effort. In this sense, unlike feelings, craving and aversion are voluntary and, with sufficient mindfulness and self-restraint, one can stop them from arising. The challenge is to be sufficiently self-aware and mentally disciplined to do this. When successful, the Buddhist severs the link between feeling and craving or aversion and experiences detachment.[49] Recognising the impermanence of all feelings, he or she

[46] *Majjhima Nikāya* I, 415–420. Trans. Ñāṇamoli and Bodhi, op. cit., pp. 524–526.

[47] *Abhidharmakośabhāṣya* V, 34. Trans. Waldron, op. cit., p. 210.

[48] For example, see *Dhammapāda* XVII, 13. Trans. Narada Thera, *The Dhammapāda: Pali Text and Translation with Stories in Brief and Notes* (Kuala Lumpur: Buddhist Missionary Society, 1978, 3rd edn.), p. 196.

[49] For example, see *Saṃyutta Nikāya* III, 127. Trans. Bodhi, op. cit., p. 942.

learns to respond to them with neither craving nor aversion, thus averting the consequent suffering.

Therapy as Sensitive to Context

A good doctor varies the medicine in relation to the precise nature of the disease, and a similar flexibility is found in most Buddhist traditions. It is believed that the Buddha did not teach the same thing to all people but adapted his message depending on the specific needs, capacities and interests of his audience. We have already seen that this is the great advantage of oral communication between teacher and pupil; it allows the teacher to assess and respond to the requirements of the individual student.

In the Pāli scriptures there are numerous examples of this context-sensitivity of the Buddhist teaching. For instance, the *Udāna* recounts the story of the monk Nanda, who considers returning to lay life because of his infatuation with a beautiful woman. Attempting to dissuade Nanda from this course of action, the Buddha guarantees him 'five hundred pink-footed nymphs' as a reward if he remains a monk under the Buddha's tutelage. Naturally enough, Nanda agrees. He subsequently realises *nibbāna* and thus no longer requires the Buddha to supply the promised nymphs. One is left wondering whether the Buddha had any intention of keeping his promise or whether he simply told a compassionate lie. The five hundred pink-footed nymphs could function here as a metaphor for the bliss of enlightenment, so superior to the sensual enjoyment that was enticing Nanda to renounce the monastic life. What is certain is that the story shows, in a particularly colourful fashion, the willingness of the Buddha to adapt his teachings as required by the situation.[50]

Another prominent example concerns the graduated teachings given to the laity and monastics, with the latter receiving higher teachings than the former. The usual presumption in Theravāda Buddhism is that lay followers will not seek enlightenment in this lifetime, but will work to ensure a good rebirth by living a good and just life in society and as family members. So, the Buddha gives instructions to the lay followers about living harmoniously by behaving with appropriate respect and consideration for other people. By contrast, the task of the monastics is to gain enlightenment, and thus sermons about the means for achieving this goal tend to be reserved for them. The *Netti Prakaraṇa* divides the

[50] *Udāna* 3.2. Trans. Ireland, op. cit., pp. 35–39.

suttas hierarchically into two primary types: those for the laity, dealing with the lower teachings about morality and those for the monastics, dealing with the higher teachings about insight.[51]

Moreover, the Pāli scriptures identify various character types, notably, the type whose conduct is dominated by greed (*rāgacarita*) and the type whose conduct is dominated by hatred (*dosacarita*). Someone with a particularly strong propensity to greed will need a different therapeutic medicine than someone whose primary disposition is towards hatred and anger.[52] Thus, the practitioner who experiences strong lust may be directed to reflect on the loathsomeness of the human body or the decomposition of a corpse. By contrast, an appropriate therapy for someone dominated by aversion will be a meditation which aims to develop loving kindness or friendliness (*mettābhāvanā*).[53] The Buddha also distinguishes between the character type dominated by a greedy temperament (*rāgacarita*) and the character type dominated by a deluded temperament (*diṭṭhicarita*). The therapy prescribed for the greedy temperament is 'calming' meditation (*samatha*), which quietens the mind through developing a highly concentrated and absorbed state of consciousness. For the deluded temperament, the Buddha prescribes insight (*vipassanā*) meditation, which entails systematic reflection on Buddhist truths such as impermanence.[54] While insight meditation is primarily aimed at combating ignorance the other major form of meditation, calming or tranquillity (*samatha*), works directly against forms of greed or craving:

> If tranquillity is developed, what benefit does it bring? The mind becomes developed. And what is the benefit of a developed mind? All lust is abandoned. If insight is developed, what benefit does it bring? Wisdom becomes developed. And what is the benefit of developed wisdom? All ignorance is abandoned.[55]

51 George D. Bond, 'The Gradual Path as a Hermeneutical Approach to the Dhamma,' in Donald S. Lopez Jr. (ed.), *Buddhist Hermeneutics* (Delhi: Motilal Banarsidass, 1993), pp. 29–45.

52 De Silva, op. cit., p. 38. The discussion of character types becomes more elaborate and systematic in later texts. For example, see *Visuddhimagga* III, 74–133. Trans. Ñāṇamoli, op. cit., pp. 101–117.

53 Étienne Lamotte, 'The Assessment of Textual Interpretation in Buddhism', in Lopez, op. cit., p. 21.

54 De Silva, op. cit., p. 30.

55 *Aṅguttara Nikāya* II, iii, 10. Trans. Nyanaponika Thera and Bhikkhu Bodhi, *Numerical Discourses of the Buddha: An Anthology of Suttas from the Aṅguttara Nikāya* (Kandy: Buddhist Publication Society, 1999), p. 42.

In Mahāyāna Buddhism, this adaptability of the Buddhist therapy is developed into the explicit doctrine of 'skilful means' (*upāya-kauśalya*). The *Saddharmapuṇḍarīka Sūtra* claims that the Buddha uses various devices to guide people towards enlightenment; they will vary depending on the individual circumstances and aptitude. In a famous parable, the *sūtra* compares the Buddha to a father who seeks to rescue his sons from a burning house. To persuade them out of the house, the father entices them with a variety of desirable toys. Similarly, the Buddha uses a range of teachings to persuade unenlightened people to leave *saṃsāra*—a metaphorical burning house of craving and delusion—and achieve the safety of *nirvāṇa*. The Buddha does not teach the truth, or the whole truth, to all people. He teaches only what will be beneficial, remaining silent as an act of merciful discretion when he judges that the revelation of the truth will have a deleterious effect. Some people are not, or not yet, sufficiently receptive and robust for the disclosure of naked reality to be helpful to them. As Nāgārjuna says in the *Ratnāvalī*:

> Just as a grammarian [first] makes
> His students read the alphabet,
> So Buddha taught his trainees
> The doctrines which they could bear.[56]

The malleability of the Buddhist therapy leads to considerable doctrinal diversity. This, in turn, creates a serious hermeneutical challenge: which of the myriad teachings of the Buddha represents his final view about reality and the highest form of cognitive therapy?

In order to address this problem, the *Catuḥpratisaraṇa Sūtra* makes a distinction between teachings of the Buddha that are of interpretable meaning (*neyārtha*) and those that have a definitive meaning (*nītārtha*), interpretive categories that are employed in many traditions of Buddhism.[57] Teachings with a definitive meaning represent the Buddha's final view and thus can be taken literally. By contrast, teachings with an interpretable meaning are therapeutic skilful means; the Buddha taught them as pragmatic concessions to those who have not progressed far enough spiritually to receive the definitive teaching. They should not be taken literally and are often taught with an ulterior motive, namely, to prepare people to become receptive eventually to the definitive teaching.

[56] *Ratnāvalī* 394. Trans. Jeffery Hopkins, *The Precious Garland and The Song of the Four Mindfulnesses: Nāgārjuna and the Seventh Dalai Lama* (London: George Allen and Unwin, 1975) p. 76.
[57] Lamotte, op. cit., pp. 16–23.

A common example of an interpretable teaching is the Buddha's reference to a self that, for instance, performs actions and is reborn in circumstances determined by its *karma*. There appear to be two prominent reasons why the Buddha sometimes gives this teaching. First, the Buddha does not literally mean that there is a real, single entity called the self; rather, he used this term as convenient shorthand for what is in reality an extremely complex web of mental and physical processes.[58] Second, the Buddha sometimes teaches the existence of the self or soul as an enduring entity that, in future lives, reaps the consequences of its action. This preparatory teaching is intended for hedonists and nihilists, who do not believe in *karma* and rebirth, in order to motivate them to live moral lives. It is only at a higher stage of the spiritual path that they will be able to comprehend that there is no such self but that this does not negate the need to lead an ethical life. In the meantime, it is better that such people lead moral lives motivated by the misconception that there is an eternal self that will be rewarded or punished.[59] These two justifications for the teaching of the self are different in an important respect. In the first case, the Buddha does not lie; rather, he intends that it should be understood that the language of the self is a pragmatic designation, not to be construed literally. In the second case, it appears that the Buddhist therapy can, in certain circumstances, entail telling benign untruths for the sake of the patient. We have already seen that this may also have been the case in the story of Nanda.

Unsurprisingly, there is considerable disagreement between the various types of Buddhism about which teachings have definitive status. For instance, writing from a Theravāda perspective, Buddhaghosa identifies the truths of impermanence, suffering, and selflessness as the definitive truths.[60] However, the Yogācāra tradition favours the teaching of mind-only (*cittamātra*) as definitive. Some Mādhyamikas criticise this Yogācāra claim, arguing that the mind-only teaching is interpretable and provisional. It is a therapeutic device taught to enable practitioners to relinquish their craving for external objects.[61] The definitive teaching is universal emptiness. Both Mādhyamikas and Yogārcārins are able to claim scriptural backing for

[58] See *Milindapañha* 25–28. Trans. Thomas William Rhys Davids, *The Questions of King Milinda, Part I*, (Oxford: Oxford University Press, 1894), pp. 41–46.

[59] See Lamotte, op. cit., p. 21; Ganeri, op. cit., pp. 107–115.

[60] Donald S. Lopez Jr., 'On the Interpretation of the Mahāyāna Sūtras', in Lopez, op. cit., p. 62.

[61] See Lopez, op. cit., pp. 52–56, 69.

their hermeneutical positions; the Mādhyamikas commonly rely on the *Akṣayamatinirdeśa Sūtra* which proclaims emptiness as definitive, whereas the Yogācārins look to the *Saṃdhinirmocana Sūtra* to support their contention that the mind-only teaching is the highest truth. Furthermore, Buddhists strongly influenced by the *tathāgatagarbha* doctrine will treat teachings about the Buddha nature as definitive, Hua yen Buddhists contend that the final teaching is of mutual interpenetration of all phenomena, as taught in the *Avataṃsaka Sūtra*. And so on. As Donald Lopez points out, the notion that many Buddhist doctrines are skilful means is used not only as a way of accommodating the variety of teachings as each having therapeutic validity but also as a 'hermeneutics of control', whereby the views of rival Buddhist traditions can be conveniently subordinated to those of one's own.[62]

A further complication occurs because some passages from various Buddhist texts appear to relegate all doctrinal formulations to the level of skilful means, declaring that they must all be relinquished eventually. For example, the *Aṭṭhakavagga* from the *Sutta Nipāta* seems to advocate that the enlightened person will hold no views whatsoever.[63] A similar claim is made by Nāgārjuna, who contends that he has no thesis (*pratijñā*) and that to treat emptiness as a view (*dṛṣṭi*) is a serious error.[64] Furthermore, the famous simile of the raft indicates that, like a raft used to cross a river, the *Dhamma* should be used for crossing to the far shore beyond the stream of birth and death (*saṃsāra*). Once one has reached the other side the *Dhamma*, like the raft, should be abandoned as it has fulfilled its purpose.[65] And Candrakīrti quotes approvingly a passage from the *Ratnakūṭa Sūtra* which likens the Buddha's teachings to a medicine that expels itself from the body as well as the poison that it removes.[66]

62 Lopez, op. cit., p. 6.

63 *Sutta Nipāta* 780–787. Trans. Kenneth R. Norman, *The Rhinoceros Horn and Other Early Buddhist Poems* (*Sutta Nipāta*) (London: Pali Text Society, 1985), p. 131.

64 *Vigrahavyāvartanī* 29. Trans. Kamaleswar Bhattacharya, *The Dialectical Method of Nāgārjuna* (Delhi: Motilal Banarsidass, 1990, 3rd edn.), p. 113.

65 *Majjhima Nikāya* I 134–135. Trans. Ñāṇamoli and Bhikkhu Bodhi, op. cit., pp. 228–229.

66 *Prasannapadā* 83b–84a. Trans. Jay L. Garfield, *Empty Words: Buddhist Philosophy and Cross-Cultural Interpretation* (Oxford: Oxford University Press, 2002), pp. 66–67. See also Christopher Gowans, this volume.

The interpretation of such passages is vexing. Taken at face value, they communicate that even the most profound Buddhist teachings about impermanence, insubstantiality and so forth fail to express adequately the way things really are. If one asserts that they are ultimately true, then one has fallen prey to a dogmatism that is inimical to the spirit of the Buddhist therapy. In effect, these passages collapse the distinction between interpretable and definitive teachings, for no teaching is in fact definitive. Even Buddhist right views of the highest order have a merely instrumental value, as means to achieving the end which is enlightenment. This is often coupled with the claim that the truth experienced in enlightenment is strictly inexpressible. In this case, even supposedly definitive Buddhist views are only true insofar as they are useful or therapeutic. It would appear to follow that the enlightened person will no longer assent to them as true, except perhaps as a means to help others achieve the same ineffable enlightenment. Once enlightenment has been achieved, these views lose their utility and thus their truth.

I do not wish to deny that some Buddhists do maintain this purely pragmatic understanding of all Buddhist views, and that this may be the intention of the cited passages. However, an alternative Buddhist position is that enlightenment does not entail giving up the views which, as various Buddhist sources claim, express the true nature of things in a definitive manner. Surely these right views are constitutive of enlightenment, rather than simply instruments for its attainment? And when they are useful, is not this because they are true, rather than vice versa? Indeed, Pāli sources describe the Buddha's enlightenment experience as an insight into, rather than the abandonment of, the four truths, dependent origination and so forth.[67] As Ganeri points out, the similes of the raft and the purgative medicine seem problematic, given that they imply that the truths expressed by Buddhist doctrine can be dispensed with once their therapeutic work has been done. He suggests the helpful alternative analogy of a man who flees from danger by climbing a large rock:

> From the top, he is safe and has an excellent view. Should he then say to himself 'This rock has served me well, and now I can dispense with it? Obviously not. The point is that we might prefer a solid grasp of the truth as helping to sustain and maintain a person in a form of life, for example, the life of a sincere

[67] *Majjhima Nikāya* I, 247–250. Trans. Ñāṇamoli and Bhikkhu Bodhi, op. cit., pp. 340–343.

Buddhist practitioner, rather than as functioning merely as a means to an end.[68]

So, the enlightened person would not give up definitive Buddhist doctrines, which are thought to be correct statements of the true nature of things. These doctrines are formulations of the truths—about impermanence, insubstantiality, the folly of craving, and so forth—to which the enlightened person is said to have become fully receptive, allowing them to reshape his or her entire cognitive and affective experience. They are not to be renounced; on the contrary, they are to be embraced and made to permeate one's every thought and action.

Perhaps, then, the raft and purgative medicine similes, and the 'no views' statements are best interpreted as not undermining the accuracy and truthfulness of definitive Buddhist doctrines, nor claiming that these teachings have a merely instrumental value and should be dispensed with once enlightenment has been attained. Rather, they are warnings that one should not get attached to these doctrines; they are pointing out that the way in which these doctrines are held is important. The enlightened person would assent to the truth of Buddhist views but without pride or arrogance. Buddhist scriptures warn against clinging to views as one of the impediments to enlightenment.[69] And right views as much as wrong views can be the focus of one's clinging. The purpose of the right view has been missed if one's understanding of it is a cause of self-satisfaction, or if one uses it to appear clever or superior to other people. Such a misguided attitude betrays the fact that one's sense of ego is still strong, and that one has not been genuinely affected by the therapeutic message expressed by the view, namely that craving and selfishness are to be given up.

Critical Reflections

It would be inaccurate to accuse the Buddhist therapy of ignoring the significance of the body and its impact on one's psychology. Physical well-being is often viewed as a prerequisite for effective spiritual training, as exemplified by the Buddha's famous rejection of extreme forms of asceticism such as self-mortification. And early Buddhist sources devote considerable attention to medicines,

[68] Ganeri, op. cit., p. 49.
[69] *Majjhima Nikāya* I, 63–68. Trans. Ñāṇamoli and Bhikkhu Bodhi, op. cit., pp. 159–163.

physical exercises and dietetics.[70] They also commonly stress the interrelatedness of body and mind, an influence that cuts both ways.[71] Buddhaghosa likens the mind and body to two sheaves of reeds which rest against one another for mutual support.[72] In conjunction with traditions such as *Āyurveda* as well as Chinese and Tibetan medicine, Buddhism often advocates a holistic approach to physical illness and psychological difficulties.[73] Nevertheless, it does seem that there is a challenge to Buddhism in modern scientific claims that some emotions could be changed only by physiological intervention, such as drugs, and that belief and behavioural modification may have little or no role to play in these cases. If these claims are true, then Buddhism might be adapted to accommodate them, but, as far as I am aware, traditional Buddhism does not usually acknowledge that physical medicinal therapies rather than cognitive and behavioural therapies are required to overcome some unwholesome desires and emotions.

Another common criticism of the Buddhist therapy concerns its ultimate objective, that is, complete nonattachment.[74] As we have seen, the Buddhists stress that attachment causes unhappiness, and lies at the root of disturbing emotions such as fear, anger, jealousy and avarice. However, it is debatable whether a life of total nonattachment is really possible. Is it not more likely that enlightenment is an ideal that one may strive towards but never realise? Buddhist therapies may be effective in reducing attachment and ignorance, but it

[70] See Mark Tatz, *Buddhism and Healing: Demieville's Article 'Byo' from Hōbōgirin* (Lanham, Maryland: University Press of America, 1985). See also Kenneth G. Zysk, *Asceticism and Healing in Ancient India: Medicine in the Buddhist Monastery* (Delhi: Motilal Banarsidass, 1998).

[71] See Peter Harvey, 'The Mind-Body Relationship in Pali Buddhism: A Philosophical Investigation' in *Asian Philosophy* Vol. 3, No. 1 (1993), pp. 29–41.

[72] *Visuddhimagga* XVIII, 32. Trans. Bhikkhu Ñāṇamoli, op. cit., p. 614.

[73] For example, see C. Pierce Salguero, *Traditional Thai Medicine: Buddhism, Animism, Ayurveda* (Holm Press, 2007) and Theodore Burang, *The Tibetan Art of Healing* (London: Robinson and Watkins Books Ltd, 1974). For a contemporary perspective on the importance of the body for Buddhist practice, see Reginald A. Ray, *Touching Enlightenment: Finding Realization in the Body* (Boulder: Sounds True, 2008).

[74] For instance, Christopher Gowans, this volume.

may seem unrealistic to believe that they can be forever eradicated. Yet Buddhist sources are replete with examples of people who are said to have achieved the goal of complete and irreversible enlightenment.

However, the apparent Buddhist optimism about the possibility of attaining complete wisdom needs to be seen in the context of frequent claims that it is extremely difficult and requires enormous effort. Moreover, it is usually maintained that enlightenment is the result of numerous lifetimes of endeavour, a process that is recorded, in the case of the historical Buddha, in many stories of his previous lives as an unenlightened Bodhisattva, working towards the attainment of wisdom. Thus, the Buddhists think that enlightenment is much more difficult and rare than might first seem to be the case. Moreover, there is a prevalent belief in various forms of Buddhism that we live in an age of decline, in which enlightenment by following the Buddhist therapeutic techniques is no longer achievable, because selfishness and ignorance have become too deep-rooted. In some Buddhist traditions, notably some of the Pure Land schools, this leads to the conviction that the traditional Buddhist therapies of mindfulness, ethical conduct, meditation and so forth have become ineffective. We can no longer achieve spiritual progress, let alone enlightenment, by our own efforts, and must rely on the saving grace of a celestial Buddha. A less extreme view is that the therapies are worth pursuing, but that, given the intractable nature of some of our attachments and ignorance, their transformative power has limitations. In the latter case, wisdom is always to be striven for but is unlikely to be attained in any final and complete sense. In this case, an important aim of therapy will be to encourage a realistic attitude of acceptance that one will have shortcomings and will not live up to one's ideals. Perhaps this is the highest wisdom that is attainable.

Whether or not the state of nonattachment is possible, it is also questionable whether the Buddhists are right to claim that it is desirable. It can be objected that the equanimous existence that Buddhism advocates sacrifices many of the desires and emotions which make life worth living—for example, the passion of the lover, sensual enjoyment in its manifold forms, the strong attachment and devotion to family and friends. A life without love, lust, grief, and anger may be calm and unperturbed but arguably it is also incomplete and emotionally impoverished. It is tempting to think that Buddhism has misdiagnosed the problem and perhaps even invented a disease that does not exist and for which, therefore, a cure is not required. The Buddhists' mistrust and devaluing of basic human instincts appears to be an example of the life-denying asceticism so despised by Nietzsche.[75] Perhaps the Buddhist therapy makes us less than fully human, alienating us from beliefs, desires and emotions that make our lives meaningful.

Aristotle (4th century BCE) is critical of the ideal of nonattachment on similar grounds. He claims that detachment does not lead to true human happiness and a genuinely fulfilled human existence is one 'rich in attachments to people and things outside the self—friendships, family loves, political ties, ties of certain sorts to possessions and property. Thus it is a life rich in possibilities for emotions such as love, grief, fear, and even anger.'[76] The self-sufficient and tranquil life of the Stoic, Epicurean or Sceptic, impervious to these emotions, may be relatively safe and secure, but sacrifices many of the things that make human life potentially so fulfilling. For Aristotle, the best human life is one that is always vulnerable to loss and requires good fortune, because many of the things on which happiness depends are to some extent beyond one's control. Bad luck can undermine human flourishing (*eudaimonia*). But it is better to take the risk of disappointment and separation and to experience the joys of appropriate attachments to family, friends and so forth, than to make oneself invulnerable through a therapy of nonattachment.[77]

On the one hand, the claim that attachments can enrich life enormously is hard to resist and probably accords with most people's 'common sense' intuitions. It is arguable that it is appropriate to value greatly things such as the love for a sexual partner and that of the parent for a child, the close bond with a friend, and the enjoyment of the delights of the senses. Indeed, the very fragility of these desires and emotions and their objects possibly contributes to their beauty and worth. On the other hand, the consequences of attachments can be devastating, which might give one reason to doubt the reliability of the dominant view. Bereavement and betrayal can shatter one's life, and attachments to tribe, race, country, ideology and territory often cause war and genocide. If we reflect seriously on the terrible suffering that attachments can cause, it is hard to dismiss outright the attraction of a life of nonattachment with its promise of peace and freedom from emotional vicissitudes.

[75] Friedrich Nietzsche, *On the Genealogy of Morals*. Trans. Douglas Smith (Oxford: Oxford University Press, 1996), pp. 95–97. See also Ansell Pearson, this volume.

[76] Martha Nussbaum, *The Therapy Of Desire: Theory and Practice in Hellenistic Ethics* (New Jersey: Princeton University Press, 1994), p. 42.

[77] Ibid, pp. 42–101.

A plausible alternative to the Buddhist position might be to condone attachments to certain things (for example, one's family) and in certain respects (for example, in moderation). Even if one rejects the ultimate Buddhist goal of complete nonattachment, the therapeutic exercises may prevent one from forming excessive or inappropriate attachments. These exercises may also be useful when dealing with the painful consequences of one's attachments. For instance, Buddhist-inspired reflections on impermanence and selflessness may ameliorate somewhat the suffering of loss; loving kindness meditation directed impartially towards all, including one's enemies, may help alleviate anger and hate. This can be the case even if one does not agree that a life without any attachments would be best. In other words, these therapeutic techniques can be of value even when divorced from the ideal of human perfection which they were originally intended to help one realise.

There is another way in which the Buddhist philosophical therapy may be thought to have important limitations. Its focus tends to be primarily on the inner changes in the individuals that are required to treat suffering. It can be objected, therefore, that Buddhism tends to neglect the role that broader problems play in causing human suffering. Buddhism strives to make the individual independent of material and economic factors by stopping the craving and attachment that one has for comfort, food, sex, wealth and so forth. Buddhists aim to withdraw from society rather than seeking to improve it. It might be objected that this is naïve, given that the individual's inner world of desires, emotions and beliefs is at least in part a product of the environment which he or she inhabits? Would not the Buddhist therapy be more effective if it turned its attention more to the social and economic conditions which shape individual attitudes?

The emphasis of Buddhist teachings has usually been placed on treating the individual rather than society, and this has led to accusations that the tradition has too little to say about solutions to social and political problems. Of course, one venerable Buddhist response is that such problems are inevitable given the nature of *saṃsāra*, and thus it is not naïve but realistic for the practitioner to concentrate his or her efforts on transcending rather than reforming this world of suffering. Thus, there is a stress in many forms of Buddhism on monasticism as a withdrawal from and renunciation of family and politics. But another response is that Buddhism has not always been and should not be silent on these issues. A central part of the Buddhist therapeutic treatment is to transcend selfishness by encouraging individuals to cultivate attitudes of loving kindness and compassion. The Buddhists think that we should extend our empathy and benevolence to include as many others as possible.[78] This is an obligation which arguably should entail an interest in social and political improvements. And there are examples of Buddhist thinkers, such as Nāgārjuna, dispensing advice to rulers about how best to govern for the benefit of society as a whole.[79] The Buddha himself offers laypeople guidance on how to build a harmonious society through living in accordance with ethical precepts.[80] There is often recognition that supportive political and social conditions are required in order for the Buddhist teachings to be transmitted and practised effectively. As reputedly exemplified by Aśoka (3rd century BCE),[81] rulers have sometimes sought to create societies governed in accordance with the ethical principles of the Buddha's teaching and in a way which supports the flourishing of the Buddhist community. Moreover, given the claim that there is no autonomous self, and that one's inner world is not separate from what lies outside it, it would seem to follow that Buddhists should recognise the influence of society on one's psychology. Nevertheless, it is fair to claim that this social aspect of the Buddhist therapy has been relatively undeveloped. Indeed, Buddhism has often tacitly or explicitly supported social injustice, discrimination, and the status quo. However, it is also the case that this deficiency is being addressed by the phenomenon widely referred to as 'socially engaged Buddhism'. Prominent recent Buddhists—including the Dalai Lama, Sulak Sivaraksa, Thich Nhat Hanh and many others—have stressed in various ways the need to treat both the individual's ills and those of the wider society as they are mutually dependent. They contend that the ultimate aim of Buddhism may be liberation from *saṃsāra* but this does not preclude the Buddhist from, in the meantime, endeavouring to make *saṃsāra* less painful and more conducive to the practice of Buddhism through addressing issues such as injustice, lack of education and poverty. They draw on and adapt central Buddhist teachings—such as those about interconnectedness, selflessness, compassion, giving, right livelihood and so forth—to develop social

[78] See *Sutta Nipāta* 143–152. Trans. Norman, op. cit., pp. 24–25; *Visuddhimagga* IX, 295–315. Trans. Bhikkhu Ñāṇamoli, op. cit., pp. 288–308; *Bodhicaryāvatāra* X, 1–58. Trans. Kate Crosby and Andrew Skilton, op. cit., pp. 138–143.

[79] *Ratnāvalī* 301–400. Trans. Hopkins, op. cit., pp. 62–77.

[80] *Dīgha Nikāya* III, 180–193. Trans. Walshe, op. cit., pp. 461–469.

[81] See Romila Thapar, *Aśoka and the Decline of the Mauryas* (Delhi: Oxford University Press India, 1997, 3rd edn.).

therapies that admittedly go far beyond anything done or said by the Buddha himself.[82]

There is a final question that needs to be addressed: To what extent is Buddhist therapy open to the charge of indoctrination, which compromises rather than develops the students' powers of critical reasoning? This is not a question to which a simple answer can be provided, given the sheer diversity of Buddhism and of Buddhists. But it is undeniable that Buddhist therapy does in some of its forms emphasise the power of the received wisdom of the exalted teacher (*guru*) in which the student must have faith. Indeed, it may be argued that this dependence on the *guru* is entailed by Buddhist teaching – if we are ignorant, then surely this applies to our thinking and reasoning processes, or at least to the way in which we put these to use. So why would one rely on these rather than the guidance of an enlightened teacher? Hence faith and trust play a vital role in many forms of Buddhist therapy.[83] Moreover, techniques such as rote memorisation and recitation of key doctrines are often employed at the expense of genuine critical engagement and questioning. If alternative views are considered, the intention sometimes seems to be only to assert the assumed superiority of the Buddhist position. Buddhist sources often give the impression that there can be no doubt about the efficacy of the Buddhist methods and the desirability of the goal of non-attachment. To this extent, it seems that Buddhism and philosophy do part company.

An important source in this context is the Buddha's famous advice to the Kālāma people of Kesaputta. He teaches them that the *Dhamma* should be accepted only 'when you know for yourselves'. It is interesting that this sermon explicitly rejects the ultimate authority of reasoning in favour of an experiential form of knowledge.[84] If the intention here is that one should rely only on one's own experiences and not at all on reasoning, then this passage seems to support the objection that Buddhism does not give sufficient attention to rational reflection. Of course, there are many problems with such epistemic dependence on personal experiences, especially when divorced from any rational scrutiny. For instance, there are the possibilities of delusion, self-deception and that the experiences may

[82] See Sallie B. King, *Being Benevolence: The Social Ethics of Engaged Buddhism* (Honolulu: University of Hawai'i Press, 2005).

[83] I am grateful to Clare Carlisle for this insight.

[84] *Aṅguttara Nikāya* III, 65. Trans. Thera and Bodhi, op. cit., pp. 64–67. It is interesting that this sermon also warns against reliance on the words of one's teacher.

be strongly conditioned by the Buddhist training that one undertakes and thus themselves a product of indoctrination.

However, a more charitable reading is that in this source the Buddha is teaching that one should not rely purely on reasoning, because such rational examination needs to complemented and confirmed by experiential verification. Reasoning on its own, unsupported by experience, can lead one into many distracting and speculative views that may or may not be true and have little bearing on the task of overcoming suffering. Questioning and rational testing of Buddhist claims is a component of the Buddhist training but there is a danger of overvaluing it at the expense of the experiential.[85] But experiences unscrutinised by reason are also unreliable. So, critical, rational assessment may be insufficient but is nonetheless a necessary requirement before one should fully assent to the *Dhamma*. Hence there are developed traditions of debate in some forms of Buddhism.[86] The *Bodhisattvabhūmi* declares that it is reasoning which ensures that one confronts truths and does not 'deviate from the meaning of reality.'[87] And Śantarakṣita (8th century CE) quotes the Buddha as having said that his words should be accepted 'after due investigation' rather than out of respect for him 'just as gold is accepted as true only after heating, cutting and rubbing.'[88]

In the contemporary Japanese Buddhist movement referred to as 'Critical Buddhism,' scholars such as Hakamaya Noriaki and Matsumoto Shirō have argued provocatively that the rational pursuit of truth is the heart of Buddhism. They contend that Buddhist traditions which have been authoritarian and unquestioning have departed from the genuine message of Buddhism.[89] Of course, this attempt to identify a single, authentic Buddhist attitude to reasoning is problematic. Nevertheless, the frequent Buddhist recommendation not to be attached to the Buddhist teachings might be

[85] For further discussion, see Gunapala Dharmasiri, *A Buddhist Critique of the Christian Concept of God* (Antioch: Golden Leaves Publishing, 1988), pp. 254–258.

[86] For example, see Dan Perdue, *Debate in Tibetan Buddhism* (Ithaca: Snow Lion, 1992).

[87] *Bodhisattvabhūmi* 257. Trans. Lamotte, op. cit., p. 12.

[88] *Tattvasaṃgraha* 3588. Trans. Ganganatha Jha, *The Tattvasangraha of Shantaraksita with the Commentary of Kamalashila* (Delhi: Motilal Banarsidass, 1986), p. 1558.

[89] See Jamie Hubbard and Paul L. Swanson (eds), *Pruning the Bodhi Tree. The Storm over Critical Buddhism.* (Honolulu: University of Hawai'i Press, 1997).

construed as requiring a reasoned receptivity to alternative points of view and, consequently, a willingness to modify or even relinquish the Buddhist views if they are demonstrated to be lacking. Non-dogmatic practitioners might deny that the Buddhist claims about the ultimate truth, and how to achieve wisdom, are incontrovertible.

At the beginning of this chapter, I raised the question whether the Buddhist therapy can rightly be considered as philosophy. If philosophy involves the exercise of critical, rational reflection in the pursuit of human fulfilment, then it seems that non-dogmatic Buddhists might engage with the Buddhist therapy in a recognisably philosophical manner. They would continually question and test the efficacy and truthfulness of the teachings and be receptive to the possibility that further enquiry and experience may require revision of the therapy and its truth claims.[90]

[90] I would like to thank Clare Carlisle, Shaun Davies, Jonardon Ganeri and Christopher Gowans for their extremely valuable comments on earlier versions of this chapter.

Patañjali's Yoga as Therapeia

JAYANDRA SONI

This chapter tries to show that there is indubitable evidence for the claim that the Yoga philosophy of Patañjali can be said to be a philosophy as therapeia. For this reference will be made particularly to the Sāṅkhya school, whose ontology and metaphysics are presupposed by Yoga philosophy.[1] The Sāṅkhya school begins with the question about overcoming three kinds of 'suffering' that torment human beings, and Patañjali himself says that the implementation of yoga, is, among other things, for the sake of minimising the afflictions (*kleśas*, YS 2, 2). The second part of the chapter will be concerned with the philosophical activity referred to in Yoga itself, namely the active yoga, or yoga in the form of action (*kriyāyoga*, YS 2, 1), in order to show how this can be seen as advancing the case for Yoga as therapeia.

The beginnings of Indian philosophy, it is often said, go back to ideas contained in the Vedas, especially in the chronologically later parts of the Āraṇyakas ('forest treatises') and the Upaniṣads ('secret teachings'), the earliest being composed perhaps before the sixth century BCE. There seems to be a fundamental difference in the Vedic *Weltanschauung* before and after Buddha and Mahāvīra (who were contemporaries around the fifth–fourth century BCE). The ancient view did not stress the idea of a recurrent cycle of existences

[1] Students of Indian philosophy know that the so-called six orthodox schools are generally classified in pairs so that when one talks of the ontology and metaphysics of Yoga philosophy reference to the Sāṅkhya school is inescapable. One way of classifying the schools of Indian philosophy is by referring to the six schools of 'Hinduism' in order to contrast these from the Cārvāka/Lokāyata or materialist school and those of Buddhism and Jainism. The pairs of the six 'orthodox' Hindu schools are: Nyāya and Vaiśeṣika, Pūrva and Uttara Mīmāṃsā (or Mīmāṃsā and Vedānta) and Sāṅkhya and Yoga. With the exception of the Sāṅkhya school all the basic works of the others are written in the cryptic and mnemonic sūtra style, making it difficult to understand them without a commentary. Although there are many commentaries to the *Yogasūtra*, it is usually read with the commentaries by Vyāsa (*Vyāsabhāṣya*) and Vijñānabhikṣu (*Yogavārttika*). The basic *sūtra* works of the schools of Indian philosophy were composed probably in the four centuries around our era (200 BCE–200 CE). However, it is generally accepted that their basic ideas are earlier.

doi:10.1017/S1358246109990324

as characterising the human situation. This emphasis might have come about through the influence of the ascetic tradition which seems to have been quite well established during Buddha's and Mahāvīra's times. With the exception of the materialist school of Cārvāka or Lokāyata, the idea of recurrent existences became one of the important presuppositions of all the schools of Indian philosophy.[2] It is well-known that in his first sermon the Buddha said that in life 'everything is suffering' (*sarvaṃ duḥkham*). It is also known that this characterisation is merely a starting point for his views on how to overcome suffering. He described many aspects of suffering common to life, including normal pain, be it physical or psychological, but sought a kind of final liberation from suffering as such, from a suffering which was seen as intrinsically linked to and a part of the human condition. What he wanted was a liberation from the cycle of existences as such, and not only from suffering in the form of birth, old age, sickness and death.[3] He said that he had himself achieved this liberation and that he wanted to share his method with his fellow human beings. This basic view of life as entailing suffering became an assumption taken over by all other Indian schools except Cārvāka school, including Yoga. *Yogasūtra* 2, 15 says 'Because of the pains (of causing suffering) in the end, because of anguish, because of subliminal impressions and because of the contrary nature of the constituents of primeval nature (*guṇas*), to the discriminating, all is pain'.[4]

Most Indian schools therefore provide pathways to liberation (*mokṣa-mārga*), each school offering its own way in the context of its own ontological presuppositions. It is Sāṅkhya which provides the basic metaphysical background for the Yoga school. The earliest work that presents the fundamental ideas of Sāṅkhya is the *Sāṅkhyakārikā* by Īśvarakṛṣṇa (before the fifth century CE). In good Indian style of the period, the beginning—here the first two stanzas—clearly establishes the programme of the undertaking:

> On account of the infliction by a threefold suffering [there arises] an investigation (*jijñāsā*) into the means of counteracting it (*tad-abhighātake hetau*). If it is said that in being [already] known

[2] For other presuppositions in Indian philosophy see Karl H. Potter, *Presuppositions of India's Philosophies* (Englewood Cliffs: Prentice Hall, Inc., 1963); Jayandra Soni, 'Intercultural Relevance of Some Moments in the History of Indian Philosophy,' *Topoi* 17 (1998), pp. 49–55; pp. 49–52.

[3] See the chapters by David Burton and Christopher Gowans.

[4] *Pariṇāma-tāpa-saṃskāra-duḥkhair guṇa-vṛtti-virodhāc ca duḥkham eva sarvaṃ vivekinaḥ* YS 2, 15 (tr. Rukmani).

(*dṛṣṭe*), it (the investigation) is useless, then [we say] no, it is not so, because [what is known] is neither absolute nor eternal (SK 1).[5]

The second line clearly implies that the means of counteracting the threefold suffering are relative and temporary, not absolute and eternal. This becomes clear when, as the commentary says, the threefold suffering refers: 1. to the infliction 'proceeding from bodily and mental causes within one's self' (the dictionary meaning of *ādhyātmika*); 2. the infliction 'belonging or related to created beings' (*ādhibhautika*), namely, the infliction caused by other beings, including people, animals and insects like mosquitoes, etc.; and 3. the infliction 'relating to or proceeding from gods or from spirits' (*ādhidaivika*). In the normal course of events, these inflictions are not eliminated once and for all, but recur over and over again.[6] What is sought, then, is a remedy that is absolute and eternal.

It is clear that the author has a specific aim in mind, and in the second stanza of the work he makes explicit his reference to a *permanent* means of overcoming the afflictions, namely, a philosophical knowledge of Sāṅkhya ontology. The stanza starts by implying an objection from a putative opponent, someone who says, 'All right, it might be so that these known means already talked about fail in their intent to cure human suffering for ever, but what about scriptural tradition?' This scriptural knowledge, namely, what is derived

[5] This and the following translations are based on Suryanarayana S. Śāstri, The *Sāṅkhyakārikā of Īśvara Kṛṣṇa*, edited and translated (Madras: University of Madras 1965), from where the original is also cited: I. *duḥkhatrayābhighātāj jijñāsā tadabhighātake hetau | dṛṣṭe sā, 'pārthā cen naikāntātyantato 'bhāvāt* ||. The text is usually read with the commentary (*bhāṣya*) by Gauḍapāda and the anonymously written *Yuktidīpikā*.

[6] In his explanation of the idea behind the objection in the stanza, Śāstri, ibid, p. 3 briefly summarizes the different remedies mentioned in the commentaries: 'Physical disease can be cured by medicine and mental distress by indulgence in pleasure. Enemies may be circumvented by diplomacy and spirits may be won over by charm. Such means are not only patent but also easy. ... The objection would be valid, if any of the means so patent in experience were either certain or final in its results. None of them, however, passes the test. Medicines fail to cure, fortifications fall and let in the enemy. Diplomacy is a double-edged weapon, and so are spirit-charms.' For a critical discussion of recent scholarship, see Roland Steiner, 'Das 'dreifache Leiden' in *Sāṃkhyakārikā* 1', in *Indica* et *Tibetica. Festschrift für Michael Hahn*, ed. Konrad Klaus and Jens-Uwe Hartmann (Wien: Universität Wien, Arbeitskreis für Tibetische und Buddhistische Studien, 2007), pp. 507–520.

from tradition or the Veda (*anuśravika*), must surely supply the eternal cure. With this objection in the background the text goes on to say:

> What is derived from tradition is like what is [already] known (*dṛṣṭavad*); it is verily linked with impurity, destruction and excess; different from this and superior [to it] is [the means derived] from the discriminative knowledge (*vijñānāt*) of the evolved, the unevolved and the knower (SK 2).[7]

The first stanza says that the known methods offer mere temporary respite from suffering; the fact that they are considered finally to be useless implies that there is a superior method, one that is quite different from the known ones, a method of overcoming suffering once and for all through a special kind of knowledge, known as 'discriminative knowledge' (*vijñāna*).

Revelant dictionary meanings of the word *vijñāna* are: 'the act of distinguishing or discerning, understanding, comprehending, recognizing'. SK2 states that if one can distinguish between the terms 'the evolved,' 'the unevolved' and 'the knower' (*vyaktāvyakta-jña*), then one is in possession of the key which ends suffering for ever. This key, in fact, is nothing other than knowledge of Sāṅkhya ontology. Although three categories are mentioned, these reduce to two because 'the evolved' and 'the unevolved' refer to a single category in two states of its existence, namely, the unevolved state of equilibrium, and the evolved state that is brought about when the equilibrium is disturbed. Let us quote the definitions of these categories given in Īśvarakṛṣṇa's *Saṅkhyakārikā*. A summary of Sāṅkhya ontology is given immediately after what was said above, in stanza 3:

> Primeval matter is not a modification; the seven, beginning with the the great one, Mahat, (or *buddhi*, intellect or 'reason')[8] are

[7] *dṛṣṭavad ānuśravikaḥ sa hy aviśuddhi-kṣayātiśaya-yuktaḥ | tad-viparitaḥ śreyān vyaktāvyakta-jña-vijñānāt* ||SK 2||

[8] The other six categories are *ahaṃkāra*, the 'I-maker', the ego, or the the category responsible for 'the sense of individuality' and the five *tanmātras* or subtle elements, as supplied by the commentaries: sound (*śabda*), touch/touchability (*sparṣa*), form (*rūpa*), taste/tastability (*rasa*) and smell (*gandha*). These are categories which not only are themselves modifications, but they are also responsible for other modifications, namely, the sixteen mentioned immediately afterwards. These sixteen are mere modifications, without themselves being responsible for other modifications. This is the difference between the terms *vikṛti* (plural *vikṛtayas*) and *vikāra* (see next note as well).

changed states/modifications of [primeval] matter (*prakṛti-vikṛtayas*); the sixteen, however, are [mere] modifications.[9] Puruṣa is neither matter (prakṛti) nor a modification [of it] (SK 3).[10]

This statement clearly distinguishes pimeval matter and its evolutes or modifications from *puruṣa*, which is neither material nor has modifications. This stanza has to be read with stanzas 10 and 11, which deal with the evolved, the unevolved and the knower mentioned in SK 2:

The evolved is caused, non-eternal, non-pervasive, mobile, manifold, dependent, mergent, conjunct, and heteronomous. The unevolved is the reverse [of all these] (SK 10).

The evolved is [composed] of the three constituents, non-discriminated, objective, general, non-intelligent and productive; so is the unevolved (*pradhāna*). The Spirit (*pumān*), though similar, is [yet] the reverse of these (SK 11).[11]

So Sāṅkhya ontology involves unevolved primeval matter (*avyakta/pradhāna/prakṛti*) and a principle of life (*puruṣa/pumān/ātman*). As ontological categories both are abstract principles and both substances. Stanza 11 states that 'the Spirit, though similar', that is, in also being a substance, 'is yet the reverse of these', insofar as it does

[9] Sixteen here refers to the *jñānendriyas*, the five organs of knowledge (like hearing, etc.), the *karmendriyas*, the five organs of sense (like speech, etc.), the five gross elements (like ether, etc.) and *manas* which is usually translated as the 'mind'.

[10] *mūlaprakṛtir avikṛtir mahad-ādyaḥ prakṛti-vikṛtayaḥ sapta* | *ṣoḍaśakas tu vikāro na prakṛtir na vikṛtir puruṣaḥ* ||SK 3||. The word *puruṣa* is best left untranslated here. Some dictionary meanings of it are: 'man, male, human being, in plural people, mankind; the personal and animating principle in human and other beings, the soul or spirit.' The specific meaning with reference to Sāṅkhya is given as: 'the Spirit as passive and a spectator of the Prakṛti or creative force' (Monier-Williams). The term can be seen as a synonym of *ātman* or *jīva*, and as an ontological category *puruṣa* or *pumān* (as in SK 11) would also refer to this defining principle, the principle of life, of human beings, without which the body would be a mere corpse. In this sense *puruṣa*, *ātman* or *jīva* can be understood in the sense of consciousness, *cit* or *cetana*, terms that are used to distinguish it from (primeval) matter in Sāṅkhya and Yoga (SK 11 uses the negative, *acetana*, to describe matter, translated here as 'non-intelligent').

[11] *hetumad anityam avyāpi sakriyam anekam āśritam liṅgam* | *sāvayavaṃ para-tantraṃ vyaktaṃ viparītam avyaktam* ||SK 10|| *triguṇam aviveki viṣayaḥ sāmānyam acetanaṃ prasava-dharmi* | *vyaktaṃ tathā pradhānaṃ tad-viparītas tathā ca pumān* ||SK 11||.

not share the elements that serve to define primeval matter, which, among other things, is non-intelligent. The evolved is an altered state of primeval matter in which the three constituents become clearly distinguished because one or the other becomes dominant.[12]

Yoga as Therapeia

The basic text of the Yoga school is Patañjali's *Yogasūtra* in 195 (or perhaps 196) *sūtras*, divided into four sections. The basic questions are dealt with in the very first chapter: What is Yoga? Where does it begin? What does it lead to? What psychological states are associated with the path of Yoga? What are its methods? What are the hindrances on the path? The eightfold Yoga discipline is dealt with in the second chapter, namely, the means which lead towards the minimisation of suffering. The third chapter describes important elements of the Yoga path given in *Yogasūtra* 2, 29; namely, *dhāraṇa, dhyāna* and *samādhi*, which Rukmani translates as 'concentration,' 'meditation' and 'oneness with [the] object of meditation.' The third chapter also describes what is achieved or the perfections attained (*siddhi, vibhūti*) as a result of successfully performing the yoga exercises. The fourth chapter, among other things, discusses and defines important philosophical terms like 'psyche' (*citta*), reason/intellect (*buddhi*), the 'I-maker' or ego (*aham-kāra*), and latent traces (*vāsanā*) in the psyche. It also gives a description of the ultimate state of liberation from suffering (*mokṣa*).

Patañjali begins his *Yogasūtra* with these six sūtras:

1. Now an exposition of Yoga [is begun].
2. Yoga is the restriction of the modifications of the psyche.
3. At that time the seer abides in itself.
4. At other times it has the same form as the modification [of the psyche].
5. The modifications are of five types and they are afflicted and non-afflicted [painful and non-painful].

[12] The constituents refer to the three guṇas: *sattva*, *rajas* and *tamas* which together make up (primeval) matter. When they are in a state of equilibrium none is dominant. When this state is disturbed, the one or the other becomes predominant and so we have the evolved state. SK 13 says what functions they fulfil: 'Sattva is considered to be buoyant and illuminating, Rajas to be stimulating and mobile; Tamas alone is heavy and enveloping; their functioning for the goal (of the Spirit) is like (the action of) a lamp' (Śāstri's translation).

6. Correct knowledge, misapprehension, mental construction, sleep and memory [are the five kinds of modifications].[13]

The first *sūtra* announces what is being undertaken in the work, namely, an exposition of Yoga philosophy. The second *sūtra* then defines what Yoga is, namely, a restriction, an arrest of the modifications or changes which take place in the psyche, changes which in the final analysis are reducible to the activity which takes place in primeval matter, *prakṛti*. When the psychical activities are under control then, as the third *sūtra* says, the seer abides in itself; this is a reference to the *puruṣa* which in a sense can be seen as the defining characteristic of human beings, or as consciousness as such. When this does not happen, when the modifications of the psyche are not under control, then, as the fourth *sūtra* says, 'it has the same form as the modification [of the psyche]'. 'It' refers to *puruṣa* which takes on the psychical change.

What are these modifications and how many of them are there? The text says that there are five such modifications, and defines each of them in subsequent sūtras: correct knowledge refers to the means or instruments of cognition or knowledge, namely, perception, inference, and the utterance of a trustworthy person (YS 1, 7:); misapprehension is the 'false knowledge [of a thing] which does not correspond to its [real] form' (YS 1, 8); mental construction 'is devoid of a corresponding object and is conjured by knowledge which arises from words' (YS 1, 9); sleep is that modification of the psyche based on the absence of any knowledge content' (YS 1, 10); and memory 'is non-loss [or, not losing] or not stealing of the objects in the psyche which have been once experienced' (YS 1, 11).

We have seen that according to Sāṅkhya the absolute and eternal cure, namely, the means of removing or counteracting suffering in any of its three forms, is by way of discriminative knowledge of the evolved, the unevolved and the knower. We also saw that this meant a knowledge of *puruṣa* and *prakṛti*. Now, here in the Yoga view, the seer (*draṣṭu* = *puruṣa*) abides in itself only when there is a restriction or an arrest of the psychical modifications (*citta-vṛtti* =

[13] The translation is largely from Rukmani, with the difference that I have rendered *citta-vṛtti* as 'the modification of the psyche' and not 'modifications of the mind'. I reserve the word 'mind' as a translation of *manas*. Patañjali's text is also quoted from her work: *atha yogānuśāsanam* ||1, 1|| *yogaś citta-vṛttinirodhaḥ* ||1, 2|| *tadā draṣṭuḥ svarūpe 'vasthānam* ||1, 3|| *vṛttisārūpyam itaratra* ||1, 4|| *vṛttayaḥ pañcatayyaḥ kliṣṭā 'kliṣṭāḥ* ||1, 5|| *pramāṇa-viparyaya-vikalpa-nidrā-smṛtayaḥ* ||1, 6||. Unless otherwise stated, the tr. and text of the *Yogasūtra* are from Rukmani's excellent study.

prakṛti); otherwise the seer takes on the form of the modification. For the removal of suffering, according to Yoga, what is needed is a clear knowledge of the difference between the intrinsic natures of *puruṣa* and *prakṛti*. Whereas Sāṅkhya merely recognizes the problem and theoretically points at the solution, Yoga now says that the remedy rests in the restriction of the modifications of the psyche through 'practice and through detachment' (YS 1, 12: *abhyāsa-vairāgyābhyāṃ tan-nirodhaḥ*). Practice is 'the effort to stay in the restricted state' (YS 1, 13: *tatra sthitau yatno 'bhyāsaḥ*) and detachment is the 'absence of greed towards objects seen and heard of' (YS 1, 15: *dṛṣṭānuśravika-viṣaya-vitṛṣṇasya vaśīkāra-saṃjñā vairāgyam*). The point becomes even more explicit in the next statement: 'That is the highest detachment which results in the absence of greed towards the *guṇas*, on account of discernment of *puruṣa*' (YS 1, 16: *tat-paraṃ puruṣa-khyāter guṇa-vaitṛṣṇyam*).

The definition of Yoga as being 'the restriction of the modifications of the psyche' is a short and clear statement. However, when one learns that these modifications entail cognition, misapprehension, mental construction, sleep and memory (as given and defined in YS 1, 6ff.), and that all of them have to be restricted (according to the definition in YS 1, 2), one wonders whether and how these common and natural human activities can be brought to a standstill. All one can say is that the Yoga view is that this can indeed be achieved, when certain obstacles are overcome. YS 1, 30 enumerates nine hindrances:

> The distractions (*vikṣepa*) of the mind are [these nine:] sickness, idleness, doubt, negligence, sloth, lack of detachment (*avirati*), misapprehension (*bhrānta-darśana*), failure to attain any stage [of concentration, *alabdha-bhūmikatva* and] inability to stay [in the stage of concentration attained, *anavasthitatva*] (YS 1, 30).[14]

If the modifications of the psyche cannot be restricted because of the distractions or hindrances, then these hindrances are responsible for suffering: 'Pain, dejection, unsteadiness of the body, inhaling and exhaling exist along with distractions' (YS 1, 31). How is one to get rid of these hindrances: 'In order to remove these [there should be] practice on a single entity' (YS, 1, 32), namely, one-pointedness.

[14] *vyādhi-styāna-saṃśaya-pramādālasyāvirati-bhrānti-darśanālabdha-bhūmikatvānavasthitatvāni citta-vikṣepās te 'ntarāyāḥ* ‖YS 1, 30‖ *duḥkha-daurmanasyāṅgamejayatva-śvāsa-praśvāsā vikṣepa-sahabhuvaḥ* ‖YS 1, 31‖ *tat pratiṣedhārtham ekatvābhyāsaḥ* ‖YS 1, 32‖.

By this is meant exercising the psyche to concentrate 'on a single entity as support', as the commentary says.[15]

The question still remains as to how exactly a 'clarity of the psyche' can be attained. The answer is given in YS 1, 33:

> The psyche attains clarity by cultivating friendliness, compassion, joy and indifference towards happiness, pain, virtue and vice (that is to say, towards those who are happy, those who are miserable, those who are virtuous and those who are evil-minded) (YS 1, 33).[16]

Then follow other suggestions for attaining a stability of the psyche, through proper breathing (YS 1, 34), meditation (*dhyāna*, YS 1, 39), etc., and the first chapter of the *Yogasūtra* ends after briefly mentioning various kinds of intense meditation (*samādhi*).[17] Chapter Two begins with the statement: 'Self-discipline, study [of the scriptures and] devotion to Īśvara [the lord] are yoga in the form of action', and they are 'for the sake of bringing about *samādhi* and for the sake of minimising the afflictions'.[18] Apart from distractions such as sickness, idleness and doubt, mentioned in YS 1, 30 above, the afflictions which torment human beings are: 'misapprehension, the sense of I, attachment, aversion and clinging to life'.[19] After briefly

[15] This one-pointedness (*ekāgratā*) is an important exercise, discussed in more detail in YS 3, 11–12: 'When there is weakening of attention to all things and there is the rise of one-pointedness, that is the change into 'samādhi' state of mind[/psyche]' (YS 3, 11) and 'Then again, when there is a similar [sequence] in the cognitive act of the past and the cognitive of the present, it is the change of one-pointed state of the mind[/psyche]' (YS 3, 12) (Rukmani's tr.).

[16] *maitrī-karuṇā-muditopekṣāṇāṃ sukha-duḥkha-puṇyāpuṇya-viṣayāṇāṃ bhāvanātaś citta-prasādanam* ||YS 1, 33||.

[17] Two basic kinds of intense meditation (*samādhi*) are given YS 1, 17–18: 'Saṃprajñāta (*samādhi*) is that accompanied by deliberation (*vitarka*) (or) by reflection (*vicāra*) (or) by bliss (*ānanda*) (or) by sense of 'I' (*asmitā*)' (YS 1, 17) and 'That preceded by the practice of cessation of modifications (knowledge) and which has (only) the subliminal impressions as residue, is the other (asaṃprajñāta-samādhi)' (YS 1, 18). *Saṃprajñāta-samādhi* may be understood as an intense meditation that is based on the help of some object of concentration, such as deliberation (*vitarka*) or reflection (*vicāra*), and the other, *asaṃprajñāta-samādhi*, would be an intense meditation without the support of any such meditation aids.

[18] *tapaḥ-svādhyāyeśvara-praṇidhānāni kriyā-yogaḥ* (YS 2, 1). *samādhi-bhāvanārthaḥ kleśa-tanū-karaṇārthaś ca* (YS 2, 2).

[19] *avidyā 'smitā-rāga-dveṣābhiniveśāḥ pañca kleśāḥ* (YS 2, 3).

defining each term in subsequent *sūtras*, YS 2, 11 then says: 'Their modifications are to be destroyed through meditation'.[20] YS 2, 28 and 29 not only say what is achieved through the help or aid of yoga, but also give the eight limbs which make up the essence of the yoga discipline:

> By the practice of the different aids to yoga, when there is destruction of impurity, there arises the light of knowledge culminating in discriminate-discernment (YS 2, 28).
>
> Restraint (*yama*), observance (*niyama*), posture (*āsana*), regulation of breath (*prāṇāyāma*), withdrawal of the senses (*pratyāhāra*), concentration (*dhāraṇā*), meditation (*dhyāna*), and oneness with object of meditation (*samādhi*) are the eight limbs (of yoga) (YS 2, 29).

Each of these limbs is then defined. Various restraints and observances are listed which have to do with conduct and behaviour in general and should be observed throughout one's life, unlike breathing and concentration exercises which are practised for a specific time. The restraints are given in YS 2, 30: abstinence from injury (*ahiṃsā*), truthfulness (*satya*), abstinence from theft (*asteya*), continence (*brahmacarya*), and abstinence from avariciousness (*aparigraha*); these make up the 'great vow' (*mahāvrata*, YS 2, 31). The observances are given in YS 2, 32: cleanliness (*śauca*), contentment (*saṃtoṣa*), austerity (*tapaḥ*), study (of the scripture, *svādhyāya*) and devotion to the lord (*īśvarapraṇidhāna*).

The last four of the eight 'limbs' are: the withdrawal of the senses (*pratyāhāra*), concentration (*dhāraṇā*), meditation (*dhyāna*), and oneness with the object of meditation (*samādhi*). They are described as follows in the *Yogasūtra*:

> When the sense-organs do not come in contact with their [respective] objects and appear to be imitating the nature of the mind it is called withdrawal of sense-organs (*pratyāhāra*, YS 2, 54). From that [is achieved] the highest control of the sense-organs (YS 2, 55). Concentration (*dhāraṇā*) is fixing the mind in one place (YS 3, 1). With reference to the same place, when there is continuous flow of the same knowledge, it is called meditation (*dhyāna*, YS 3, 2). When the same *dhyāna* shines as the object alone [in the mind] appearing to have lost its reflective

[20] *dhyāna-heyās tad-vṛttayaḥ* (YS 2, 11).

> nature, it is called oneness with the object of meditation/ intense meditation (*samādhi*, YS 3, 3).[21]

With an intensification of concentration a deeper state of the psyche is reached, ending with the state of becoming one with the the object of concentration. In other words, a withdrawal of the sense-organs from their respective objects enables one not only to concentrate better but also to learn to intensify this concentration through proper exercise. The state of oneness with the object has two main stages, one with the aid of an object of meditation and the other without such an aid (YS 1, 17 and 18 mention two broad kinds of intense meditation, *saṃprajñāta* and *asaṃprajñāta-samādhi*). The first of these has four kinds: *savitarka, nirvitarka, savicāra* and *nirvicāra*, translated respectively as 'deliberative,' 'super-deliberative,' 'reflective' and 'super-reflective' (YS 1, 42–44).

The 'deliberative' is a kind of logical thinking as an aid for meditation. This exercise involves an intensive internal argumentation and presupposes a preparation for it, so as to enable the psyche to experience the object in 'its essential or intrinsic whole.' In a sense, this intense meditation is a state based on what is 'gross' (*sthūla*; Rukmani vol. 2, p. 213; solid, thick, compact). Further, as YS 1, 17 says, the state entails the sense of 'I' as in 'I recognise this object,' or 'this object of meditation is mine.' The 'super-deliberative,' a state without such internal deliberation, though arising out of it, is no longer concerned with what is gross and is without the sense of 'I'. It is a condition in which the object which serves as an aid is seen in its essence, without a name and without its previous form (YS 1, 42–43).

The other two kinds of intense meditation which are aids to concentration are the reflective and super-reflective. Whereas the first two states are based on what is 'gross,' these two are based on what is 'subtle' (*sūkṣma*, Rukmani vol. 1, p. 230–1). In the first of these states time and space are realised in their subtle forms, and take on a qualitatively different relevance from the one they have in daily experience. The super-reflective state, one 'without or beyond' reflection, is literally beyond anything that can be reflected upon; the practitioner 'sees' the subtle object which serves as an aid to meditation in its 'ideal form'. It is a state in which thoughts are in their

[21] *sva-viṣayāsaṃprayoge cittasya sva-rūpānukāra ivendriyāṇāṃ pratyāhāraḥ* ||YS 2, 54|| *tataḥ paramā vaśyatendriyāṇām* ||YS 2, 55|| *deśa-bandhaś cittasya dhāraṇā* ||YS 3, 1|| *tatra pratyayaikatānatādhyānam* ||YS 3, 2|| *tadevārtha-mātra-nirbhāsaṃ sva-rūpa-śūnyam iva samādhiḥ* ||YS 3, 3||.

'pure form'. Feelings such as sadness, happiness, violence and sloth are no longer present.

The aim of these exercises is, step by step and with practice, to arrive at a balanced state (*samāpatti*) of the psyche. The idea is to become adept—thoroughly proficient and skilled—in entering any state at will. The four states of intense meditation or oneness with the object of meditation that help concentration are a preparation for a second kind of *samādhi*, which is a state without such an aid. All the four states involve controlled modifications or fluctuations of the psyche because an attempt is being made through these exercises to arrest or restrict the activity of the psyche. When the practitioner has mastered the fourth state, then even this activity will have to be restricted and arrested in order that the practitioner continue steadfastly and maintain the state of concentration. In the state of intense meditation without a meditation aid, the practitioner is devoid of any help to limit or support the psyche. Then the true nature of the psyche is ready to be manifested. A manifestation of the true nature of the seer, or observer (*drastu*, YS 1, 3), goes in tandem with it. In other words, with a knowledge of 'the evolved, the unevolved and the knower', as Sāṅkhya puts it, and an arrest or restriction of psychical activity, as Yoga says, the goal of both schools is arrived at.

The eight limbs of Yoga, and within these the successive stages or states of meditation constitute a discipline based on ascetic exercises. There are practical instructions to help the practitioner on the path of yoga in several places of the text. So, for example:

> When perverse thoughts oppose [the restraints and the observances] (YS 2, 31–32]) there should be the cultivation of opposite [thoughts] (YS 2, 33). Perverse thoughts such as causing injury, etc., whether done by oneself or caused to be done or approved, preceded by greed, anger, and delusion which is mild, moderate, or intense, result in endless pain and ignorance—this [kind of thought] is an opposite thought (YS 2, 34).[22]

Following the restraints and observances, the practitioner proceeds in logical sequence. He or she learns to practice a steady and comfortable posture (*āsana*, YS 2, 46); to regulate the breath, that is, to suspend the movement of inhalation and exhalation (*prāṇāyāma*, YS 2, 49); and to withdraw the senses from their respective objects

[22] *vitarka-bādhane pratipakṣa-bhāvanam* ||YS 2, 33|| *vitarkā hiṃsādayaḥ kṛta-kāritānumoditā lobha-krodha-moha-pūrvakā mṛdu-madhyādhimātrā duḥkhājñānānanta-phalā iti pratipakṣa-bhāvanam* ||YS 2, 34||.

(*pratyāhāra*, YS, 2, 54). The last three stages belong together very closely and are a more subtle kind of control of and mastery over the modifications and fluctuations of the psyche. Beginning with concentration, each step involves a further intensification and together they make up the final stages of the path to self-knowledge in which the seer then abides in his or her self.[23]

Conclusion

We have seen that Yoga is defined as the restriction or arrest of the modifications or fluctuations of the psyche, and that its aim is to show how suffering may be minimised, if not completely eradicated. YS 2, 15 says that everything is indeed suffering (*duḥkham eva sarvam*), a point emphasising what was said in YS 1, 31, namely, that if the modifications of the psyche, which cause distractions, are not steadied or stabilised, then there is pain, dejection, and so forth. Suggestions for stabilising the psyche are given. Afflictions and distractions are a sign of an uncontrolled, erratic psyche and they need to be overcome. YS 2, 29 gives a summary of the eight limbs of Yoga, which, in fact, constitute an ascetic discipline requiring meditation exercises in order to control the psyche. Two main

[23] Despite its brevity and conciseness the *Yogasūtra* devotes a relatively large number of *sūtras* (altogether at least 46) to the enumeration of so-called achievements, perfections or powers (*siddhi, vibhūti*, YS 3, 16 to YS 4, 6). These powers may be seen as unavoidable consequences of the ascetic discipline. So, for example, YS 3, 19 says that by meditating on ideas or notions 'then [there follows] knowledge of other minds'; by meditating on the moon 'there is knowledge of the arrangement of stars' (YS, 3, 27); by meditating on 'the pit of the throat there is the cessation of thirst and hunger' (YS 3, 30). YS 4, 1 clearly says that these perfections or powers are achieved not only through intense meditation but can arise also by birth, through drugs (*auṣadhi*), from spells (*mantra*) or through strict asceticism (*tapas*). However, already in YS 3, 37 it is clearly stated that 'These powers are obstructions (*upasarga*) in *samādhi*...,' and YS 3, 50 clinches the argument in favour of disregarding these powers as hindrances: 'As a result of passionlessness even with regard to these [perfections] there follows, after the dwindling of the seeds of the defects, Isolation'; James Haughton Woods, *The Yoga-System of Patañjali or the Ancient Hindu Doctrine of Concentration of the Mind* (Cambridge, Mass.: Harvard University Press, 1914), p. 284. It is precisely this isolation which is the goal of Saṅkhya and Yoga because it is a knowledge of the essential natures of consciousness (*puruṣa*) and primeval nature (*prakṛti*).

types of intense meditation—one involving an object of meditation as an aid, and the other without such an aid—are distinguished. The latter is seen to be the aim of Yoga. This state of intense meditation without an aid or a support leads finally to an arrest or restriction of psychical activity, as Patañjali says, and a knowledge of 'the evolved, the unevolved and the knower', as Sāṅkhya puts it. Thus both schools set out to arrive at the goal of overcoming suffering and pain, and the means to this end is philosophy as therapeia par excellence.

Bibliography

Abbey, Ruth, *Nietzsche's Middle Period* (Oxford: Oxford University Press, 2000).

Alt, Wayne, 'There Is No Paradox of Desire in Buddhism', *Philosophy East and West* 30.4 (1980), pp. 521–528.

Annas, Julia, 'Epicurean Emotions,' *Greek, Roman and Byzantine Studies* **30** (1989), pp. 145–64.

——, 'Philosophical Therapy, Ancient and Modern,' in Mark G. Kuczewski and Ronald Polansky, eds., *Bioethics: Ancient Themes in Contemporary Issues* (Cambridge, MA: The MIT Press, 2000), pp. 109–127.

Apte, V., *A Practical Sanskrit Dictionary* (Delhi: Motilal Banarsidass, 1959).

Aristotle, *Nikomachische Ethik* (gr. rec. Immanuel Bekker, Berlin: Reimer, 1831).

Āryadeva, *Āryadeva's Catuḥśataka: On the Bodhisattva's Cultivation of Merit and Knowledge*, Karen Lang, tr., (Copenhagen: Akademisk Forlag, 1986).

Aurelius, Marcus, *Meditations*, translated by C. R. Haines, *Marcus Aurelius*, Loeb Classical Library (Cambridge, MA.: Harvard University Press, 1916).

Bartuschat, Wolfgang, *Baruch de Spinoza* (Munich: C. H. Beck, 1996).

Bhattacharya, Kamaleswar (trans.), *The Dialectical Method of Nāgārjuna* (Delhi: Motilal Banarsidass, 3rd edn. 1990).

Birnbaum, Raoul, *The Healing Buddha* (Boulder: Shambala, 1979).

Bittner, Rüdiger, 'Spinozas Gedanke, dass Einsicht befreit', *Deutsche Zeitschrift für Philosophie* **42** (1994), pp. 963–971.

Blake, William, *Complete Writings*, ed. G. Keynes Oxford University Press: London, 1966).

Bodhi, Bhikkhu (trans.), *The Connected Discourses of the Buddha: A New Translation of the Saṃyutta Nikāya* (Boston: Wisdom Publications, 2000).

Boland, Vivian O. P., *St. Thomas Aquinas* (London: Continuum, 2007).

——, ' The Healing Work of Teaching: Thomas Aquinas and Education,' in Gabrielle Kelly, O. P. and Kevin Saunders, O. P. eds, *Towards the Intelligent Use of Liberty: Dominican Approaches in Education* (Adelaide: ATF Press, 2007), pp. 32–41.

Boethius, *The Consolation of Philosophy*, trans. V. E. Watts (Middlesex: Penguin, 1969).

Bond, George D., 'The Gradual Path as a Hermeneutical Approach to the Dhamma', in Donald S. Lopez Jr. ed., *Buddhist Hermeneutics* (Delhi: Motilal Banarsidass, 1993), pp. 29–46.

Boyle, Leonard O. P., *The Setting of the Summa Theologiae of Saint Thomas* (Pontifical Institute of Medieval Studies: Toronto, 1982).

Bibliography

Buddhaghosa, Bhadantācariya, *The Path of Purification (Visuddhimagga)*, Bhikkhu Ñāṇamoli, tr. (Seattle: Buddhist Publication Society Pariyatta Editions, 1999).

Burang, Theodore, *The Tibetan Art of Healing* (London: Robinson and Watkins Books Ltd, 1974).

Burke, Edmund, *A Philosophical Enquiry into the Origin of our Ideas of the Sublime and Beautiful* (Oxford: Oxford University Press, 1998).

Burton, David, *Buddhism, Knowledge and Liberation: A Philosophical Study* (Aldershot: Ashgate, 2004).

Cabezón, José Ignacio (trans.), *Dose of Emptiness: An Annotated Translation of the sTong thun chen mo of mKhas grub dGe legs dpal bzang* (Albany: State University of New York Press, 1992).

——, *Scholasticism: Cross-cultural and Comparative Perspectives,* (Albany, New York: State University of New York Press, 1998).

Candrakīrti, *Lucid Exposition of the Middle Way: The Essential Chapters from the Prasannapadā of Candrakīrti*, Mervyn Sprung, tr., (Boulder CO: Prajñā Press, 1979).

——, *Four Illusions: Candrakīrti's Advice for Travelers on the Bodhisattva Path*, Karen C. Lang, tr., (New York: Oxford University Press, 2003).

Carlyle, Thomas, *Sartor Resartus*, K. McSweeney and P. Sabor eds. (Oxford: Oxford University Press, 1987).

Caygill, Howard, 'The Consolation of Philosophy or 'Neither Dionysus nor the Crucified', *Journal of Nietzsche Studies* **7** (1994), pp. 131–51.

Chari, S. M. Srinivasa, *Vaiṣṇaivism: its Philosophy, Theology and Religious Discipline* (Delhi: Motilal Banarsidass, 1994).

Chesterton, G. K., *Heretics* (John Lane: New York, 1905).

Cicero, *On Moral Ends*, Raphael Woolf, tr., (Cambridge: Cambridge University Press, 2001).

——, *Cicero and the Emotions: Tusculan Disputations 3 and 4*, Margaret Graver, tr., (Chicago: University of Chicago Press, 2002).

Clark, Gillian, 'In the Foreskin of Your Flesh: The Pure Male Body in Late Antiquity', in *Roman Bodies*, A. Hopkins and M. Wyke eds. (Rome: British School at Rome, 2005), pp. 43–54.

Clark, Maudemarie and Leiter, Brian, 'Introduction' to F. Nietzsche, *Daybreak: Thoughts on the Prejudices of Morality*, trans. R. J. Hollingdale, Cambridge: Cambridge University Press, 1986).

Clark, Stephen R. L., *Aristotle's Man: Speculations upon Aristotelian Anthropology* Clarendon Press: Oxford, 1975).

——, 'A Plotinian Account of Intellect', *American Catholic Philosophical Quarterly* **71** (1997), pp. 421–32.

——, 'Going Naked into the Shrine: Herbert, Plotinus and the Constructive Metaphor':, in D. Hedley & S. Hutton, eds., *Platonism at the Origins of Modernity* (Springer: Dordrecht, 2008), pp. 45–61.

Clooney, Francis S. J., 'Binding the text: Vedānta as Philosophy and Commentary,' in *Texts in Context: Traditional Hermeneutics in South Asia*, Jeffrey R. Timm ed. (Albany, New York: State University of New York Press, 1992), pp. 47–68.

——, *Theology After Vedānta* (Albany, New York: State University of New York Press, 1993).

——, 'Scholasticisms in Encounter: Working through a Hindu Example,' in Cabezón, José Ignacio ed., *Scholasticism: Cross-cultural and Comparative Perspectives*, (Albany, New York: State University of New York Press, 1998), pp. 177–200.

Colebrooke, Henry Thomas, *The Sánkhya Káriká of Íswara Krishna, tr. from the Sanskrit with the Bháshya or commentary of Gaudapáda* (Bombay: Tookaram Tatya, 1887).

Collins, Steven, *Selfless Persons: Imagery and Thought in Theravāda Buddhism* (Cambridge: Cambridge University Press, 1982).

Cook, Thomas J., 'Affektive Erkenntnis und Erkenntnis der Affekte. Ein Problem der spinozistischen Ethik,' in *Affekte und Ethik. Spinozas Lehre im Kontext*, ed. A. Engstler and R. Schnepf (Hildesheim: Georg Olms Verlag, 2002), pp. 164–181.

Coward, Harold, *Mantra* (Albany: State University of New York Press, 2004).

Crosby, Kate and Skilton, Andrew (trans.), *The Bodhicaryāvatāra: A Guide to the Buddhist Path to Awakening* (Oxford: Oxford Paperbacks, 1998).

Cumont, Franz, *Astrology and Religion among the Greeks and Romans* [1912] (Dover: New York, 1960).

Cushman, Robert Earl, *Therapeia: Plato's Conception of Philosophy* (Chapel Hill: University of North Carolina, 1958).

Damasio, Antonio, *Looking for Spinoza: Joy, Sorrow, and the Feeling Brain* (New York: Harcourt, 2003).

De Silva, Padmasiri, *An Introduction to Buddhist Psychology* (London: Palgrave Macmillan, 4th edn. 2005).

Dharmasiri, Gunapala, *A Buddhist Critique of the Christian Concept of God* (Antioch: Golden Leaves Publishing, 1988).

Dumoulin, H., *History of Zen Buddhism*, tr. Paul Peachey Faber: London, 1963)

Edelstein, Ludwig, 'The Relation of Ancient Philosophy to Medicine,' in *Ancient Medicine: Selected Papers of Ludwig Edelstein*, Owsei Temkin and C. Lilian eds., (Baltimore: Johns Hopkins University Press, 1967), pp. 349–66.

Eckhart, Meister, *Deutsche Predigten und Traktate*, edited and translated by J. Quint, (Munich: Hanser), 1963.

——, *Meister Eckharts Predigten*, edited and translated by J. Quint, *Die deutschen und lateinischen Werke*, Sermons vol. 3 (Stuttgart: Verlag W. Kohlhammer, 1976).

Edwards, Mark J., 'In Defense of Euthyphro', *American Journal of Philology* **12** (2000), pp. 213–224.

Epictetus, *The Discourses of Epictetus*, Christopher Gill, ed., Robin Hard, tr. (London: J. M. Dent (Everyman), 1995).

——, 'Letter to Menoeceus,' in *Hellenistic Philosophy: Introductory Readings*, second edn, Brad Inwood and L. P. Gerson eds. and trs., (Indianapolis: Hackett Publishing Company, 1997), pp. 28–31.

Erikson, Erik H., *Identity: Youth and Crisis* (New York: W.W. Norton, 1968).

Falk, Harry, 'The Galits in the Ṛg Veda *Padapāṭha*: On the Origins of the *Samhitapāṭha* and the *Padapāṭha*', in Axel Micheals, ed., *The Pandit* (Delhi: Manohar, 2001).

Falkner, John Meade, 'After Trinity' (1910): *Collected Poems* (John Meade Falkner Society: Kings Newton 2008).

Feinstein, Howard, *Becoming William James*, with a new introduction, (Ithaca: Cornell University Press, 1999).

Ganeri, Jonardon, *The Concealed Art of The Soul: Theories of Self and Practices of Truth in Indian Ethics and Epistemology* (Oxford: Clarendon Press, 2007).

Garfield, Jay L., *Empty Words: Buddhist Philosophy and Cross-Cultural Interpretation* (Oxford: Oxford University Press, 2002).

Genova, Judith, *Wittgenstein: A Way of Seeing* (London: Routledge, 1995).

Gethin, Rupert, *The Foundations of Buddhism* (Oxford: Oxford University Press, 1998).

Ghose, Lynken, '*Karma* and the Possibility of Purification: An Ethical and Psychological Analysis of the Doctrine of *Karma* in Buddhism,' *Journal of Religious Ethics* **35** (2007), pp. 259–90.

Goethe, Johann Wolfgang, *Wilhelm Meisters Lehrjahre* (München: Insel, 1980). Translation: *Wilhelm Meister's Apprenticeship*, ed. and trans. Eric A. Blackall in cooperation with Victor Lange (Princeton: Princeton University Press, 1995);

Goldfarb, Warren, 'I Want You to Bring Me a Slab. Remarks on the Opening Sections of the *Philosophical Investigations*,' *Synthese* 56 (1983), pp. 265–282.

Golomb, Jacob et al., *Nietzsche and Depth Psychology* (Albany: SUNY Press, 1999).

Gombrich, Richard, *Theravāda Buddhism: A Social History from Ancient Benares to Modern Colombo* (London: Routledge, 1988).

Gonda, Jan, *Change and Continuity in Indian Religions* (The Hague: Mouton, 1965).

Griffiths, Paul, 'Scholasticism: The Possible Recovery of an Intellectual Practice,' in Cabezón, José Ignacio ed., *Scholasticism: Cross-cultural and Comparative Perspectives,* (Albany, New York: State University of New York Press, 1998), pp. 201–235.

Hacker, Paul, 'Śraddhā', in *Wiener Zeitschrift fur die Kunde Sud-und Ostasiens*, Band III (1963), p. 151–189.

Hadot, Pierre, *Philosophy as a Way of Life: Spiritual Exercises from Socrates to Foucault* (Oxford: Blackwell, 1995); translated by Michael Chase from the original *Exercices spirituels et philosophie antique* (Paris: Etudes Augustiniennes, 1987).

——, *What is Ancient Philosophy?*, trans. Michael Chase (Cambridge, Mass.: Harvard University Press, 2002).

Hagberg, Garry L., *Meaning and Interpretation: Wittgenstein, Henry James and Literary Knowledge* (Ithaca: Cornell University Press, 1994).

——, *Art as Language: Wittgenstein, Meaning and Aesthetic Theory* (Ithaca: Cornell University Press, 1995).

——, *Describing Ourselves: Wittgenstein and Autobiographical Consciousness* (Oxford: Clarendon Press, 2008).

Halbfass, Wilhelm, 'The Therapeutic Paradigm and the Search for Identity in Indian Philosophy,' in his *Traditions and Reflection: Explorations in Indian Thought* (Albany: State University of New York Press, 1991).

Hampe, Michael, 'Der Körper von innen. Zur Wahrnehmung des Körpers in Spinozas Doppelaspekttheorie der Affekte', in *Affekte und Ethik: Spinozas Lehre im Kontext*, ed. A. Engstler and R. Schnepf (Hildesheim: Georg Olms Verlag, 2002), pp. 129–148.

——, 'Baruch de Spinoza – Rationale Selbstbefreiung,' in A. Beckermann and D. Perler, *Klassiker der Philosophie heute* (Stuttgart: Reclam, 2005), pp. 230–250.

Hampe, Michael and Schnepf, Robert eds., *Baruch de Spinoza: Ethik in Geometrischer Ordnung Dargestellt* (Berlin: Akademie Verlag, 2006).

Hara, M., 'Note on Two Sanskrit Religious Terms: bhakti and śraddhā', *Indo-Iranian Journal* 7 (1964), pp. 124–145.

Harris, William V., *Restraining Rage: The Ideology of Anger Control in Classical Antiquity* (Cambridge, MA: Harvard University Press, 2001).

Harvey, Peter, 'The Mind-Body Relationship in Pāli Buddhism: A Philosophical Investigation', *Asian Philosophy* 3.1 (1993), pp. 29–42.

Havelock, Eric, *Preface to Plato* (Oxford: Clarendon Press, 1963).

Hegel, G. W., *Lectures on the History of Philosophy* (Lincoln: University of Nebraska Press, 1995).

Herman, A. L., 'A Solution to the Paradox of Desire in Buddhism', *Philosophy East and West* 29.1 (1979), pp. 91–94.

Hopkins, Jeffery (trans.), *The Precious Garland and The Song of the Four Mindfulnesses: Nāgārjuna and the Seventh Dalai Lama* (London: George Allen and Unwin, 1975).

Horner, Isaline B. (trans.), *The Book of Discipline*, volume V (London: Luzac, 1963).

—— (trans.), *The Book of Discipline*, volume IV (London: Luzac, 1971).

Hubbard, Jamie and Paul, L. Swanson, Paul, L. eds., *Pruning the Bodhi Tree. The Storm over Critical Buddhism.* (Honolulu: University of Hawai'i Press, 1997).

Hubbeling, H. G., *Spinoza* (Freiburg and Munich: Verlag Karl Alber, 1978).

Hutter, Horst, *Shaping the Future: Nietzsche's New Regime of the Soul and Its Ascetic Practices* (Lanham: Lexington Books, 2006).

Inwood, Brad and Gerson, L. P., *The Epicurus Reader* (Indianapolis: Hackett, 1994).

Ireland, John D. (trans.), *The Udāna: Inspired Utterances of the Buddha and The Itivuttaka: The Buddha's Sayings* (Kandy: Buddhist Publication Society, 2007).

James, Henry (brother of WJ), *A Small Boy and Others* (London: Gibson Square Books, 2001).

——, *Notes of a Son and Brother* (London: MacMillan, 1914).

James, Henry (son of WJ), ed., *The Letters of William James*, vol. 1 (Boston: Atlantic Monthly Press, 1926).

James, William, *Essays in Philosophy* (Cambridge: Harvard University Press, 1978).

——, *The Will to Believe and Other Essays in Popular Philosophy* (Cambridge: Harvard University Press, 1979).

——, *Essays in Religion and Morality* (Cambridge: Harvard University Press, 1982).

——, *Essays, Comments, and Reviews* (Cambridge: Harvard University Press, 1987).

——, *Manuscripts, Essays, and Notes* (Cambridge: Harvard University Press, 1988).

——, *The Varieties of Religious Experience* (Cambridge: Harvard University Press, 1985).

Jha, Ganganatha (trans.), *The Tattvasangraha of Shantaraksita with the Commentary of Kamalashila* (Delhi: Motilal Banarsidass, 1986).

Jordan, Mark, *Rewritten Theology: Aquinas after His Readers* (Oxford: Blackwell Publishing, 2007).

Joyce, Richard, 'Theistic Ethics and the Euthyphro Dilemma', *Journal of Religious Ethics* (30) 2002, pp. 49–75.

Kajihara, Meiko, *The Brahmacārin in the Veda: The Evolution of the 'Vedic Student' and the Dynamics of Texts, Ritual and Society in Ancient India* Harvard University Thesis, 2002).

Kane, P. V., *History of Dharmaśāstra* (Poona: Bhandarkar Oriental Research Institute, 1975).

Kant, Immanuel, *Critique of Judgment*, trans. Werner S. Pluhar (Indianapolis: Hackett, 1987).

Kerr, Fergus O. P., *After Aquinas: Versions of Thomism* (Oxford: Blackwell, 2002).

King, Richard, *Indian Philosophy: An Introduction to Hindu and Buddhist Thought* (Edinburgh: Edinburgh University Press, 1999).

King, Sallie B., *Being Benevolence: The Social Ethics of Engaged Buddhism* (Honolulu: University of Hawai'i Press, 2005).

Klever, W. N. A., 'Spinoza's Life and Works', in Don Garrett ed., *The Cambridge Companion to Spinoza* (Cambridge: Cambridge University Press, 1996), pp. 13–60.

Kofman, Sarah, 'Beyond Aporia', in Andrew Benjamin, ed., *Post Structuralist Classics* (New York: Routledge, 1988).

Lamotte, Étienne, 'The Assessment of Textual Interpretation in Buddhism', in Donald S. Lopez Jr. ed., *Buddhist Hermeneutics* (Delhi: Motilal Banarsidass, 1993), pp. 11–28.

Lane, Melissa, 'Honesty as the Best Policy: Nietzsche on *Redlichkeit* and the Contrast between Stoic and Epicurean Strategies of the Self', in Mark Bevir, Jill Hargis, and Sara Rushing eds., *Histories of Postmodernism* (London: Routledge, 2007), pp. 25–53.

Lang, Karen C., *Four Illusions: Candrakīrti's Advice to Travellers on the Bodhisattva Path* (New York: Oxford University Press, 2003). See Candrakīrti.

Larson, Gerald J., *Classical Sāṃkhya: An Interpretation of its History and Meaning* (Delhi: Motilal Banarsidass, 1979).

Lash, Nicholas, *The Beginning and the End of 'Religion'* (Cambridge University Press: Cambridge, 1996).

Lester, Robert, *Rāmānuja on the Yoga* (Madras: Adyar Library and Research Centre, 1976).

Levy, Oscar ed., *Friedrich Nietzsche. Selected Letters*, trans. A. N. Ludovici (London: Soho Book Company, 1921)

Loizzo, Joseph (trans.), *Nāgārjuna's Reason Sixty (Yuktiṣaṣṭikā) with Chandrakīrti's Commentary (Yuktiṣaṣṭikāvṛtti)* (New York: American Institute of Buddhist Studies, 2007).

Long, A. A. and Sedley, D. N., eds. and trs., *The Hellenistic Philosophers, vol. 1: Translations of the Principal Sources, with Philosophical Commentary* (Cambridge: Cambridge University Press, 1987).

Longinus, *On the Sublime*, trans. T. S. Dorsch (Harmondsworth: Penguin, 1965).

Longrigg, James, *Greek Rational Medicine: Philosophy and Medicine from Alcmaeon to the Alexandrians* (London: Routledge, 1993).

Lopez, Donald S. Jr., 'On the Interpretation of the Mahāyāna Sūtras,' in Donald S. Lopez Jr. ed., *Buddhist Hermeneutics* (Delhi: Motilal Banarsidass, 1993), pp. 47–70.

——, *Buddhism in Practice* (Princeton: Princeton University Press, 1995).

Löwith, Karl, 'Gott, Mensch und Welt in der Metaphysik von Descartes bis zu Nietzsche' [1967], in his *Sämtliche Schriften 9: Gott, Mensch und Welt – G.B. Vico – Paul Valery* (Stuttgart: Metzler, 1986), pp. 3–194.

Lubin, Timothy, *Consecration and Ascetical Regimen: A History of Hindu Vrāta, Dikṣā, Upanayana and Brahmacārya* (Columbia University Thesis, 1994).

Lucretius, *On the Nature of Things*, Martin Ferguson Smith tr. (Indianapolis: Hackett Publishing Company, 2001).

Mace, Ch. ed., *Heart and Soul: The Therapeutic Face of Philosophy* (London: Routledge, 1999).

Machiavelli, Niccolo, *The Prince* [1513], tr. Paul Halsall (*Internet Medieval Sourcebook*, http://www.fordham.edu/halsall/basis/machiavelli-prince.html, accessed 1st September 2008).

MacIntyre, Alasdair, *After Virtue: A Study in Moral Theory* (London: Duckworth, 1981).

Maimonides, Moses, *The Guide of the Perplexed* [1190], tr. Chaim Rabin, ed. Chaim Rabin, Hackett: Indianapolis, 1995).

Malcolm, Norman, 'Language Game (2),' in his *Wittgensteinan Themes: Essays 1978–1989* (Ithaca: Cornell University Press, 1995), pp. 172–181.

McEvilley, Thomas, *The Shape of Ancient Thought: Comparative Studies in Greek and Indian Philosophies* (New York: Allsworth Press, 2002).

McPherran, Mark L., 'Socratic Piety in the *Euthyphro*', *Journal of the History of Philosophy* **23** (1985), pp. 1–30.

——, 'Piety, Justice, and the Unity of Virtue', *Journal of the History of Philosophy* **38** (2000) pp. 299–328.

Milinda-pañhā, translated by I. B. Horner, *Milinda's Questions* (Oxford: The Pali Text Society, 1996 repr.).

Murdoch, Iris, *Acastos* (Penguin: Harmondsworth, 1987).

Nāgārjuna, *The Fundamental Wisdom of the Middle Way: Nāgārjuna's* Mūlamadhyamaka-kārikā, Jay L. Garfield, tr. (New York: Oxford University Press, 1995).

——, *Buddhist Advice for Living and Liberation: Nāgārjuna's* Precious Garland, Jeffrey Hopkins, tr., Ithaca (New York: Snow Lion Publications, 1998).

Ñāṇamoli, Bhikkhu (trans.), *The Path of Purification: Visuddhimagga by Bhadantācariya Buddhaghosa* (Kandy, Buddhist Publication Society, 1991, 5th edn.).

Ñāṇamoli, Bhikkhu and Bodhi, Bhikkhu (trans.), *The Middle Length Discourses of the Buddha,* (Boston: Wisdom Books, 1995).

Nārada, Mahāthera and Bodhi, Bhikkhu (trans.), *A Comprehensive Manual of Abhidhamma. The Abhidhammattha Sangaha of Acariya Anuruddha* (Kandy: Buddhist Publication Society, 1993).

Nietzsche, F., *The Anti-Christ*, trans. Judith Norman (Cambridge: Cambridge University Press, 2005).

——, *Beyond Good and Evil*, trans. and ed. Marion Faber (Oxford: Oxford University Press, 1998).

——, *Dawn: Thoughts on the Prejudices of Morality*, trans. Brittain Smith (Stanford: Stanford University Press, forthcoming); also *Daybreak: Thoughts on the Prejudices of Morality*, trans. R. J. Hollingdale (Cambridge: Cambridge University Press, 1986).

——, *On the Genealogy of Morality*, trans. Carol Diethe (Cambridge: Cambridge University Press, 2006); also trans. Douglas Smith (Oxford: Oxford University Press, 1996).

——, *The Gay Science*, trans. Walter Kaufmann (New York: Random House, 1974).

——, *Human, All too Human* (in two volumes), trans. R. J. Hollingdale (Cambridge: Cambridge University Press, 1984). Includes *Assorted Opinions and Maxims* and *The Wanderer and His Shadow.*

——, *Nietzsche contra Wagner*, trans. Judith Norman (Cambridge: Cambridge University Press, 2005).

——, *Sämtiche Werke: Kritische Studienausgabe* in 15 Bänden (München, Berlin & New York,: dtv/de Gruyter, 1988).

——, *The Will to Power*, trans. Walter Kaufmann & R. J. Hollingdale (New York: Random House, 1968).
Neumann, Karl Eugen [Übers.], *Buddha: Die Reden des Buddha* (Stammbach: Beyerlein & Steinschulte, 1995).
Norman, Kenneth R. (trans.), *The Rhinoceros Horn and Other Early Buddhist Poems (Sutta Nipāta)* (London: Pali Text Society, 1985).
——, *Poems of Early Buddhist Monks: Theragāthā* (Oxford: The Pali Text Society, 1997).
Nussbaum, Martha, *The Therapy of Desire: Theory and Practice in Hellenistic Ethics* (Princeton, NJ: Princeton University Press, 1994).
——, *Upheavals of Thought: The Intelligence of Emotions* (Cambridge: Cambridge University Press, 2001).
Olivelle, Patrick, *Dharmasūtras* (Oxford: Oxford University Press, 1999).
O'Rourke Boyle, Marjorie, 'Pure of Heart: From Ancient Rites to Renaissance Plato', *Journal of the History of Ideas* **63** (2002), pp. 41–62.
Patton, Laurie, ed., *Jewels of Authority: Women and Text in the Hindu Tradition* (New York: Oxford University Press, 2002).
Perdue, Dan, *Debate in Tibetan Buddhism* (Ithaca: Snow Lion, 1992).
Perry, Ralph Barton, *The Thought and Character of William James*, vol. 1 (Boston: Little, Brown, 1935).
Peterman, J. F., *Philosophy as Therapy: An Interpretation and Defense of Wittgenstein's Later Philosophical Project* (Albany: State University of New York Press, 1992).
Philodemus, *On Frank Criticism*, David Konstan et al. trs. (Atlanta: Scholars Press, 1998).
Plant, B., 'The End(s) of Philosophy: Rhetoric, Therapy and Wittgenstein's Pyrrhonism', *Philosophical Investigations* **27** (2004), pp. 222–257.
Plato, *Complete Works*, ed. John Cooper (Indianapolis/Cambridge: Hackett, 1997); also *The Dialogues of Plato*, tr. Benjamin Jowett (Oxford: Oxford University Press, 1892), 5 vols.
Plotinus, *Enneads*, tr, A. H. Armstrong in the Loeb Classical Library edition (Cambridge, Mass.: Harvard University Press, 1966).
Potter, Karl H., *Presuppositions of India's Philosophies* (Englewood Cliffs: Prentice Hall, Inc., 1963).
Rāmānuja, *Śrī Bhāṣyam Bhagavad-Rāmānuja-viracitam Śārīrakamīmāṃsābhāṣyam*, the critical edition (Melkoṭe: The Academy of Sanskrit Research, 1985).
Ray, Reginald A., *Touching Enlightenment: Finding Realization in the Body* (Boulder: Sounds True, 2008).
Rhys Davids, Thomas William (trans.), *The Questions of King Milinda* (Oxford: Oxford University Press, 1894), 2 Parts.
Richardson, Richard D., *William James: In the Maelstrom of American Modernism* (Boston: Houghton Mifflin, 2007).
Rorty, Richard, *Contingency, Irony, and Solidarity* (Cambridge: Cambridge University Press, 1985).
Rosen, Frederick, 'Piety and Justice: Plato's Euthyphro', *Philosophy* **43** (1968), pp. 105–16.

Rukmani, T. S., *Yogavārttika of Vijñānabhikṣu. Text with English translation and Critical Notes along with the Text and English Translation of the Pātañjala* Yogasūtras *and* Vyāsabhaṣya (Delhi: Munshiram Manoharlal Publishers, 1981–1999, 4 vols).
Rhees, Rush, 'Assessments of the Man and the Philosopher', in K. T. Fann, ed., *Ludwig Wittgenstein: The Man and His Philosophy* (New York: Dell, 1967), pp. 13–29.
——, 'Wittgenstein's Builders,' in *Discussions of Wittgenstein* (London: Routledge and Kegan Paul, 1970).
Safranski, Rüdiger, *Nietzsche: A Philosophical Biography*, trans. Shelley Frisch (New York: Norton, 2002).
Salguero, C. Pierce, *Traditional Thai Medicine: Buddhism, Animism, Ayurveda* (Prescott, Ariz.: Holm Press, 2007).
Śāntideva, *The Bodhicaryāvatāra*, Kate Crosby and Andrew Skilton, trs. (Oxford: Oxford University Press, 1995).
Sartre, Jean-Paul, *Nausea*, trans. R. Baldick (London: Penguin, 2000).
Śāstri, Suryanarayana S. S. ed. and trans., *The Sāṅkhyakārikā of Īśvara Kṛṣṇa* (Madras: University of Madras, 1965).
Scharfe, Harmut, *Education in Ancient India* (Leiden: Brill, 2002).
Sen, Joseph, 'Good Times and the Timeless Good,' *Journal of Neoplatonic Studies* **3** (1995), pp. 3–25.
Seneca, *Epistles 1-65*, Richard M. Gummere, tr. (Cambridge, MA: Harvard University Press, 1917).
——, *Epistles 66-92*, Richard M. Gummere, tr. (Cambridge, MA: Harvard University Press, 1920).
——, *Epistles 93-124*, Richard M. Gummere, tr. (Cambridge, MA: Harvard University Press, 1925).
——, 'On Anger,' in Seneca, *Moral and Political Essays*, John M. Cooper and J. F. Procopé eds. and trs. (Cambridge: Cambridge University Press, 1995).
Sextus Empiricus, *Outlines of Scepticism*, Julia Annas and Jonathan Barnes trs. (Cambridge: Cambridge University Press, 1994).
Siderits, Mark, *Empty Persons: Personal Identity and Buddhist Philosophy* (Aldershot: Ashgate, 2003).
Simon, Linda, *Genuine Reality: A Life of William James* (New York: Harcourt Brace, 1998).
Skrupskelis, Ignas K., and Berkeley, Elizabeth M. eds., *The Correspondence of William James*, vol. 1 (Charlottesville: University Press of Virginia, 1992).
——, *The Correspondence of William James*, vol. 4 (Charlottesville: University Press of Virginia, 1995).
——, *The Correspondence of William James*, vol. 6 (Charlottesville: University Press of Virginia, 1998).
Soni, Jayandra, 'Intercultural Relevance of Some Moments in the History of Indian Philosophy', *Topoi* **17** (1998), pp. 49–55.

——, 'Stufen der klassischen Yoga-Meditation', *Yearbook of the European College for the Study of Consciousness 1977* (Berlin: Verlag für Wissenschaft und Bildung, 1988), pp. 47–60.

Sorabji, Richard, *Emotion and Peace of Mind: From Stoic Agitation to Christian Temptation* (Oxford: Clarendon Press, 2000).

——, *Self: Ancient and Modern Insights about Individuality, Life and Death* (Oxford: Clarendon Press, 2006).

Spinoza, *Opera*, ed. C. Gebhardt, (Heidelberg: Carl Winters, 1925).

——, *Ethics*, trans. from the Latin by R. H. M. Elwes [1883] (New York: Dover, 1955).

Śrīdhara, *Nyāyakaṇḍalī: Praśastapādabhāṣyam of Praśastapāda with the Commentary Nyāyakaṇḍalī by Śrīdhara Bhaṭṭa*, ed. Durgādhara Jhā (Varanasi: Sampurnanand Sanskrit University, 1997).

Staal, Frits, *Agni: the Ritual of the Fire Altar* (Berkeley: University of California Press, 1982).

——, *Nambudiri Veda Recitation* (S'Gravenhage: Mouton and Co, 1961).

Steiner, Roland, 'Das 'dreifache Leiden' in *Sāṃkhyakārikā 1*', *in Indica et Tibetica: Festschrift für Michael Hahn*, ed. Konrad Klaus and Jens-Uwe Hartmann (Wien: Universität Wien, Arbeitskreis für Tibetische und Buddhistische Studien, 2007), pp. 507–520.

Stephan, Achim, 'Psychoanalyse und Konnektionismus', in *Ethik und Sozialwissenschaften* **4** (2001), pp. 543–554.

Suhr, Martin, *Jean-Paul Sartre zur Einführung* (Hamburg: Junius, 2001).

Suter, Ronald, *Interpreting Wittgenstein: A Cloud of Philosophy, a Drop of Grammar* (Philadelphia: Temple University Press, 1989).

Sukthankar, Vishnu S., Belvalkar, S. K. et al., *Mahābhārata*, critical edition (Poona: Bhandarkar Oriental Research Institute, 1933–66).

Suzuki, D. T., *Zen Buddhism*, ed. William Barrett (Doubleday: New York, 1956).

Szabados, Bela, *In Light of Chaos* (Saskatoon: Thistledown Press, 1990).

Tagore, Rabindranath, *Thought Relics* (New York: The Macmillan Company, 1912).

Tatz, Mark, *Buddhism and Healing: Demieville's Article 'Byō' from Hōbōgirin* (Lanham, Maryland: University Press of America, 1985).

Thapar, Romila, *Aśoka and the Decline of the Mauryas* (Delhi: Oxford University Press India, 1997, 3rd edn.).

Thera, Narada (trans.), *The Dhammapāda: Pali Text and Translation with Stories in Brief and Notes* (Kuala Lumpur: Buddhist Missionary Society, 1978, 3rd edn.)

Thera, Nyanaponika and Bodhi, Bhikkhu (trans.), *Numerical Discourses of the Buddha: An Anthology of Suttas from the Aṅguttara Nikāya* (Kandy: Buddhist Publication Society, 1999).

Thoreau, Henry David, *Walden, or, Life in the Woods* [1845] (New York: Pocket Books, 2004).

Uddyotakara, *Nyāyabhāṣyavārttika of Uddyotakara*, critical ed. Anantalal Thakur (Delhi: Indian Council of Philosophical Research, 1997).

Ure, Michael, *Nietzsche's Therapy: Self-Cultivation in the Middle Works* (Lanham: Lexington Books, 2008).
Vātsyāyana, *Gautamīyanyāyadarśana with Bhāṣya of Vātsyāyana*, critical ed. Anantalal Thakur (Delhi: Indian Council of Philosophical Research, 1997).
Waldron, William S., *The Buddhist Unconscious: The Ālaya-Vijñāna in the Context of Indian Buddhist Thought* (London: RoutledgeCurzon, 2003).
Walshe, Maurice (trans.), *Thus Have I Heard: The Long Discourses of the Buddha* (London: Wisdom Publications, 1987).
Webster, David, *The Philosophy of Desire in the Buddhist Pāli Canon* (London: Routledge, 2005).
Weil, Simone, *Intimations of Christianity*, tr. E. C. Geissbuhler Routledge & Kegan Paul: London, 1957).
Wezler, Albert, 'On the Quadruple Division of the Yogaśāstra, The *Caturvyūhatva* of the *Cikitsāśāstra* and The 'Four Noble Truths' of the Buddha,' *Indologica Taurinensia* **12** (1984), pp. 289–337.
Wharton, Kate, *Philosophy as a Practice of Freedom in Ancient India and Ancient Greece* (SOAS, University of London Thesis, 2008).
White, Victor O.P., *Holy Teaching: The Idea of Theology According to St Thomas Aquinas* (London: Blackfriars Publications, 1958).
Whitlock, Greg, 'Concealing the Misconduct of One's Own Father: Confucius and Plato on a Question of Filial Piety', *Journal of Chinese Philosophy* **21** (1994), pp. 113–137.
Williams, Bernard, 'Do Not Disturb,' review of Nussbaum's *The Therapy of Desire: Theory and Practice in Hellenistic Ethics, London Review of Books* **16** (October 20, 1994), pp. 25–26.
Wilson, Catherine, *Epicureanism at the Origins of Modernity* (Oxford: Oxford University Press, 2008).
Wilson, E. O., *On Human Nature* (Cambridge, Mass.: Harvard University Press, 1978).
Wittgenstein, Ludwig, *Culture and Value*, ed. G. H. von Wright and Heikki Nyman, trans. Peter Winch, Oxford: Basil Blackwell, 1980).
——, *Philosophical Investigations*, trans. G. E. M. Anscombe (Oxford: Basil Blackwell, 1958, 3rd edn.).
——, *Philosophical Remarks*, trans. Raymond Hargreaves and Roger White (New York: Harper and Row, 1975).
Wollheim, Richard, *The Thread of Life* (Cambridge, Mass.: Harvard University Press, 1984).
Woods, James Haughton, *The Yoga-System of Patañjali or the Ancient Hindu Doctrine of Concentration of the Mind, embracing the mnemonic rules, called Yoga-sūtras, of Patañjali and the comment, called Yoga-Bhāshya, attributed to Veda-Vyāsa and the explanation, called Tattva-Vāiçaradī, of Vāchaspati-Miçra translated from the original Sanskrit* (Cambridge: Harvard University Press, 1914).
Woodward, F. L. (trans.), *The Book of the Gradual Sayings (Anguttara-Nikāya)*, vol. 5 (London: Luzac & Company, Pāli Text Society, 1961).

Xenakis, Iason, *Epictetus: Philosopher-Therapist* (The Hague: Nijhoff, 1969).
Yovel, Yirmiyahn, *Spinoza and other Heretics: The Marrano of Reason* (Princeton: Princeton University Press, 1989).
Zhu, Rui, 'What if the Father Commits a Crime?', *Journal of the History of Ideas* **63** (2002), pp. 1–17.
Zysk, Kenneth G., *Asceticism and Healing in Ancient India: Medicine in the Buddhist Monastery* (Delhi: Motilal Banarsidass Publishers, 1998, corrected edn.).